INSIDE THE STATEHOUSE

Lessons from the Speaker

Ralph G. Wright

Former Speaker of the Vermont House of Representatives

CQ PRESS

A Division of Congressional Quarterly Inc.
Washington, D.C.

CQ Press
1255 22nd Street, NW, Suite 400
Washington, DC 20037

Phone, 202-729-1900; toll-free, 1-866-427-7737 (1-866-4CQ-PRESS)

Web: www.cqpress.com

Interior photo credits: Page 39 photo by former Vermont State Senator Will Hunter. All other photos by AP/Wide World Photos and reprinted with permission.

Cover design: TGD Communications, Alexandria, VA

♾ The paper used in this publication exceeds the requirements of the American National Standard for Information Sciences—Permanence of Paper for Printed Library Materials, ANSI Z39.48-1992.

Printed and bound in the United States of America

09 08 07 06 05   1 2 3 4 5

Library of Congress Cataloging-in-Publication Data

Wright, Ralph G.
    Inside the statehouse : lessons from the speaker / Ralph G. Wright.
        p. cm.
    Includes index.
    ISBN 1-56802-949-7 (pbk. : alk. paper)
    1. Wright, Ralph G. 2. Vermont. General Assembly. House of Representatives—Speakers—Biography. 3. Legislators—Vermont—Biography. 4. Governors—Vermont—Biography. 5. Vermont—Politics and government—20th century. I. Title.
    F55.22.W75A3 2005
    974.3'043'092—dc22

                                                                    2005009627

Contents

Preface

Everyone has a book in them. It just takes a good memory and a whole lot of courage to write it.

When I first went to the Vermont legislature, as a naive and more than a little frightened freshman, I hadn't the faintest clue that someday I would be revealing in book form my experience over sixteen eventful years. But that's what I have tried to do in the following pages.

Actually, this is not my first effort at being an author. A memoir of sorts, *All Politics Is Personal,* preceded this endeavor. Many of the wonderful characters I hope you get to know here were originally introduced to a little wider world in that book. What is different about this effort is that I am trying not so much to share my observations and adventures as to lead the reader to a better understanding of how state government works—to take you inside the statehouse, if you will. Toward that end I have introduced to you in the following pages a cast of characters; some you'll love, others— well, that's the reader's determination. Whatever your taste in people, I have written every word with the hope that the reader is able to take away the understanding that it is people, in all their shapes and forms, that make our system of representative democracy work. This grassroots understanding of one state legislature has made me so much more tolerant of the sausage-like nature of lawmaking: It may, at times, be a less-than-appetizing procedure, but if done right, the result is extremely satisfying. The cooks always make the difference. With the legislative process it is no different. It is people, just like you and me, who make it work—heroes and cowards; the bright and the not so; the movers and shakers, and the sheep that follow.

Vermonters like to think that their government is unique, but it really is different only on the fringe—much like people. These hardy citizens are different only in their forbearance to somehow endure those long and harsh winters in America's smallest capital, Montpelier. The truth of the matter is that the system by which the people rule in the Green Mountain State is cast from the same mold that the Founders of our representative government first instituted during that hot and sultry summer of 1787. It is a governmental structure designed for people to do with what they will. To understand it all, one has to dig beyond the material remains and focus on those who built it. The political science student has to re-create what it was truly all about by focusing on those souls who came, did what it is they do, and passed on.

This is not only a text, but a story—a story about everyday folks, driven by whatever motivation, who find themselves in a legislative body. Most enter the halls of government knowing little or nothing about the business of making law. Some get to work and learn quickly; others struggle with the social nature of several hundred people working together for the common good and disappear almost unnoticed. Still others never bother and somehow manage to survive through their ability to stay out of the line of fire—what "ol' Corps grunts" once labeled "candy-ass Marines." Here again, I'll let you be the judge as to the ones who made a difference.

Finally, I feel it a duty to thank a handful of folks without whose aid and encouragement I probably never would have put this wonderful experience over sixteen years into writing. First among many equals is Alan Rosenthal, of Rutgers University's Eagleton Institute of Politics, who convinced me that I had a good tale that should be told. It was he who introduced me to our publisher, CQ Press.

Things sort of fell into place, but not without a massive infusion of help from CQ's staff. Most prominent of course was my editor Colleen Ganey. Her patience and guidance throughout kept me from calling it quits more often than she knows. How many times—that she has been too polite ever to mention—she must have hung up the phone with raised eyebrows. I'm lucky to know her, if only by satellite. Thanks also to Charisse Kiino, Brenda Carter, Nancy Geltman, Joanne Ainsworth, and Gwenda Larsen. A hearty thank you is also due to the manuscript reviewers: Burdett Loomis of the University of Kansas, John A. Straayer of Colorado State University, Anthony Gierzynski of the University of Vermont, and Susan B. Hansen of the University of Pittsburgh.

Well, enough with the preliminaries, as now I would consider it a privilege if you would come with me through that grand arched doorway, under the golden dome, and "Inside the Statehouse."

Introduction
Beyond Vermont's Golden Dome

by Alan Rosenthal

THIS IS A book about the Vermont legislature and the men and women who serve in it. Vermont is one of the smallest states in the nation, dwarfed by giants such as California, Texas, and Florida. Vermont's legislature has 150 members in the House and 30 members in the Senate. Nearly all of the members are "citizen" legislators—that is, people who work for a living at other professions or jobs while serving in the legislature. The Vermont legislature is different from the rest, but so are they all different from the rest.

Differences and Similarities

All told, there are ninety-nine state legislative bodies in the nation, if you consider senates and houses separately (only Nebraska is unicameral, with a senate but no house). Some legislative bodies are larger than Vermont's, although none comes close to the 400-member New Hampshire House. Some are smaller, such as the 41-member Delaware House or the 42-member Nevada House. A number of legislatures are controlled by the Democratic Party, and a number by the Republican Party; others have divided control, with Democrats a majority in one chamber and Republicans a majority in the other. The legislatures range from the professional ones—distinguished by large staffs, impressive facilities, and full-time members—to the citizen ones—distinguished by small staffs, limited facilities, and part-time members. California, New York, and Illinois are among the most professional; Vermont and Wyoming exemplify the citizen type. Most legislatures are hybrids, somewhere between the professional legislatures on the one hand and the citizen legislatures on the other.

There are also a total of 7,382 state legislators in the nation, including Vermont's 180. About half happen to be Democrats and about half Republicans, with a sprinkling of independents scattered around and a few Progressives in Vermont. About one out of five of the nation's legislators is, or has been, in business of one sort or another, and almost as many are attorneys. Another fifth or so are homemakers, retired, or not otherwise employed outside the legislature. Many of the legislators in some of the larger states—California, Illinois, Massachusetts, Michigan, New York, and Pennsylvania—work virtually full time in their legislative jobs, whereas those in smaller states work outside the legislature to earn a living.

Questions for Discussion

After you read this book about the Vermont legislature, you might give some thought to how your own state and your own legislature compare. What about the size of the state, the number of legislators, the partisan division in the legislature? Is it better to have a smaller legislative body or a larger one, and why? Is the legislature in your state more of a professional one or more of a citizen one? What are the advantages and disadvantages of each type?

Each and every legislature is different, and indeed, the same legislature differs from senate to house, from session to session, and from issue to issue. As Ralph Wright recalls in this book, "I never had a day in the legislature that was the same as any other." So, what can be learned from reading *Inside the Statehouse*? A lot can be learned from looking closely at Vermont, or at any other particular state for that matter, because all legislatures have roughly similar kinds of people as members, and not only in Vermont, but everywhere, politics is personal, as well as ideological, partisan, practical, and more. A lot can be learned because all legislatures have very similar statuses and jobs. The legislative branch in every state is constitutionally established, along with the executive and judicial branches, in a governmental system of separated powers. The major jobs of legislatures everywhere are representing constituents and constituencies, lawmaking, and balancing the power of the executive.

A lot can be learned from the case of Vermont because all legislatures face the same kinds of problems and engage in the same processes. One fundamental problem legislatures face is that the people in the state have competing values, interests, and priorities, and therefore their elected representatives do, too. Thus, on some major issues conflict is inevitable, and healthy. Another fundamental problem is that public needs and demands almost always exceed the resources available to meet them, so the budget that all legislatures must enact either annually or biennially almost always presents a challenge.

Approaches to the Study of Legislatures

If the reader can get a good sense of the Vermont legislature in action, then he or she will have a better sense of the legislative species in general. Note that I use the word "sense." Much of my career as a political scientist has been spent trying to understand state legislatures and legislators. If I have learned one thing from years and years of effort, it is that legislatures and legislators cannot really be understood. Therefore, I am now content with trying to approach an understanding of these elusive phenomena, and I am gratified when I think I have achieved a better sense of them.

How does one go about acquiring a better sense of them? A recent book I wrote is illustrative. In *Heavy Lifting: The Job of the American Legislature* (Washington, D.C.: CQ Press, 2004), I focused on how legislatures do their work and also attempted to figure out what a "good" (as opposed to a "poor") legislature is. To do this, I relied on a number of methods of inquiry. First, of course, I consulted the political science literature, that is, the research published by legislative scholars. It makes little sense to reinvent the wheel, so it is always useful to look at the array of research findings that have already been produced. Second, I conducted interviews with participants in the legislative process in five states—Maryland, Minnesota, Ohio, Vermont, and Washington—that were the focus of much of my attention. Third, I mailed structured questionnaires to all 848 legislators in those five states; almost half of them responded. Fourth, I observed the legislature in action in each of these states, having been permitted to shadow legislative leaders as they engaged in the lawmaking process.

Finally, I relied on memoirs, biographies, and firsthand accounts such as diaries. They added flesh to the muscle and bone of the legislative process. One book along these lines is Frank Smallwood's *Free and Independent* (1978), in which Smallwood, a Dartmouth University political science professor, describes the two years he spent in the Vermont Senate. His book is a sheer delight. The former Speaker of the Wisconsin Assembly, Tom Loftus, recounted his experiences with honesty and wit in *The Art of Legislative Politics* (Washington, D.C.: CQ Press, 1994). Harriet Keyserling's *Against the Tide: One Woman's Political Struggle* (1998) shows how a legislator, who was raised in New York City, was able, with a steady stroke and stamina, to buck the tide and get things done in the South Carolina House. In *Experiencing Politics: A Legislator's Stories of Government and Health Care* (2000), John McDonough provides an inside look at the process of lawmaking on a number of issues in which his involvement was critical. Then there is the biography *Willie Brown* (1996), by James Richardson, which details the career of the illustrious, and somewhat outrageous, Speaker of the California Assembly and at the same time provides a contemporary history of the California legislature.

Writing as a veteran of sixteen years in the Vermont House, including ten years as Speaker, Ralph Wright presents a book that is very much in the tradition of the memoirs and biography mentioned above. He is keenly insightful on the strategies and machinations of the legislative process and remarkably candid about the people involved. Moreover, the book offers the best stories that I have come across. Wright is a natural storyteller, whose tales convey the human nature of legislatures and legislative life. No reader will be able to forget the account of Rep. Frank DaPrato and his insistence that Gov. Madeleine Kunin owed him an apology. Just as memorable is the greeting from a die-hard opponent whose door Wright knocked on during a campaign, or the story about the

Speaker of the House being mistaken for a building custodian when he took a family visiting from Kentucky on a tour of the State House.

Legislative People

Tip O'Neill, D-Mass., the former Speaker of the U.S. House of Representatives, hit the nail on the head when he wrote, "All politics is local." Ralph Wright banged in another nail when he said, "All politics is personal." Not only do his memoirs bring us up close to the people in and around the legislature, but most of all, they allow Wright to reveal much about himself throughout the narrative. A liberal Democrat and strong partisan, Wright grew up in Massachusetts. When he was elected in Vermont, he began to transform the traditional style of legislative politics in the Green Mountain State. A canny politico, Wright also had a commitment to a number of causes and was always ready to scrap for what he felt was right for Vermont. Although a few Republicans had several times joined with his Democratic colleagues to elect him Speaker, the Republican Party targeted Wright and defeated him in 1994. Wright is introspective about his defeat, recognizing that his aggressive style didn't help. And he admits to having lost touch with his district. If the capital becomes more important than his or her district, any legislator will be at risk. In Wright's case, as Speaker he focused on the issues and legislation and paid too little attention to his constituency. People also were upset that the legislative session had run too long, as legislators struggled with some difficult matters, and the public wondered why they didn't go home.

In this book other individuals share the stage, and their personalities prove to be critical elements in the legislative process. Consider Edgar May, who chaired the standing committee on which Wright first served, or John Murphy, a totally different type of individual, who chaired another committee of which Wright was a member early in his career. Then there is Tom Candon, leader of the good ol' boys in the House, who didn't like Wright or his positions on issues, but still helped him get elected Speaker. Timothy Corcoran was Wright's good buddy, but when he voted against the tax bill Wright wanted, Wright threw him out of the condo they shared. In a few weeks, however, Wright let him move back in. The positions that many (but not all) legislators take on the big issues may be predictable, but their behavior in the trenches is anything but.

The intriguing question, which is mainly implicit in these memoirs, is, Why do people run for the legislature, and how do they put up with the rigors of legislative life once they are there? In many states the legislature is not a person's first elective office—30, 40, or 50 percent have already served as county executives or on county commissions, town councils, or local school boards. In Vermont, before their election to the legislature a whopping 67 percent have held prior office in the district where they live. Wright himself had served on the board of selectmen in his town. When most members get to the legislature the demands on their time increase. In Vermont the legislative session normally runs four months each year. During that period nine out of ten members spend forty hours or more a week at their legislative jobs, which is similar to what legislators in other states spend. Between sessions, however, Vermont legislators can return almost full time to their jobs outside the legislature; they are not expected to spend much time on legislative or constituency business. Only one-third spend fifteen hours a week or more during the interim period on matters to do with their legislative jobs. In states with more professionalized legislatures, the time commitments are much heavier.

The compensation that Vermont legislators receive is low, about $10,000 a year for rank-and-file members. That compares very poorly with the $99,000 that California pays its legislators and the $79,500 and $61,900 that New York and Pennsylvania, respectively, pay. But it compares pretty well with the $100 per year that legislators receive in Vermont's neighboring state of New Hampshire. Still, a rough calculation would indicate that Vermont legislators put in about 125 days a year for compensation of about $10 an hour.

In addition to the financial sacrifice legislators make in Vermont and practically everywhere else, they have to withstand other stresses and strains as well. They have to put their careers outside of the legislature on hold. They have to take time away from their families and cut way back on leisure activities. They must live with the frustration that is endemic to lawmaking, and they have to realize that they will always make some people unhappy. And every two years (or four years, as is the case of senates in most states, but not Vermont) they brave the tender mercies of their constituency electorate and can be rejected by their neighbors.

But since a large percentage of incumbents choose to run for reelection, they must be deriving satisfaction from their legislative jobs. There must be something about being in a state legislature that is appealing.

Questions for Discussion

Wright's sketches of people from Vermont touch on a number of questions about what makes legislators tick.

Would you consider running for the legislature in your state? If you did, what would your motivations be? What do you think motivated Ralph Wright? What about legislators in your state?

What skills and characteristics did Wright have that helped him adapt to the legislature? What were his weaknesses? What skills and characteristics do you have that would help you adapt to the legislature in your state?

If Wright hadn't enjoyed the legislature, he would have left voluntarily. What did he appear to like most about it? What didn't he like? What do you think you would like about serving in the legislature? What would you find the toughest to put up with? Finally, what does Wright recall most fondly about his stint in the Vermont legislature?

Legislative Performance

These memoirs enable the reader to watch the legislature doing its job—representing constituents and constituencies, lawmaking, and balancing the power of the executive. It is a very human, quite complicated, and fairly unpredictable business. In Vermont, as in other states, it is representative democracy at work.

First, and probably foremost, for members of any legislature is the job of representation. Vermont is extremely different in this respect from nearly all other states because each member of the House represents as few as 4,000 people (or in the case of two-member districts, such as Wright's in Bennington, 8,000). New Hampshire's 400 House members represent only 3,000 people each, but at the other extreme, members of the California Assembly represent as many as 423,000 people.

The small size of their districts makes the job of representation easier in a number of respects. A representative, as Wright points out, can know on a personal basis just about everyone in his or her constituency. Add to this the fact that representatives in Vermont have lived in their districts for many years: 23 percent of them have lived all their lives in the district they represent, and another 41 percent have lived twenty-five years or longer in their district. All told, four out of five have lived in their districts for at least twenty years.

The relationship between constituents and their representative is a particularly intimate one in Vermont. Legislators stay in close touch with the people back home during the session, as well as during the interim period when their work lessens. They handle requests from constituents who have encountered a problem with an executive agency and need help. Like Wright, they write to constituents in longhand or wait to use a phone in the State House when it becomes available. Vermont legislators may have fewer requests from constituents than legislators in other states, but they have neither a secretary nor other staff to assist them in the casework and other matters they handle. Like legislators elsewhere, those in Vermont try to serve the interests of the people who send them to Montpelier by getting projects for the district included in the state budget and by ensuring that state funding formulas are as generous to their district as possible. And they serve to connect constituents—at least those who want some connection—to state government.

No doubt the most difficult part of representation is expressing the public-policy views of their constituents. Here representatives face a dilemma. But it is not ordinarily one of deciding between conscience and constituency, that is, between the representative's own judgment on the one hand and the prevailing views in the constituency on the other. Rather, the dilemma is that on the overwhelming number of issues with which the state legislature deals, constituents have no views, and so there is no prevailing view. In Vermont, for example, 66 percent of the legislators responding to my survey reported that only on five or fewer bills during the biennium did their constituency have a position, a position that was prevailing. But interest groups and their lobbyists have positions and are not hesitant to make them known.

In those instances in which a prevailing view exists in the constituency, the representative ordinarily shares the view and has no trouble expressing it. But on occasion, albeit rare occasion, the views of representative and constituency come into conflict. In Vermont, struggles over gay rights and civil unions were among those rare occasions, ones that saw representatives voting their consciences rather than their constituencies. A number of those representatives paid the price when they ran for reelection.

The campaign for reelection is the linchpin of representation. Candidacy and campaigning are a large part of the work of any elected public official, and Wright gives us a real sense of what getting elected entails. In Vermont, at least, it doesn't require many votes—a thousand or so will do it. But getting them is harder than it may appear. People expect candidates to go door to door and also not to forget them between elections. Wright quickly discovered that people want to be asked for their vote before they bestow it. Campaigning in Vermont is a face-to-face endeavor, requiring shoe leather rather than a lot of money. Wright, for example, would walk his district nine times but never spent more than $200 on any of his nine campaigns—not even his last, when about $14,000 was spent to defeat him.

The second part of the legislature's job is lawmaking. Most people are aware of how a bill makes its way from introduction to committee to the floor in one house and then travels a similar route in the other house. As far as bills introduced, Vermont's legislature has a much lighter load than others. In 2001, for instance, 711 bills were introduced in Vermont. This compares with the 522 introduced in Wyoming and 668 in Ohio, but it is substantially fewer than the 16,892 in New York and the 7,924 in Massachusetts. Wright takes the reader behind the scenes generally, and specifically on issues of gay rights, taxes, and health care. We see how major bills, and also minor ones (which constitute the overwhelming majority of bills introduced), are handled.

Especially helpful are Wright's comments on and accounts of the work of standing committees. Here is where bill sponsors, interest group lobbyists, and member-specialists make their greatest efforts. If a bill gets solid support in committee, its chances of passing on the floor are extremely good. If it doesn't get out of committee, its chances of passage are slim.

In my own explorations of lawmaking in legislatures, I have focused on what seem to me to be the principal components of the lawmaking process: first, hearing the arguments; second, studying the problem; third, deliberating the merits of the case for and the case against; fourth, negotiating; fifth, compromising; and sixth, persuading in order to win support and votes. These activities take place simultaneously, but each can be thought of as distinct in the process. Throughout the book, Wright touches on these components.

The third part of the legislature's job is balancing the power of the executive. This function is embedded in the separation-of-powers provisions and the checks-and-balances implications of state constitutions. Wright allows that Vermont's citizen legislature could not compete with the governor. Still, as a legislative leader he believed that the legislature had to operate vis-à-vis the governor with as much strength as it could summon. And Wright put his belief into practice in his dealings with three Vermont governors—Madeleine Kunin, Richard Snelling, and Howard Dean.

Wright's comments on each of these chief executives could hardly be more frank (surely the sign of someone who is retired from politics and not wondering about reentry). His favorite among the three was Dick Snelling, a Republican. Wright's admiration and respect for Snelling easily overcame their partisan differences. Among the three governors, it was only with this Republican that Wright had a personal as well as a professional relationship.

The harmony with Snelling was not matched in Wright's relationship with Madeleine Kunin. Although the two shared basic beliefs, the way they practiced politics and their approaches to getting things done were quite different. The two did not feel comfortable with each other; it was what the author calls a "disconnect."

Wright respects a number of Howard Dean's qualities but appears put off by this governor's restlessness and ambition and is critical of his unwillingness to spend political capital that he had amassed. In Wright's judgment, the Vermont governor, who in 2004 sought the Democratic nomination for president, was too quick to abandon both causes and people. Wright's experience with Dean was that he would cut and run, in contrast to Snelling who would stand tall.

Questions for Discussion

In several places in this book Wright touches on the representative and his or her constituency. Representing constituents and constituencies in Vermont is similar to, and also different from, representing constituents and constituencies elsewhere. Compare the job of representing in Vermont with that of representing in your own state.

The process by which laws are made involves a number of activities: (1) hearing the arguments; (2) studying the problem; (3) deliberating the merits of the case for and the case against; (4) negotiating; (5) compromising; and (6) persuading, to win support and votes. Identify in Wright's memoirs examples of each and comment on the ones to which he seems to devote most of his attention.

Wright points out, as have many political scientists and other observers, that it is easier to kill a bill than to pass one. Why is this so?

In the executive-legislative relationship, the governor in Vermont and in most states has the upper hand. Why? What powers does the governor have when it comes to dealing with the legislature? What powers does the legislature have when it comes to dealing with the governor?

Legislative Leadership

Throughout these memoirs, Wright's observations are those of a legislative leader, specifically the Speaker of the House. A partisan Democrat, he became Speaker in a body that had not yet become especially partisan. On three occasions when he was elected to the top position in the House, the Democrats were in the minority. But Wright added to the votes from his own caucus those of ten to twelve Republicans. Six of them, according to him, were die-hard supporters; the others got something in return for their support. Bipartisan coalitions are by no means unique to Vermont; they are fashioned on occasion in other states, and even in partisan states Democrats and Republicans coalesce in choosing leaders from time to time. But the ability of a member of the minority to hold the speakership for several years is testimony to Wright's leadership skills—and his willingness to cut a deal when necessary.

Wright certainly knows what legislative leadership entails, and in this book he spells out the requirements. Something of an anomaly in this citizen legislature, Wright was a professional. He professionalized legislative politics and the leadership role. He made an indelible impression on Vermont's citizen legislature. When he left it, Vermont's legislature had become, because of him, somewhat more like other legislatures around the country and somewhat less like the politically low-key place it used to be. Some Vermonters would call that progress; some would consider it regression.

Questions for Discussion

Throughout the book, Wright touches on the various tasks of legislative leadership. Can you identify and discuss various tasks that legislative leaders are expected to carry out? How does legislative leadership compare with executive leadership?

Legislative Appreciation

Americans tend to be cynical about their political institutions, political processes, and political people. They like the idea of representative democracy, but they do not like the nitty-gritty of representative democracy, the way it works in practice. Legislatures are easy targets. They never provide enough by way of services, and they always tax more than citizens wish to pay. Democratic-controlled legislatures are likely to produce results that displease people who affiliate with the Republican Party, and Republican-controlled legislatures are likely to produce results that displease people who affiliate with the Democratic Party. The positives about legislatures are elusive, but the news media drum constantly on the negatives (for what is negative is news, and what is positive is not). The more negative, the better, from the media's point of view. Add to all of this that legislatures are messy institutions that operate in very unpredictable ways—not a pretty picture.

America's legislatures are in need of support or, at the very least, appreciation. Legislative appreciation does not come naturally. Like music appreciation or art appreciation, it has to be taught.

The best way to develop an appreciation of legislatures is to serve in one—as a member, on the staff, or possibly as an intern. Next best is probably to spend a career studying legislatures, as I have. Not many people, however, will work in legislatures or study them for years. Unless things change, if people are to come to appreciate legislatures they will have to be taught—in schools, colleges, and elsewhere. My own research and writing are intended, in part, to teach legislative appreciation. Accounts about insiders, such as Willie Brown of California, or by insiders, such as Harriet Keyserling of South Carolina and Tom Loftus of Wisconsin, can accomplish much the same. Ralph Wright's memoirs are definitely a good read, and an educational one as well. The question is, What do they say about representative democracy and the legislature?

Questions for Discussion

In thinking about Wright's book, what is your reaction? What effect did it have on your views of American legislatures and legislators? If other people read this book, do you think their appreciation of representative democracy would increase and their cynicism would decline?

1

My First Campaign

Making the Decision

DON'T BELIEVE ANY of these guys that try to tell you that they ran for office because a lot of folks begged them. It's probably the first in a career based on lies.

I ran nine times, and though I was aware of lots of people who wished I hadn't, including my wife and half of my kids, I never recall being begged. So don't expect any ticker-tape parades outside your window, clamoring for you to throw your hat in the ring. It's not likely to happen.

You want to run—run.

Everyone has his or her own reasons for running for office. The only advice I would give in making the decision is, don't be afraid to lose. Expect to win, hope to win, even pray to win—but recognize getting your backside beat is a distinct possibility.

I made the decision to run for the Vermont legislature in 1978 because I wanted to be a player in the great American game of politics. To me it was an opportunity to get involved in an arena that offered the chance to make people's lives more rewarding—including my own. I had been directing an alternative school for high school dropouts for fifteen or so years, and though I never articulated it intellectually, I guess I just wanted to do something different. I mulled over joining a local bowling league or taking up membership at the VFW. But I can't bowl and I'm not overly fond of beer. It was an impulsive decision and one that I never regretted. So politics it was.

I had problems right from the get-go.

First, I had to get the green light from my wife, Cathy. I knew she'd give me the OK, but she did it with the resignation that I had heard many times before. "If that's what you want, go ahead."

A second problem was that I decided this on the very last day for filing to run for state office. The deadline was five in the afternoon and it was now two o'clock. I needed to gather fifty signatures on my petition in a little under three hours. I scurried up and down Main Street buttonholing folks, and at five minutes to five I rushed into the clerk's office with sixty-four signatures. I was an official candidate on the Democratic ticket.

It wasn't as if I were running for an open seat. I happened to reside in a two-member district, which already had two well-entrenched incumbents. One, a fellow Democrat named Larry Powers, was running for his third two-year term; the other was the longest-serving member in the Vermont House of Representatives, Joe Caracciolla, a Republican, who was pursuing a thirteenth consecutive term. "Little Joe" and Larry were both local merchants and native Vermonters. And being a native was a distinct advantage in a state that often looks with suspicion on "outsiders." As far as the natives were concerned I was "down-country folk," and I often got teased about my heavy Boston accent; no matter that I had spent half my life in the Green Mountain State, I would forever be what Vermonters referred to as a "flatlander." My opponents had been born and reared, and had prospered, in the district they represented. In addition, Larry and Little Joe were respected members of the community and very highly regarded. They had run unopposed in the last election, and as they liked each other just fine, my last-minute entry into the race was an unpleasant surprise to them. I was to find out later that they had quietly agreed not to seek a running mate in hopes that they would win the big prize all candidates long for—a *free ride,* which is to say, an unopposed run for office. It was immediately apparent that I wasn't going to get any help from either of them. My entry meant one of us was going to lose, and I suspect they were hoping it would be me.

It wasn't going to be an easy race. Though I had some experience in politics, having served an abbreviated term on the local board of selectmen four years earlier, my tenure had a double edge to it, as I had resigned abruptly because of family problems with a year left on my term. Previous experience, no matter how brief, might have been something of an asset, but I worried that many people felt I was a quitter. I'm happy to report that the issue never did surface in the campaign.

Getting Started

The first thing I did was to get a checklist (an official list of eligible voters in a district) from the town clerk's office.[1] As my district was wholly within the town of Bennington, one checklist would serve the purpose. It cost me fifty dollars. Next I needed a map of the streets and back roads. This I procured from the local chamber of commerce. It was free.

All I had to do now was get a thousand or so votes.

Campaigning is like love. It gets very personal, and that's how it should be. And though every campaign looks much like every other campaign, the would-be officeholder molds his or her campaign to fit what he or she feels most comfortable with. Vermont's small population and reasonable-sized districts mean that ordinary citizens as well as career politicians can feel the temptation to throw their hats in the political ring. There is no IQ test to be a politician. Praise be.

No state has many requirements to run for state representative. To qualify to run in Vermont you have to be eighteen years of age, live at least one year in the district that you want to represent (other states have even shorter time limits), and obtain a certain minimum of signatures on a petition. Voilà—you're a full-fledged candidate. That's the good news. The bad news is that if you want to be truly competitive, you will have to work harder and be more organized than you've probably ever been in your life.

And it's a lonely endeavor. I don't ever remember being so alone. It's a solitariness that leaves you anxiety-ridden throughout the long weeks leading to election day, and it's something that requires acceptance if the candidate is to find the perseverance to plod on through a campaign that can, at times, seem endless. The problem is that the vast majority of voters are extremely stoical. I found that almost without exception they were exceedingly polite at the door but very cautious not to let their feelings be known. I've reflected as to the reason and surmised that most folks want to give the candidate credit for entering the political arena, and they want to express a friendliness that is encompassed in the words I most often heard, "Good luck!" But what on earth does that mean?

"Good luck" because you're obviously so hopeless a dork that only the smile of good fortune could possibly bring you out a winner? Or "Good luck. I hope you win"?

More important, I believe, is that Americans look upon their franchise as their inherent right, even though nearly half will opt not to use it, and they will protect the privacy of that right vehemently. As most people would consider intrusive your asking them how much money they make, asking them how they're going to vote will likely get you the same response.

So I trod from door to door, seldom having a clue as to how I was doing. It didn't take me long to figure out that the campaign trail was unlike any game I had ever played. No one keeps score until the very end—election day.

But we're getting ahead of ourselves.

The Green Mountain State

Vermont is a small state. It has 242 towns spread over its hills and valleys, each a little democracy, with an average of 2,400 citizens. And it likes to boast that its General Assembly is still considered a "citizen's legislature." That may be true, but I'm convinced that what it takes to get elected in a small state like Vermont is just what it takes to get elected in California. For the latter you just do pretty much the same thing magnified fifty times. That, of course, requires staff, money—lots of it—and additional organizational headaches. The core of any campaign is meeting people and convincing them that you're an "all right guy." In California, with districts fifty times larger than Vermont's, you would be forced to use the media. In Vermont you simply have to get a new pair of sneakers, a handful of leaflets, and set out to meet people. It's a "people game" whichever coast you're on.

Vermonters are also very independent minded. They were the first to outlaw slavery in their state constitution, a long time ago, and just recently the first to allow same-sex civil unions (gay marriage). Once thought of as having more cows than people, the state has witnessed an amalgamation of a majority of its small, threadbare farms into huge dairy conglomerates and an influx of a new counterculture of transplanted flatlanders from down-country urban areas. This has changed not only the state's culture but its politics. Once rock-ribbed Republican—it and Maine were the only states to vote for the Republican Alf Landon (and against Franklin D. Roosevelt) in 1936—Vermont is now, arguably, the most liberal state in the Union.

Beautiful Bennington, Vermont

I was lucky because the town I lived in, Bennington, was big enough to encompass four full legislative districts and the major part of a fifth. District 2-1, the district I lived in and hoped to win, had been reapportioned in 1972 to require two representatives.

Bennington, located in the southwest corner of Vermont, is bordered to the south by Massachusetts and to the west by New York. It is frequently referred to as the "Gateway to Vermont" or more caustically the "Banana Belt," a reference to the slightly colder temperatures endured 120 miles north in Montpelier, the state capital. Let me assure you there may be a difference of ten or fifteen degrees, but when the temperature goes below zero, who cares? Benningtonians, with great resignation, simply look upon themselves as the "Forgotten County."

A town of 16,000 in 1978, Bennington had experienced much of what the rest of New England had undergone in the 1950s—abandonment by the huge cotton factories in their quest for cheaper, nonunion labor offered by our brethren to the south. (Ironically, those same jobs have fled once again, this time offshore and for the same reason.) And one had to be careful in describing Bennington, as the residents, quick to disparage themselves, were somewhat sensitive as to how others looked on them.

Years earlier, poor Ted Bird, a local businessman running for selectman, while being interviewed by the local daily made the cardinal political blunder of referring to Bennington as a "blue-collar mill town."

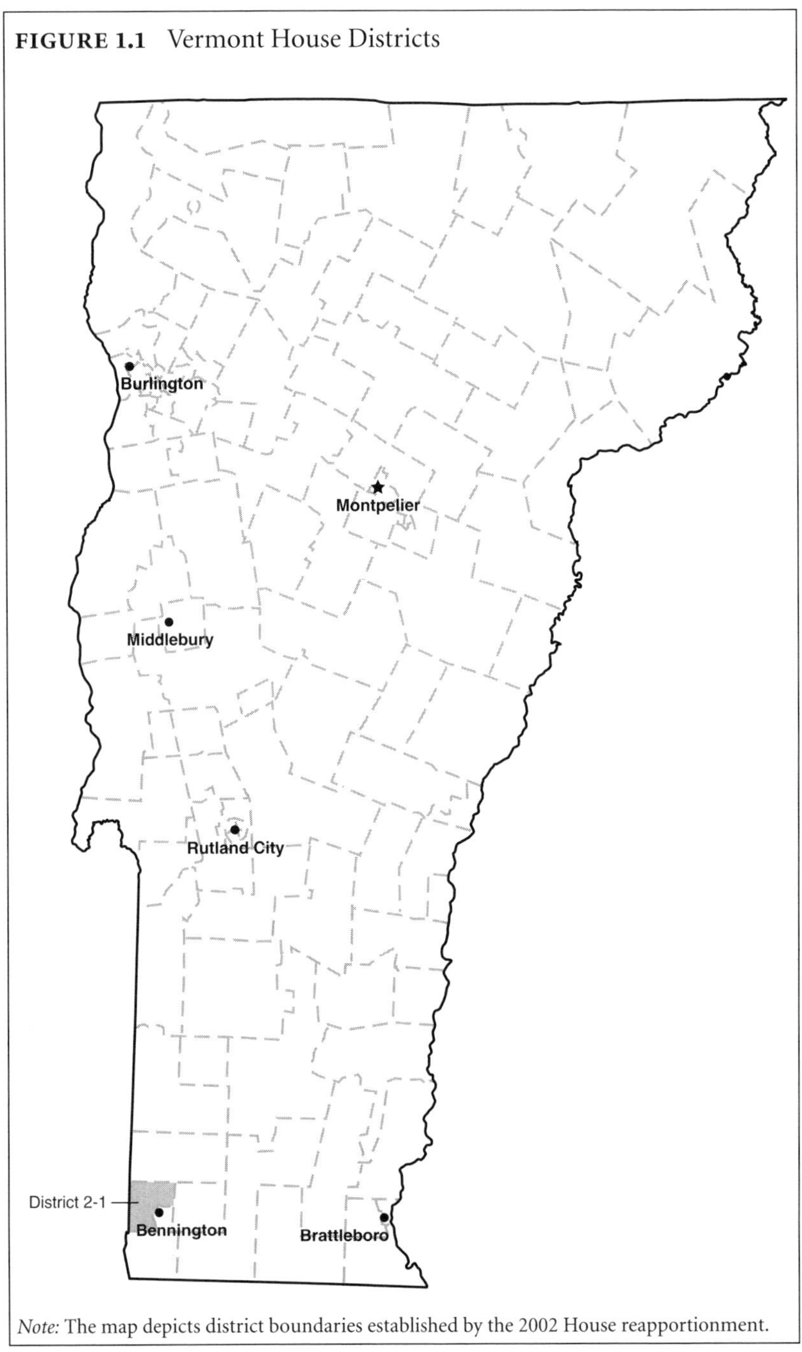

Note: The map depicts district boundaries established by the 2002 House reapportionment.

Several weeks later he was trounced in the election and a year later sold his business and followed the old cotton mills south. I often wondered what happened to Ted—perhaps he, too, is now offshore.

The moral of the story is, if you're running for office, be careful what you say, and perhaps more important, how you say it. It's not like talking to your cronies at a tailgate party.

Being in a two-member district can get complicated. It has its rewards and its drawbacks. An obvious drawback is that it means you have twice as many constituents and, consequently, twice as many doors to knock on. Not an insurmountable problem with eight thousand people, but obviously it takes more work and more organization.

The upside of this is that you may have a running mate. Or at least you'd better hope you have a running mate. I would like to have a dollar for every new candidate who, later when I was recruiting Democratic candidates throughout the state, thought it was a plus to be the only Democrat running in a two-member district. How often I heard, "Well that means, if I'm the only candidate, I get every Democratic vote." Maybe that's true, but unless you're from Boston or Chicago, you're not supposed to vote twice for the same guy. Given this rule and the fact that everyone in a two-member district can vote for two candidates, you don't want to overlook the unwillingness of voters to forgo spending what they have. The presence of another Democrat running on the same ticket (Larry Powers) was to prove invaluable. I'm convinced that Little Joe had the disadvantage; at least I had another Democrat on the ballot to absorb the die-hard Democratic second vote. He ran as the only Republican on the ticket, which meant that voters, if nothing else, had Larry and myself as a second option should they decide that party was not the be-all and end-all of choosing their representatives. But Little Joe and Larry had made the deal, and it was too late to do anything about it. Little Joe would be on his own.

Campaigning in My District

I was lucky. I could literally jog from one end of my district to the other. Don't try this in Texas. The district was only six miles end to end.

Of the eight thousand inhabitants, the number eligible to vote might total but four thousand or so. In a presidential election year, an 80 percent turnout would cause celebration among those trying to keep democracy alive. Off-year elections—and 1978 was an off-year election—are more likely to draw about half that percentage. Sounds like a piece of cake, right? Wrong.

You still have to get yourself organized and work your tail off.

I walked my district nine times—neighborhood after neighborhood, street after street, door after door. And I did it in as organized a manner as was possible. This meant crossing out areas covered and planning, at least a week ahead of time, areas that I intended to cover. And yes, I used the town map.

Part of my strategy was to jump from one section of the district to another, the premise being that the word would begin to circulate that Ralph was everywhere—working hard and leaving no potential voter behind. I found that in six or seven weeks of knocking on thirty or so doors a day, I could fairly well cover the entire district I needed to reach. I maxed out of places to go at about twelve hundred houses.

Of course, there were doors that I chose not to knock on. After the initial campaign I became fairly adroit at knowing where the voters were, thus avoiding some I knew to be rock-ribbed Republicans or just plain "anybody but Ralph" voters. Not knowing whose door you're knocking on can lead to embarrassments. One time I mistakenly knocked on my opponent's door. Amazingly, he politely teased me by promising to consider me for his second vote. Frankly, I was delighted to find him at home while I was out knocking on doors, though it took another three or four doors for the redness in my face to dissipate.

Thomas P. "Tip" O'Neill of Massachusetts, the Democratic Speaker of the U.S. House of Representatives from 1976 to 1986, once wrote a memoir titled *All Politics Is Local.* I offer that it's closer than that—it's a very personal business. Of course, it matters whether you're a candidate in a mega-state such as California, with fifty-five electoral votes, or Vermont, with three. Candidates in California would have to raise hundreds of thousands of dollars to promote themselves via the insatiable demands of television, mailings, and other forms of advertisement to reach a constituency of over a quarter-million souls. A candidate in Vermont could do it for far less in a state with only a little more than 600,000 folks, broken into 150 House districts, which provided at least the opportunity to make personal contact with the majority of the voters.

My good friend Billy Bulger, the former president of the Massachusetts Senate, once remarked after hearing the size of my constituency, "My God! I could take that many to lunch."

Creating a Leaflet

My leaflet changed little over sixteen years and nine campaigns for the legislature. It was a simple, four-by-ten-inch handout printed on heavy paper and with a hole punched at the top.[2] Of course, I changed the photo from time to time, eventually adopting one that included Cathy and our four kids. It was meant to convey the impression, "Here is a politician who has priorities and responsibilities just like everyone else." To send the message that I was a multifaceted lover of all life forms, I prodded O'Callaghan, our recalcitrant golden retriever, with Milk Bones to sit up front looking loyal and well behaved.

I was never sure that the leaflet had much use other than to serve as a reason to be at a door. People, without exception, always politely accepted it—the problem was getting them to keep it long enough to read what I had to say. I was certain, right from the start, that a leaflet with page after page explaining my stand on every conceivable issue would only get "round filed" shortly after I left the door. I was also sure that the abbreviated nature of these door-to-door encounters forced potential supporters to decide instantly whether I passed the first impression test and would get their consideration for future support.

"You gotta make the cut" before you get to play: It was important that I make a good first impression. Thus my presentation, always emitting an air of humility coupled with a neat appearance, was vital.

Few things are simple in a campaign. There still existed the problem of how to figure out a way to remain in a voter's memory long after I was gone. Here I hit on the idea of printing on the back of the leaflet a list of emergency numbers. These included the telephone numbers of the local hospital, the police and fire departments, the poison center, and the local school, and several blank lines labeled "Baby sitter," "Nearest neighbor or relative," and "Work number." At the very bottom were my name and my home phone number. This was all before the advent of the emergency number 911, and it proved to be a useful handout for my constituents. I would joke that they could turn my ugly face and post the leaflet on the refrigerator door. My hope was that, in the days to come, every time someone opened the fridge they would see my name. It must have worked, because in later visits I would see my yellowed leaflet still where they had placed it years earlier.

The front of the leaflet was embarrassingly brief. Below the photograph I simply listed personal information and achievements. The details varied from campaign to campaign, but I typically included such things as my undergraduate education at Boston University (I never mentioned graduate degrees—I didn't want to be looked at as an intellectual); my military service in the U.S. Marine Corps (in case the guys at the VFW thought I might be a sissy); my directorship of the Bennington Program (this was a program for potential high school dropouts that I ran at the high school); and the names of my wife, Cathy, and my children, Rick, Cathy, Sheila, and Suzanne (I hoped that my wife and kids might help me connect). And, I also included this commitment: *"No promises...but a pledge to do my best."* In small print at the very bottom was the name of the union print shop that had printed up the two thousand leaflets. Nowhere did the leaflet say which party I belonged to.

Registering Voters

America is a very mobile society. People come and go. My district must have had at least a 15 percent turnover every two years. Thus I always carried voter registration forms in my daily rounds. There's a good deal of satisfaction in registering a new voter. You get a good feeling that you've got another player in the game. Or at least you've put him or her on the field in uniform. Whether they chose to play, or not, was up to them.

I was always delighted to return to my kitchen table each night with a handful of new voter registrations. The multicopy form allowed me to keep one copy for my records, the others to be turned in to the town clerk's office for addition to the checklist. This afforded me the opportunity to contact the new voters a second time with a brief note informing them that I had seen to it that their names had been added to the checklist. In effect, I was telling them that they had made the team—I only hoped it was my team.

Staying Organized

I was determined to do my best to stay as organized as my disorderly habits would allow. Therefore, each night when I arrived back home, I would meticulously list on three-by-five cards the names of my new registrants, their telephone numbers, and

Besides sporting a new photo, the leaflet for my sixth reelection campaign in 1990 had two minor changes from my first leaflet in 1978— it didn't mention my occupation, and it included the slogan, "Working for Bennington." Not wanting to boast about being Speaker, I let the reader gather it from the photo, which was taken at the House podium. The "Campaign to Re-Elect Ralph G. Wright" amounted to little more than $100, which I paid personally to print the leaflets.

whatever bit of information would help me recall my visit at their door.

To this "vote box" (Cathy called it the "hope box") also were added the names of folks who requested absentee ballots, known friends and acquaintances, "solid" Democrats who frequented political events, colleagues that I taught school with, and more important, those I had met knocking on doors who I felt had sent a signal that they would support me. Deciding on the latter, I caution the reader, is not a science.

Obviously, maintaining my hope box required a good deal of discipline, because it was the last thing I wanted to face after teaching all day and campaigning until eight o'clock or so. But I knew that campaigning was a "contact sport," and the more contacts the better. Thus I arranged for a small group of family and friends to help me with a telephone campaign scheduled the last weekend before election day. This is where the hope box names and phone numbers would be put to use. After nine weeks of campaigning I had accumulated a little over one thousand cards.

I invited the twenty or so supporters to a pizza-and-beer gathering at my house. It took two gatherings to distribute all the cards to those in the group who could identify family or friends whom they would not be embarrassed to call. The calls were to be made from the offices of a friend who owned a large car dealership in town, who allowed me to use his bank of eight or nine phones the weekend before the election. Thus the small platoon of helpers manned the phones for two hours on Friday night from seven o'clock, Saturday from five to nine, all day Sunday, and the Monday night before the polls opened the next day.

I did my best to qualify which cards each of the crew agreed to call. My criteria were, "Don't take anybody you couldn't borrow $50 from or anybody who would turn you down if you asked them to bring their cables and help you jumpstart your car." In other words, they were to pick people they could ask outright to vote for me without getting an embarrassing response or losing a friend.

The purpose of having them all gather at one phone bank, with a specific two-hour block of time, was twofold: First, it created a party atmosphere because they were calling friends who respected them, even loved them, and the responses would not be of a nasty nature. The goal was to have them spend the time hearing positive results. (I worried that had I asked them to make the calls from home, the first time they heard "Ralph Wright? You gotta be kidding. I wouldn't vote for that jerk if he was the only name on the ballot" would turn out to be their last call.) They supported me, but I didn't expect them to lose any friends trying to get me elected.

Second, not only did I ensure that the calls would be made, but I would obtain the first real inkling as to how I was doing. Perhaps it would be too late in the game to do anything about it, but still, it would potentially allow me to rest a little easier, if only for a couple of days.

As I was still knocking on my last few doors, I asked the captain of each group of callers to be sure to have the members of his or her team jot down a brief response from each call. From this I could make a final, if a wee bit smaller, list identifying my strong supporters for election day, when I hoped to assign poll watchers at the two voting locations. I was well aware of the importance of poll watchers, as they could, by six o'clock on election evening, provide the names of supporters who had failed to show up. As Larry and Little Joe had chosen not to have them, I mused over the thought that I had the more sophisticated and thorough campaign strategy. Once again, though, I ran into a road to nowhere; it turned out that no poll watchers were allowed at the polls, at the whim and crankiness of the town clerk. Her simple response was, "I won't have a bunch sitting at my check-in tables pestering the life out of my helpers asking to repeat names and begging for votes. When I say no I mean no, and that's for everybody." I was smart enough not to argue with a town clerk who had been overseeing elections since the 1920s. That's all changed today, as even omnipotent clerks have had to concede that poll watching is part of the process and, within rigid rules of propriety, has to be allowed.

I'll still opt to offer no opinion as to whether Bennington is a blue-collar town, but it did have two Section 8 federal housing communities, referred to rather crassly as the "low-income housing projects." When it came time for me to cover those neighborhoods in my door-to-door efforts I thought I had come upon the lost Garden of Eden. Here was apartment after apartment with no one registered to vote. I was the first politician ever to knock on the inhabitants' doors, and they appeared elated that somebody wanted them for something. It would prove to be but a mirage, as I was to find out down the road.

I must have spent two full weeks covering the same number of homes that I normally would have been able to race through in two nights. I would joyfully trek down to the town clerk and drop my stack of new voter registrations on her counter. Her look of disdain forewarned of what I was to discover two years later when I sat in the clerk's office recording who had voted in the previous election. Of the eighty or ninety I had so laboriously taken the time to register in those projects two years earlier, not ten had actually gone to the polls.

Beyond the satisfaction of bringing a new player into the game, registering someone might be seen as a service provided. I hoped that would translate into a future vote. So I registered folks wherever I found them. I learned something far beyond the mundane knowledge that day-to-day campaigning taught. As stated, indelicately, by a former governor, "If the poor in America voted with the same exuberance as the rich, there would never again be a Republican sitting in the Oval Office."

And that's a pretty good reason why they're so often left behind.

Absentee Ballots

Many states, in their effort to increase turnouts, are doing all they can to make it easier for the voter to cast a ballot prior to election day. Workers, people who will be out of town, and those who just don't want to fight the lines on election day find it a whole lot less hassle to be able to vote at their convenience.

If you were a candidate in Bennington you were wise to learn the value of the absentee ballot early on. Bennington would always raise eyebrows in the state capital with its propensity to register as high as 20 percent absentee votes in a hotly contested election. Absentee votes are like money in the bank, and that makes them different from votes promised to someone at the door. The promise at the door may be sincere, but whether the people actually get out and vote in November is less than guaranteed.

Absentee voters actually vote. If you are a politician who runs across someone who would like you to request that they get an absentee ballot in the mail, make it a point to see that it happens.

For my part, I would have a list of people who had voted absentee in the previous election, and I would know enough at their door to ask if they wanted to vote absentee once again.

Bullet Votes

Asking voters for a "bullet vote" (a vote for only one candidate on a ballot that instructs, "Vote for not more than two") is a risky venture. First, not every voter is a Democratic voter who would break out in hives at the thought of casting a vote for a Republican. (I confess, for the first time publicly, that my first vote, at the age of twenty-one in 1956, was for Ike.) Some lean toward the Democrats but will never fail to argue that they vote for the best person. Many younger voters consider themselves independents who look over a ballot much as a kid looks over his choices at the penny candy counter. Still others arrive at the polls not focused on party at all but on criteria only they and their priest will ever know.

The one thing I'm absolutely sure of is that the last thing people do is throw away a vote. That's why we have attics, cellars, and garages. To a voter behind that curtain, those two votes are a two-for-one. To drive home this point I would ask, when's the last time you ever bought one of something and got one free and refused to take the second? I was certain that throwing away a vote happened as often as washing a rental car. Your supporters most probably will carry out their word and vote for you, but they'll also most likely carry out their God-given right to cast their second ballot. Guess who's going to get that one? So you must have, absolutely have to have, the "sponge"—a running mate.

It may turn out that even with a running mate you opt to go it alone on the campaign trail. A partner's work schedule or family responsibilities may make it impossible to coordinate your campaign hours. Vermont's citizen legislature pays less than $10,000 a year, has a four-month session running from January through April, and thus requires that most legislators have a day job. Some candidates simply prefer to campaign alone. If two candidates of the same party decide to run their own campaigns separately, it is assumed that even though they're not working together on a daily basis one would help the other where he or she could. It is pushing the ethical envelope to request outright that the constituent "bullet-vote" you, or even hint at it. People are innocent and may not see the skullduggery of the request at the moment, but what goes around comes around, and it would be an unusually short and lucky campaign that failed to bring to light what you had been doing. It can, justifiably, get your so-called partner pretty ticked-off.

Raising $$$$$ and Using the Press

I never spent more than $168 on any of my campaigns. In my final campaign, which ended in my only defeat over a sixteen-year political career, I was outspent two hundred to one. I was defeated for a multitude of reasons, but being outspent was not the major one.

It wasn't that I couldn't raise money; I raised tens of thousands of dollars during ten years as Speaker. It was just that I found asking people to open their wallets as distasteful an act as the political world presents. Beyond the ugliness of trolling for dollars there is the absolute certainty that very few people donate to campaigns without expecting something in return. I taught public school, so I wasn't rich. Some close friends tried to push a few dollars into my hand because they liked my issues or they simply wanted to lend a hand. But I always politely thanked them and returned their checks.

I was lucky I happened to live in Vermont, with its small and homey political culture, and that I was in a district that didn't require reaching tens of thousands of voters. We had a local daily newspaper, the *Bennington Banner,* in which I took out a couple of forty-dollar advertisements just before election day.

Our local radio station went off the air at darkness. Radio ads were even cheaper than a one-eighth-page ad in the *Banner.* I remember buying some thirty-second ads that would be played over and over during a three-day period. The problem I found was that thirty seconds is an eternity when you're attempting to voice your stand on an issue without alienating some segment of the community. After great labor, and a shortening of my messages to fifteen seconds, I managed to create five ads. Each was carefully worded so as to avoid getting me in trouble. I did that only in my first campaign because I couldn't shake the feeling of hypocrisy involved in creating messages that said little or nothing. I have since reflected that the real hypocrisy was the fear of risking defeat by daring to state my beliefs. It would prove to be another of those unanticipated crossroads that one comes upon in an election. Regardless, I never bothered with radio ads again.

As far as news interviews went, or press conferences, there were none, other than a brief portrayal of each of the candidates a week or so before election day. Some years the *Banner* issued endorsements and some years not, depending on the editor. In my first campaign it endorsed no candidates.

Pressing the Flesh

My routine was to hit doors when people were likely to be home; there's nothing more frustrating than climbing two flights of stairs, or traversing a long driveway, only to find no one at home. That meant that I would head out around five in the afternoon and not return home until eight-thirty or so. These would be the most bountiful hours because people would be coming home from work and preparing supper. As I never began campaigning until after Labor Day it meant that I could get in three hours or so of door knocking before darkness fell—at least through September. As the days got shorter so did my work hours—and for two good reasons.

First, you can get shot roaming around Vermonters' driveways after dark. I think I was the last guy in Vermont not to have a gun hanging over the fireplace. Second, it's bad politics to be rapping on someone's door after dark, because inevitably the kids have just been wrestled into bed upstairs, and Mom and Dad are luxuriating in their moment of peace. All hell breaks loose when they hear someone at the door. It's not a good way to start a relationship.

Weekends made more time available to canvass, but even here one had to plan carefully. I never went out on Sunday mornings; they were reserved for matters more important than getting into the legislature. And even on Sunday afternoons I trod lightly; next to God, Vermonters love the NFL New England Patriots. Saturdays were my favorite time, especially during the gorgeous days of a New England autumn. Often I'd get seven or eight hours in, meeting neighbors who were raking leaves, sweeping out the garage, or puttering around simply enjoying a glorious Indian summer day.

My routine seldom varied and always had one underlying purpose: Make a contact; if at all possible, a positive contact. It went something like this:

"Hi. I'm Ralph Wright and I'm running for representative here in *our* district. I just wanted to drop by and say hello, and perhaps answer any questions you might have. I know you're busy and I don't want to take up too much of your time, so if you don't mind I'd like to leave with you a little brochure that has my number on it and if I can ever answer any of your questions or be of *help,* please don't hesitate to give me a call at any time."

The response could be one of many:

1. "Hi, Ralph. Must be that time of year again." *Good. Maybe!*
2. "Thank you, I'll keep you in mind." *Hmmn! I wonder what that means?*
3. "No problem. How's the campaign going?" *Good. Hope he votes.*
4. "Are you a Democrat or a Republican?" *Keep ya fingers crossed.*
5. "What's the sense in voting. You guys never get anything done. You're all the same." *Bad. Hope he doesn't vote.*
6. "You didn't have to stop here, Ralph. You know I always vote for you." *Super. Cloning has its points.*
7. Silence. *Bad, bad. Get on your way.*

And the getaway might be, "Well I'll let you get back to what you were doing. Thanks, again. I forget the folks next door. What's their name?"

"That's Jim and Joan Weeks. They should be out back in the yard."

This last response allowed me to go through a neighborhood knowing the next person's name as I approached their door. The problem was that I would inevitably forget it in the twenty steps to the door (another reason to have a partner).

Amazingly, very few people ever asked me about an issue. Whether this was because they didn't want to embarrass me or because I never wanted to embarrass them by asking them what they thought I can't be sure. When I was asked a question, I learned early on—tell the truth. The truth always stays the same—lies require a good memory.

Don't get me wrong. Issues do matter; it's just that they take a while to surface. The longer you serve the more certain it is that what you stand for will bob to the top—catching people's attention. You can perhaps avoid, certainly delay, this public knowledge, if you remain low key or fail to rise up the legislature's pyramid of power. And many legislators are satisfied to do just that. But that was not the case with me.

I might not have sought my first election with illusions of power or advancement, but one didn't have to have a degree in psychiatry to guess that I would not be one to let the legislative world pass me by. I wore my liberal agenda on my sleeve, and though my first campaign amounted to simply getting acquainted with my constituents, later campaigns became more than first impressions, as people in the district became more informed through the press and coffee shop gossip of my voting record and what I stood for. The longer I served, the more enemies I made. I often equated it to being a Marine second lieutenant somewhere in the Pacific in 1943.

One soon realizes politicians aren't like diamonds—they're not forever. This was brought home to me in a later campaign.

Not All Doors Say "Welcome"

In 1988 I had been Speaker of the Vermont House for four years, and during the campaign for reelection was doing my normal thing of going door to door. About halfway through the routine I received a call from an Associated Press reporter asking permission to accompany me on my rounds. Her objective was to write a special story about "a day in the life of a Speaker's campaign." I agreed, and I think she was truly impressed at the reception I received door after door. Actually, I was pretty impressed, myself, with the apparent love my constituents had for their legislator. When I noticed that she was beginning to wonder if she had been set up, I purposely took her into an area that would set the record straight. As we approached the door of a longtime political foe, Dwight Lorenz, I nonchalantly cautioned my guest, "We may not get a very welcome reception here. This guy's to the right of Attila the Hun."

I knocked on the screen door, and we both were startled by the roar of a very large dog. My door-to-door experience kicked in, and I pressed my foot up against the bottom part of the door, though it occurred to me that the beast from whose throat the warning had emanated probably would not have given a second thought to the flimsy protection we now relied on to keep from being eaten. Suddenly the largest Doberman pinscher I had ever seen came racing out of the kitchen and across the dining room. Thankfully, Dwight happened to be on the other end of the leash. Doing his best to control his pet, he beckoned us to enter, "Well, well, if it isn't Ralph Wright. The Speaker himself." With a warped grin he added, "Come in, come in. The dog hasn't eaten all day."

After Dwight had informed both of us of my failings we managed to escape and moved on down the road—she with her story, I with a tad more humility.

Campaigning with a Partner

During my last three campaigns I had as my Democratic district mate a wonderful partner in Dick Pembroke. Though he was a little more conservative than I, we hit it off right away and soon grew to be fast friends. Dick was to prosper in the legislature, later rising to a position of power—chairman of the Transportation Committee in the House.

Dick was easy to campaign with, as he was game for anything. Always willing to use his truck on our daily rounds, he never failed to show up no matter rain, snow, or dark of night. Inevitably, I would have to share the front seat with the ton of munchies that always accompanied him. Dick liked to eat, and he's got to be the only guy I know who actually gained weight during a campaign. He never missed a meal of his own and seldom turned down someone else's. I recall campaigning in one kitchen where Dick actually accepted a pork chop. It happened to be dinnertime, and the couple politely, if only perfunctorily, asked us to sit and join them. Dick, never hesitating, pulled up a chair and sat. They were a little more than surprised. I was shocked and hustled Dick, pork chop in hand, out the door. I insisted he sit in the truck and finish the chop before I would accompany him to the next door. The dog in the next yard got the bone.

Being Lied To

I know this all sounds so routine that you might think one would get bored to death on the campaign trail. But there were days that were testy. Confrontations weren't common by any means, but they happened. Dick and I didn't have the same hot buttons. He was easygoing and nonchalant, but you could touch him off.

Our routine didn't vary much. We had a pretty organized setup in that we shared duties once on the campaign trail. On alternating nights one of us would be in charge of the paperwork, which meant carrying the leaflets, registration forms, and absentee ballot requests on the clipboard. The other's responsibility was taking care of getting to the door. He would be the first out of his truck and up the stairs.

Vermonters never use their front doors. Don't ask me why. It's a historical thing. It was never difficult to decipher which door they used, as there would be myriad clues to lead us to the payload. The obvious door would be that closest to the family vehicle. If there was no vehicle, we'd look for where the kid dumped his bike, and if that wasn't evident, we'd look for the chain that held the two-thousand-pound family pet. Pembroke was great with dogs, and unlike me, he never showed any fear of them. I feared all but aging golden retrievers and as a defense always armed myself with a pocketful of Milk Bones before setting out—bribe money, so to speak.

We exited the truck, me fumbling with the clipboard and Dick nonchalantly pushing himself past the dog and tapping on the door. Because this evening I was in charge of the paperwork, it was my job to inform Dick who lived here, how many in the house, who voted, and how often—all, we hoped, before the door opened. It was important to get good at this, and we did, with each passing election, because this was the vital information that determined whether we would spend seconds or minutes with the person who answered. As it happened, at this particular door I wasn't fast enough and the door swung open. We knew the name—it was on the mailbox—but not whether they voted or not.

"How's it going, Joe?" Dick would be casual when a familiar face opened the door. The eternal optimist, he always thought everyone he met was a long lost friend who couldn't wait to vote for us. His spiel at a door was, to say the least, more abrupt and direct than mine. "It's that time of year again," he'd inform them. And avoiding small talk, he would quickly add, "We're looking for support come November." The leaflets would be almost thrust into Joe's hand through the half-opened screen door.

"Hey, no problem in this house. You guys always get my vote. Wife, too. Don't vote, don't complain. That's what I always say."

Still desperately fumbling through the checklist, I hadn't said a word.

"OK. We'll be on our way. See you at the polls down at St. Francis Parish Hall."

I had climbed back into the truck and Dick was backing down the driveway headed for the next house down the road when I finally realized that Joe's name wasn't on my checklist. I hesitated saying anything, as we were pulling into the next driveway, and besides I was certain Joe was a voter and what he had told us was money in the bank. Perhaps I was just confused, and his name was somewhere else on the checklist. But something piqued my curiosity and I asked, "Isn't Joe's last name Morgan?"

"Yeah! Why?"

"Well there isn't any Joe Morgan on this list."

"He's got to be there, somewhere."

"Not."

"Look again. You heard him. He's a big supporter, and he votes. He's gotta be there somewhere."

"Look, I'm telling you. The bum's not on here. He's conned us. He probably never voted in his life. Ya live and learn, Dick." I chuckled. That was the end of it as far as I was concerned, but not for Pembroke. He had certain principles he wouldn't compromise, and not being "taken" was one of them. He reacted like a man whose wallet had just been lifted.

Pembroke threw the truck in reverse and spun out of the driveway. Before I could get any more out of my mouth than "Where are we going?" we were in the driveway we had just left, and he was out of the truck. Pembroke is a giant of a man who, at six feet six, towered over me. I usually didn't worry about his temper because I had never known him as anything but a big, pleasant puppy dog. But now I was worried, as he pounded extra hard on the door and stood red-faced, awaiting Joe's arrival at the door. "Uh-oh!" I thought.

"Hi, again. You forget something?" Joe, our leaflet still in hand, had no idea that his small sin had struck my running mate with such force.

"No, I didn't forget anything, but you apparently forgot to tell us you're not registered. You or your wife. Neither on our checklist. You can't vote if you're not on the damn checklist."

"Well, it must be some mistake. I know I'm registered. Can I see that?" He was pointing to Dick's leaflets, verifying that he didn't know a checklist from his Adam's apple. Pembroke's face turned another shade of red.

"Never mind; it's a mistake," Pembroke huffed. "Mary isn't the one who made it." He was now referring to Mary Hodeck, the superefficient and revered Bennington town clerk. "Mary would have had you on the checklist if you had registered. You're not registered and you couldn't have voted for anyone, let alone us."

"Well, where can I register?" he stammered.

"It's too late. New registrations are closed." The deadline for registering, usually about three weeks before election day, had in fact come and gone.

With that he snatched the leaflet from Joe's hand and stormed back to the truck. I wasn't sure that this was the time to say anything, so I just shut up.

Pembroke's only response was, "The guy's a liar. He lied to us."

Ya can't win 'em all.

Election Day

So off I went. Night after night—weekend after weekend. There were times when, after teaching five classes during the day, I would have to fight the urge to take a night off. But the fear of losing because I hadn't done all I could managed to overcome both my fatigue and that dreaded aloneness that hovered menacingly over the eight-week campaign. This was my first effort to enter the State House, and there were times I swore I'd never undertake it again.

The first Tuesday following the first Monday in November dawned cold and blustery. The polls weren't scheduled to open until seven in the morning, but I was up and ready to go at five. Of course the whole town was still fast asleep when I entered Dunkin' Donuts for coffee and perhaps some last-minute campaigning. This idea was quickly discouraged when I found that, except for a tired over-the-road truck driver drinking coffee at the counter, I was the only one there. I ordered coffee to go and retreated back home to my warm kitchen table—alone with my thoughts and anxiety.

Standing at the polls is a political ritual that probably has little merit. Perhaps politicians do it simply because the other guys are going to do it, and you don't want them to have the edge, no matter how nebulous that may appear. I certainly don't think it ever won a single vote. Voters come to the polls pretty much knowing what they are going to do. Some half-frozen candidate may conjure up sympathy, but I don't think pity ever translated into many votes.

The day dragged and I thought it would never end. I don't believe I had ever been colder in my life. But I must tell you that I don't think there are many experiences to equal in pride and "sense of America" the amazing scene of watching thousands of Americans going to the polls. It made real all that Miss Cheney, my seventh-grade civics teacher, had tried to unveil to me so many years earlier. It still sends chills up my spine as I reflect back on that day. I remember thinking, "Democracy works." I also remember thinking, "Pray, Lord, it works for me."

All the candidates crowded as close to the main entrance as was possible—often, in their anxiety to be seen, blocking easy access for the voters.

From time to time a poll worker would ask us to move out of the way of the folks trying to enter. The embarrassment, brought on by desperate eagerness to push one last leaflet into a hand, smile one final time, and leave one last impression, made asking and groveling appear synonymous to me.

But more frustrating was trying to decipher how I was doing. Time after time I would flush with joy as obvious supporters smiled or shook my hand on the way in to the polling booth to determine my fate. As my opponents chose to stay but an hour or so, I only passively felt sorry for the other candidates running for various local offices who experienced the sense of aloneness of being unnoticed. As voters exited through the same door they entered through, I was just as eager to try to catch their eye. This was even more encouraging. I was certain from the smiles, waves, and thumbs up that poor Joe and Larry were about to be the first candidates ever to be shut out in an election.

I won that day, but I sure didn't throw a shutout. Of the three of us, I finished first with 836 votes. Larry came in second with 791 votes. Poor Joe, the dean of the Vermont House, finished back in the pack with 704. I'm convinced that had Little Joe made the effort to get any semblance of a Republican running mate to siphon off those second rigid Republican votes, he'd still be in the House.

A political career had come to an end.

Another had just begun.

Notes

1. Checklists can be obtained at one's town or city hall. There usually is a charge to purchase, but public access is granted at no charge.

2. The hole punched in the card was so I could avoid having to cram it in the door that went unanswered. Before leaving the house each evening, I would make up a couple of dozen that had rubber bands looped through the hole. That made it easy to hang one on the doorknob. The last thing you want is to have your leaflet blowing about the backyard when the residents come home and open the door. I would write on these, "Sorry I missed you when I dropped by. Ralph"

2

Life in the Legislature

The Learning Curve

I DIDN'T GO to the legislature with any notion of rising to a level of leadership or power. It never occurred to me that someday I would be Speaker. Just getting elected was such a high that I gave little thought to what I might do there, and I was more than content to serve on any committee the Speaker assigned me to. Besides, my freshman naiveté led to an amusing ambivalence when it came to my first impressions of the importance of the Speaker.

The Speaker, to me, was simply a traffic cop, a person at the podium who had the rather uninteresting task of presiding over our deliberations. Though he occasionally had visitors, he was a lonely sort of figure, the only member isolated by post and obligations high above the well of the House where members sat. The rest of us legislators were at liberty to wander wherever we desired, enjoying the luxury of visiting with our seatmate when bored or getting up and leaving when we had something better to do. The Speaker, in contrast, appeared chained to his post. In addition, I began to realize that the title of "Speaker" was a misnomer. Speakers never spoke. They "chanted" in that fast staccato that makes it all but incomprehensible to the uninformed onlookers sitting in the galleries. No ad-libbing and no interjecting of their own opinions. More than once I felt I was attending Mass, listening to Father.

When I first took my seat I had no conception of the power amassed above and to the right of where I sat. Years later, when I personally would be doing the "chanting," I came to realize that this was the very heart and

26

soul of all that occurred in the building. It was the traffic control center for a busy international airport. Nothing could take off or land without at least the knowledge and often the OK from the controlling officer.

And there were stringent rules. The Vermont legislature used Mason's Rules (akin to Robert's Rules of Order) as its guide to maintaining order and controlling debate.[1] Mason's Rules weren't complicated, but they were extensive, and a Speaker had to know the rules well if he wanted to avoid chaos in often heated debate. He also had to be quick on his feet concerning procedure or run the risk of appearing confused, or worse, inept. I wouldn't understand either the complexity or the difficulty of all that until later.

For now I was content to believe that as a legislative member from Bennington, occupant of seat 23, I was an equal partner in that great American experiment—democracy.

Getting to Committee

Every member of the House serves on a single committee. The Senate, with but thirty members, assigns each to at least two committees, and the responsibility of committee assignment in the Senate rests in the hands of the lieutenant governor, the elected president pro tempore, and a third member chosen by the first two. The House rules give a single individual, the Speaker, total license to assign and reassign all members. It's a prerogative of great power and is perhaps the Speaker's greatest weapon in his vast arsenal of authority.

In our "newcomers" packet we had been given a form asking us to list our first three committee choices. The form was accompanied by a note from the Speaker informing us that he would do all he could to satisfy one of those choices. I remember writing, "Put me anywhere you think I might be of some help." I learned, later, that that was a very risky—some said idiotic—thing to do because it invited the Speaker to take advantage of my naive nonchalance and put me where no one else wanted to go. I was also to learn later just how tough a job committee assignment is for the Speaker to perform; it is impossible to please all 149 members. My carelessness was an opportunity that, fortunately, the Speaker, Timothy O'Connor, D-Brattleboro, didn't take advantage of. And, though I wasn't privy to the behind-the-scenes complaining, I was aware that a lot of members were unhappy with their assignments.

As a public school teacher I felt that the Education Committee would be the natural place for me, but the Speaker, as he explained later, felt that I would become exasperated sitting with ten other members whose last educational experience was as a student. So I had the good luck of being assigned to the Health and Welfare Committee, chaired by Edgar May who, unbeknownst to me, had made a personal request that I be assigned to his committee.

Life on a Committee

It turned out to be the best thing that could possibly have happened to me. Each day, each hour, with Chairman May I felt I was in a classroom with a dynamic professor. It was a whole new world. The committee received bills dealing with children, the poor, the elderly, the mentally disabled, and health issues. In other words, we dealt with all the people and programs about which I cared the most. The new language and jargon often escaped my comprehension, and I struggled in the beginning trying to keep up. But it wasn't long before I became adept enough to join in the debate. With this came additional responsibility, as May believed in "inclusion." When you were ready to play he saw to it that you were in the lineup. It was to be a great and enriching four years.

A New Frontier Democrat, Edgar May had worked with Sargent Shriver in the Kennedy administration, sometimes hobnobbing with the Kennedy clan. Earlier in his career as a journalist, May had won the Pulitzer Prize and eventually, for reasons I never asked, had found his way to Vermont and then to the legislature. He was an amazing guy, who proved the perfect model and teacher for me. Moreover, he was also half of a remarkable brother-and-sister act; his sister Madeleine Kunin became Vermont's first female governor in 1985, the year I became Speaker.

Here was one smart guy—not just intellectually but street-smart as well. He never liked to admit that he, like most chairpersons, always had two agendas. I never questioned his commitment to the right causes, nor did it ever bother me that May was a master at manipulating people—OK, using people. "Used" was exactly what I wanted to be.

Everyone on the committee felt the May magic. The committee was always under Edgar's control, and he would find a way to obtain consensus. If we showed initiative and interest, he would give us encouragement and all the free rein we wanted. I learned a ton about the nuts and bolts of the process during this period, which proved to be a valuable foundation for the future. Marking up bills, referencing them to the present statute, amending them, totally rewriting them (called "strike-alls"), became second nature. The give-and-take in committee could get heavy at times, but Edgar always maneuvered to keep us working together to produce a bill and eventually move it on out of committee to its next station along the road to passage. Bringing people with divergent views into harmony for a common cause was not an impossible task, especially in a committee filled with people who were committed and, not incidentally, as devoted to the chair as I was, but it took a special talent.

Each member, over time, took on his or her special role in the group of eleven that made up the committee. Mine was to report bills out onto the floor and, when the occasion called for it, to play the role of "bad cop." Of course, Edgar got the choice role—"good cop."

In addition, his showman's attitude made it seem that we were center stage as each bill was brought up and the whole world was watching. My memories of the small committee room are of people crammed into every conceivable corner waiting to testify—often with their nervousness showing in their sweat-stained garb.

As bills were assigned to our committee by the Speaker, May would go around the conference table in the tiny committee room asking each of us to prioritize the myriad bills gathering on the bulletin board. The bills would cover a gamut from so-called housekeeping bills (making minor changes in present law) to potentially explosive measures such as ones dealing with abortion or sterilization of the mentally disabled. The latter would necessitate not only a good deal more caution and time but also closed-door meetings between Edgar and the Speaker that few of us were ever privy to.

Once prioritized, a weekly schedule would be drawn up that pinpointed the time and amount of discussion the committee would devote to each bill (perhaps half a day) and scheduling testimony for and against by those we felt were affected by it. These would include the sponsor of the bill, by necessity a fellow House or Senate member, as Vermont has no avenue for a citizen to introduce a bill; lobbyists for and against; the governor's staff—they always wanted to let us know what the executive branch felt about any proposed change to law; and finally any outside interest group or citizen that wanted to testify.

Housekeeping bills would be whisked through with only a commissioner or department head giving us his or her thoughts as to changes or additions. More controversial bills could be debated over weeks or months; the committee might hedge by bringing the proposal up, postponing action (called "laying on the table"), and bringing it back up before taking a straw vote (an unofficial and nonbinding vote) to read the feelings of the eleven members.

For a bill to emerge from the committee would most often require a majority vote; 11–0 was what May always strove for, but 10–1, 9–2, even 8–3 votes were enough to warrant passage from the committee to the floor. If a bill went forth with a 7–4, or worse still a 6–5, majority it signaled a precarious future on the floor because it would be recognized by the full membership as controversial. A committee did have the option to send a bill out when the committee had voted against it, but such an "adverse" vote almost always augured failure.

Chairman May absolutely refused to allow adverse votes out of the committee. If he couldn't persuade, finesse, or cajole a positive vote out of us, he always found a way to table the bill.

Committees are a trusted entity in any legislature, and because it is the committee that gives birth to a bill it is vital that the reporter—the member designated by the chairman to report the bill out—not try to cut corners or, worse, deceive or dupe the members on the floor. When the rest of us are hearing a bill and its import for the first time, the reporter is expected to be articulate, forthright with the pros and cons, and preferably as brief as possible. If a bill is only one page long, most members will take the time to read it prior to the committee report on the floor.

I reported my share of bills on the floor, and I always made an effort to be as knowledgeable as I could. This meant not just being well versed on the bill itself but making every effort to anticipate questions from other members, as well as deciphering who those members might be and their agendas. But there were a small number of members who were lazy and often totally unprepared when they stood up to report a bill. They invariably ran into trouble during interrogation and often had to be rescued, usually by their chair or another member of the committee. I recall a few who bragged that they never read a bill.

Danny DeBonis, D-Poultney, who sat to my left in seat 131 during my second term, didn't brag but never failed to chuck the daily pile of bills delivered to our desk each morning into a recycling box off to the side of the aisle. At first I didn't know what to make of this veteran with the blasé attitude. When the occasion arose that he had to report a bill or get involved in debate, he would ask me to tell him what the bill said. We were seatmates for the better part of a year before I realized that Danny, a third-generation Vermont farmer, couldn't read, at least not very well.[2]

Bills of considerable length took a more dedicated sort to drag through page after page. Most members are loath to do this, and thus it is in consideration of the lengthy bills that being able to trust in the reporter to highlight the significant points is most appreciated.

No matter the length or complexity of a bill, the first thing a member would look for would be the last line—how the committee voted. This was the clue that uninformed members would use as their starting point to determine whether they would support the bill or not. A trusted reporter, supported by a unanimous vote by a trusted committee, was a signal that all was OK. Should a member have some problem with a specific bill, he or she was wise to search out the member who may have voted against it in committee. Delivering information in this person-to-person manner was within the unwritten code of conduct, and it happened often. What wasn't accepted was for members of a reporting committee to stand on the floor and oppose their committee openly. That was a transgression that was not soon forgotten.

Several years later, while Speaker, I was surprised to hear John Murphy, D-Ludlow, chairman of the General and Military Affairs Committee, after reporting an innocuous bill on the floor, end his brief summary by informing the members that his committee had voted 9–2 in favor of its passage. I had to interject and remind him from the podium that the General and Military Affairs Committee only had nine members. Murphy may have been a little confused, but I wasn't, because I had appointed those nine people to his committee.

Murphy, being Murphy, stood at his desk looking befuddled and apparently wondering what happened to the two members of his committee that never existed. Finally he looked up at me, staring down on him from the podium with a look that said, "Well, Mr. Murphy, how are you going to get out of this?" And then in a most humble tone, he said, "You're right, Mr. Speaker. I stand corrected as the vote was 7–2." He paused and then went on, "But Mr. Speaker, if I may?"

Smiling, I queried, "Yes, member from Ludlow."

"If I had had eleven members on my committee, my guess is it would have been 9–2."

Though we dealt with all levels of bills, the committee, under the steady tutelage of Chairman May, seemed to be successful in passing bills out of committee, through the House, and on to the Senate. It helped that Edgar was respected by Democratic Speaker O'Connor and was given great discretion. And though I was hardly aware of the Senate, as they seemed a rather stuffy and far-off body in those days (they would remain stuffy but much too close when I became Speaker), I was cognizant of Edgar's ability to schmooze with them, whether in the hallways and cafeteria or at small dinner parties that he would have from time to time. I was never invited to these, but it never bothered me because I believed he was entitled to his private life and I to mine.

My first two years in the legislature flew by. I couldn't imagine wanting to be anyplace else. The Health and Welfare Committee was the center of my universe, and I never longed to be on any of the lesser planets. Even a new Speaker drew only the faintest interest from me.

The Changing of the Guard

One learns early in the legislative life that people come and go but the system goes on. There's no place like a legislature. I say this with admiration in the sense that if continuity is the essence of life, then the legislature is eternal. Personalities may color the General Assembly with different tints, but we're all just passing through. It's the process that is forever. The historic parameters of conduct and process allow us to continue to move forward in our efforts to provide for our people. The history also helps explain why we are so reluctant to change our country's Constitution.

By the end of my first term Speaker O'Connor had decided to venture out in the world of statewide politics. His decision to run for the Democratic nomination for governor, after serving as the longest-reigning Speaker in state history (six years), proved ill-fated. O'Connor was a great guy to work for—an opinion shared by members on both sides of the aisle—but he was an eclectic sort. As a politician, he was of a conservative bent, and his agenda (though some argued he had none) alienated no one. What he did have was the endearing quality of not taking himself, or politics, too seriously. Consequently his campaign for governor had the air of casualness that inevitably spelled disaster. He was defeated in the Democratic primary in 1980, returned home to practice law, and was never to enter politics again. That was it—another political career ended. It all seemed so heartless—to serve so long and then to have a single defeat appear to bring on a pox that made one all but an outcast. But, as I related earlier, like buses leaving a Greyhound depot, people come and go, and the rest of us that remained went on with our legislative lives.

And so it was during my second term; the beat went on. I had, as an incumbent, won reelection with some ease, and I returned for my second term feeling very much like a seasoned veteran. Things were changing, but I was slow to recognize what the impact was to be on my life in the legislature.

Our new Speaker, Stephen Morse, a young Republican from Newfane, was sworn in on the first day of the session in 1981. His election was no surprise. The Republicans had a comfortable majority of 85 seats, to 64 Democrats and 1 independent. Though O'Connor had managed to do what no other Democrat in the history of the Vermont legislature had ever done—be elected as a minority candidate—the Republicans, this time around, were not going to take any chances, and they chose one of their own to lead them.

Morse had risen quickly, first to be majority whip after just his second term and then to the speakership at the beginning of his third. He was handsome, thirtyish, and from a small, picturesque town in the southern part of the state. I didn't vote for him, but I remember he won by a much larger margin than his majority. A large number of Democrats obviously had crossed over to be with the winner; their rewards soon followed. (I made a mental note of this ultimate in bipartisanship.) I don't regret having voted against Morse, but I do have some misgivings about telling him that I was going to vote for his Democratic opponent, Norrie Hoyt, D-Norwich. It was the honest answer but perhaps not the most politically adroit one.

I was still naive enough to assume that my vote was mine to do with as I saw fit—not a reasonable conclusion in the Speaker's mind. I was to discover that a vote against the Speaker too often becomes thought of as a political stab to the heart. The personal affront that it represents at times may be forgiven, but in the political world it is seldom forgotten.

Still, I was somewhat surprised when Edgar informed me that though Speaker Morse had followed O'Connor's custom of discussing with him the Health and Welfare Committee membership for the next two years, he had had to "fight" (Edgar's word) to see to it that I remained on the committee. I know now that this should have served as a dire warning that things were not going to be the same—a shot across the bow, if you will—but I still clung to the naive notion that I was elected by the same number of folks as everyone else, and that made me an equal with just a different job.

We all got used to the new Speaker. Morse settled into his new role with facility as he rode the crest of acceptance that a new Speaker generally experiences. Everyone was paying deference to the newly crowned king. Bipartisanship was rampant.

This Speaker was no single-vote winner. Accompanying his victory was the reelection of Gov. Dick Snelling, not only of the same party as Morse but a father figure who several years later was to administer the vows of marriage to Steve and his new bride. This tandem, coupled with an overwhelming Republican majority in the House and Senate, placed the Speaker in the enviable position of a two-thousand-pound gorilla. He could, as the Republican chieftain, do anything he pleased.

Meanwhile, in the Health and Welfare Committee, we kept pumping out "dopey-do-gooder" bills. They weren't moving as fast, or as far, as I remembered in my first term, but that change was expected. I didn't yet have a broad agenda—my agenda was Edgar's agenda—and I felt little responsibility for any bill once it left the committee and passed on the floor. The rest, it seemed to me, was always the chairman's responsibility. What wasn't anticipated was the diminishment of Chairman May's enthusiasm and forbearance. One had to look closely, but it was noticeable. He just didn't seem to be as happy a warrior as in the past. His liberal agenda was being stifled by a much more aggressive Speaker who, unlike Speaker O'Connor, exerted his authority. Edgar no longer had access to the vortex of power that was the Speaker's office.

During those second two years the committee spent less time on committee work, and I spent more time doing constituency work. Representatives can pretty much determine on their own how busy they want to be responding to the folks back home. I knew members who did next to nothing in the way of responding to constituents asking for help back in their districts. Not surprisingly, their tenure usually was brief. But I was not one of them. What attention members paid in reaching out to serve their constituents' requests for assistance in matters large and small depended on their willingness to get in the trenches and do the work necessary. Vermont provides no funds for staff, nor expenses for phone or stationery. So I made my calls often after waiting in line for an available phone, and I wrote my own correspondence in longhand.

The Citizen Legislature

A whole lot of other states rush to lay claim to the humble title of "citizen legislature," but only a few can truly claim it. Vermont is one.

The 150 members of the House and the 30 members of the Senate have no staff—only the Speaker and the Senate president pro tem have a secretary, that is, a secretary who answers the phone, files, types, and keeps a schedule, not a "secretary" who serves as a political servant. The rest of the members have the availability of the Legislative Council.

The council has a staff of fifteen or twenty clerical workers who will service members' requests for typing mail concerning official state business, general legislative copying, and other matters relating to a legislator's duties. There is a hard-and-fast rule that prohibits them from performing personal or business matters for the members. This means that legislators make their own calls and write their own constituency mail. They have access to a WATS line for calls directly connected to legislative matters, though this unwritten rule was often breached. As there were only three of these lines available, one was often required to stand in line and wait his or her turn. Legislators paid for their official business outside the statehouse. Stationery was provided, but it was limited. And woe to those who used official stationery for personal or business purposes, campaign mailings included.

In addition, the council has a battery of fifteen lawyers whose main duty is to assist members, on a first come, first served basis, in drafting bills. You want to introduce a bill to make all red lights purple. No sweat! Without question, they'll transform it from everyday jargon to legalese in a jiffy. (What they say about you after hours, over a beer, I can only imagine.) They also will do research in the law and be of any general help within their time restraints and expertise. They are bipartisan and are so conscious of being perceived that way that it took me years, through numerous personal discussions—sometimes over bills and sometimes over drinks—to figure out who in the council was liberal leaning and who was of a conservative bent. They hid their political persuasions well. And whatever a member asked them to do, he or she could be well assured, would be kept confidential.

Of course, they weren't stupid. They knew which legislators were members of the power structure and which were not. They also were aware that among the Speaker's duties was setting *their* budget for entry into the Appropriations Bill, their pay included, an advantage if you were

FIGURE 2.1 Vermont General Assembly Salary for Members, 1967–1997

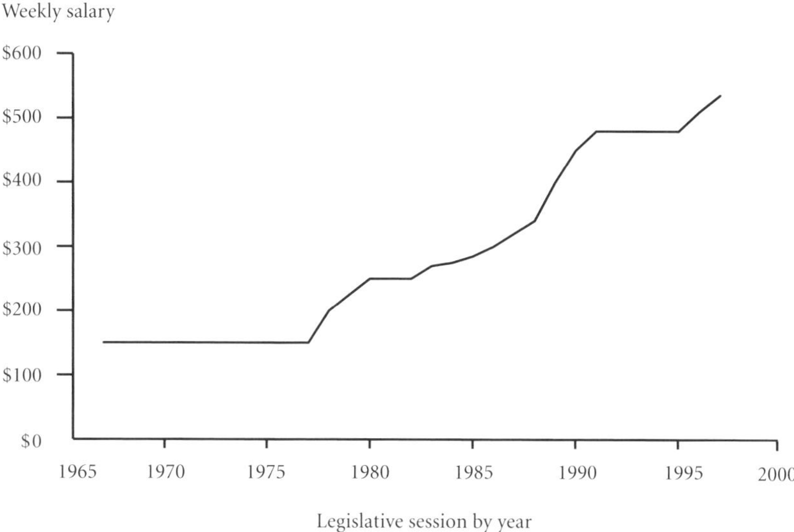

the Speaker, but because of their fairness not necessarily a disadvantage if you were only a member.

Remuneration

If you were one of the idle rich the pay didn't matter, but for most members of the legislature it was a financial hardship to serve. When I entered the legislature in 1978 the pay was $200 per week. When I left in 1994 it had risen, after a good deal of hard work and political heat, to $480 per week (Figure 2.1). Automobile mileage was paid for commuters who traveled back and forth each day, and mileage for one round trip a week was paid for those who lived too far away to commute daily. The noncommuters (those of us who stayed in the capital Tuesday through Thursday night) also received a per diem of $84 that covered meals and a hotel room. Members often took advantage of this latter sum by renting an apartment for two or three to share, thereby saving a few dollars each week. The

Speaker got a little more—$57 each week and a lump sum of $9,172 in addition to the weekly salary—as he was expected to be available during the eight months a year that the House is not in session.

The leader of the Senate, the president pro tem, for some unknown reason received the $57 while in session but no extra stipend for out-of-session responsibilities. As the annual session only lasted about sixteen weeks, from January to the first of May, most people had a "day job." (Sessions have grown progressively longer as the years have gone by, required for managing ever-increasing budgets and ever-increasing demands for services.)

As for office space, we had none, other than our cramped seat at the committee room conference table and our desks, with a small shelf beneath, on the floor of the House—no file cabinet and no privacy. When the two-year session ended we were required to pack everything up and take it home in anticipation of some of us not returning.

This sparse legislative life earned us the satisfaction of calling ourselves a citizen legislature. But it also placed us at a distinct disadvantage in the system of checks and balances.

Drawbacks to the Citizen Legislature

We could never compete with the executive branch. The governor, with a full-time staff of perhaps fifty commissioners, department heads, personal staff, and the inevitable handful of political gurus (to say nothing of the 7,500 state employees), always had the edge. They were all on the job fifty-two weeks a year, and even the lowest-paid clerk made more than a legislator. (A more humbling statistic is that when I became Speaker my secretary always took home a bigger paycheck than I did.) In addition, being well aware who signed their paycheck, they usually worked as a team. That the legislative branch ever came out on top on any issue opposed by the executive branch still amazes me.

Governors are elected by all the people and consequently are looked upon as "our" governor—"our" being the entire population of the state. We only have one. Governors hold weekly news conferences, and statewide newspapers and television and radio stations faithfully record every word

I worked with many exceptional people in the legislature. Let me introduce the most important players in friendship and collaboration (about whom you will read more in the following pages). Pictured here in the governor's ceremonial office are "my lieutenants" (from left to right): Rep. Paul Poirier (D-Barre City), myself, John Murphy (D-Ludlow), and Tim Corcoran (D-Bennington). In Vermont, the Speaker serves as acting governor when the governor and lieutenant governor are out of the state. To the horror of her staff, we gathered in Madeleine Kunin's office on one such occasion.

they utter. Statewide name recognition is a given, even for the modest personality who might hold the title, and whether one voted for the incumbent chief executive or not, he or she is recognizable and important.

Legislators, in contrast, are elected by a tiny segment of the population and seldom are recognized by name or sight beyond their district. With 180 of us, who could keep track? Even as a long-serving Speaker I could travel to the most remote corners of the state and usually not be recognized. Governors traveled in four-door Lincolns driven by burly guys who were armed. A state trooper was always assigned to be by the governor's side. If he traveled overnight on business or vacation, several would be assigned.[3] Legislators carpooled to make a few extra dollars on the mileage expenses and took turns driving. How many were armed I don't know.

Add to all these advantages the pomp and ceremony that followed a governor wherever he or she traveled, and certainly in any squabble the governor had a distinct edge over what amounted to a gang of unknowns in the legislature.

Obviously, the easiest, if not the only, route to success was for the legislature to find a way to get on the same page as the governor. This was less painful if the majorities in the legislature were of the same party as the governor, but even that stroke of electoral luck didn't always guarantee success: A majority sometimes can be too much of a good thing when the bravado that comes with an expanded majority brings on the infighting that eventually divides.[4]

Combine all these factors with the divisions between House and Senate, majority and minority, conservative and liberal, and one begins to make sense of what Mary Evelti, D-Burlington, once told me:

"You know Ralph, I had eight children, not one an easy pregnancy, and none was as long or painful a route as this darn bill has taken."

Notes

1. These were written by Paul Mason, a clerk in the California Assembly in the 1930s. Most of the states use Mason's, as Robert's rules are geared for smaller groups such as PTAs or town governments, whereas Mason's are specifically for larger groups such as state legislatures. The system has been adopted by the National Association of State Legislators.

2. Danny was a veteran legislator who was very much a part of the in-crowd that hung with the Speaker and his cohorts. He was a good man who always appeared to have another agenda beyond the legislature. Very proud and at times sullen, Danny was found dead from a gunshot wound in his cornfield in 1987. It was ruled an accident.

3. The driver is a state trooper. There is no governor's residence or mansion in Vermont, but the new office, built in 1989, does have a pull-out couch for winter nights that might find him or her snowbound.

4. In 1993 the Democrats in the House had the first comfortable majority since before the Civil War—eighty-six members. Almost immediately internal war broke out. Liberals wanted to do everything; moderates wanted to do a little; conservatives wanted to do nothing.

3

The Committee Process

Learning the System

THE REAL GUT work in any legislature is done in the committee. It is here that the amazing web of law ebbs and flows until (one prays) it makes its way out onto the floor for general debate. One hopes that it has stood up to changes and additions and can withstand the onslaught of criticism that is almost guaranteed to come.

Moving a Bill

Bills are assigned by the Speaker to the appropriate committee, and the committee as a whole decides what its priorities will be as to taking action. It is also within the committee's prerogatives not to take action, simply to refuse even to bring a bill up for discussion—and thereby effectively kill it. To *move* or *kill* a bill requires a good deal of give-and-take on the part of each committee member and not a little political adroitness. The chair usually will reserve the right to have final say as to which bills move and which bills die. The only authority above the chairperson is the Speaker of the House, and he will have made his priorities known prior to any committee discussion.

Once it is decided that a bill is to be moved, witnesses for or against it will be notified by the committee clerk (a voluntary position filled by a member of the committee) to appear at a certain time and date to testify. Witnesses can often be long-winded, and there were lots of times that I felt I had heard more than I ever wanted to know about a particular sub-ject. This is where a member hopes that the chairperson is highly orga-nized and adheres to a schedule. Edgar May was a champ at this. The next committee chairman that I was assigned, John Murphy, wasn't.

After perhaps hours of testimony and a score of witnesses, or simply after we'd heard all we wanted to know, the bill would be voted on and, if a majority was in favor, passed on to its next stop—to the floor or to an-other committee. If it cost money or affected taxes, it would, by rule, have to be sent to the Appropriations Committee or the Ways and Means Committee, respectively.

As I've already mentioned, a bill that had no majority wasn't a good bet, and often the chair would just end its life by keeping it in committee. Chairman Murphy would signal the fate of these nonsurvivors by simply tacking the three-by-five card bearing the title of the bill face-first to the "bill board," thereby leaving any interested party to guess about its disap-pearance.

Occasionally there were bills that the committee may not have liked but that the larger body wanted on the floor. In this case the committee would have the unenviable chore of voting it out "adversely." A bill ac-companied by an adverse vote faced the predicament of trying to make it on the floor without the endorsement of the very committee that knew it best. This was like your mother telling the judge that you've always been a rotten kid.

A bill hung up in committee has one last and desperate avenue to reach the floor, but it is seldom used. Any member can rise on the floor and ask the body to relieve a committee of a bill. This is called *pulling a bill.* The request will be met with an explosion of resistance; it is considered an af-front to the sanctity of the committee chair's authority to decide which bills move and which don't. In my sixteen years in the House I witnessed this act of what is considered treason only once. A liberal Democratic group of rebellious members succeeded in getting a bill out on the floor, but I, then Speaker, moved quickly to call a recess and ask my Democrats to gather in the caucus room, where I explained in a somewhat angry tone that if they began this process of usurping a committee's authority, it would soon become a weapon of the Republicans to pull bills that we all agreed shouldn't see the light of day. Here I was talking about the handful of abortion restriction and parental notification bills that these same liberals were grateful were assigned to a decidedly pro-choice Health and Welfare Committee. The caucus finally agreed that it was, in fact, a dangerous precedent, returned to the floor, and overturned the vote. The bill in question was returned to committee and died there, but the animosity that the attempt aroused lingered for months.

Committees and Levels of Prestige

The Vermont House had fourteen standing committees. Speaker Stephen Morse added a fifteenth—Energy—but that really served as a dumping ground for recalcitrant members. Within two years (and with a new Speaker) it disappeared as a standing committee and was amalgamated into the new Natural Resources and Energy Committee.

Committees can be rated from "most prestigious" to "least desirable," and it doesn't take the newly elected very long to know the difference. All committees have eleven members assigned to them, with the exception of two of the least desired: Fish and Wildlife and General and Military Affairs. The choicest committees are the money committees—Appropriations and Ways and Means.

The Money Committees

The Appropriations Committee is where the action is. Not only is the appropriations bill, that is, the single bill encompassing each and every expenditure the state makes annually (appropriately labeled the "Big Bill"), constructed here, but any other bill that hopes to make it along the line of process and costs a single dollar has to fight its way through this ring of fire to emerge on the floor. And it draws a constant audience of lobbyists, governor's staff, general public, and legislators who can steal away from their own committee, all fighting for a seat in the room. The heat and overcrowding often push the limits of human tolerance.

Members assigned to this select group of eleven are always being buttonholed in the corridors by folks hoping to push their issues, or in the case of most lobbyists, hoping to kill an issue.

The Ways and Means Committee—the tax committee—runs a close second in prestige. Any bill that would even slightly affect Vermont's taxing structure, which includes thirty-three different taxes, has to be referred to this committee. And as with the Appropriations Committee, any of the thousand or so bills introduced in any given year that directly or indirectly influences the committee's taxing jurisdiction must be referred here sometime during the long journey to the floor, even if assigned initially to one of the nonmoney committees.

These committees have immense legislative power, and the members, by association, become important players in the halls of the capital. The reward of being assigned to these is a signal to outsiders that the member has the love and trust of the Speaker, for unlike the system in Congress, the Speaker has total authority to make all committee appointments. Not only can he (or she—to date there have been two women Speakers in the Vermont House[1]) appoint, he can "un-appoint" without restriction. Those prestigious and "made" members must never forget Newton's law—what goes up can also come down.

Obviously, only twenty-two lucky people get to report to these two prestigious committee rooms. The rest of us spent our two years in committees that, though important, never drew the crowds of the top two. (Bills speaking to controversial issues such as abortion, reapportionment, and the like, would bring relevant commotion, but they amounted to not much more than fifteen minutes of fame for any of us.)

Middle-Prestige Committees

The middle committees were Health and Welfare; Natural Resources (environment); Education (schools); Government Operations (all government agencies and their structure and, every ten years, reapportionment); Judiciary (the courts and any change in the legal statutes); Transportation (highways, bridges, and so forth); Commerce (business);

and Institutions (state buildings and prisons). On these committees sat members who usually had requested their assignment and felt comfortable spending the legislative session debating the corresponding issues.

Where you were assigned depended on your party affiliation, political or personal closeness to the Speaker, longevity (to a degree), and talents (not a given).

Speaker Morse once punished a very wealthy and proper, but rebellious, woman of his own party by assigning her to the Institutions Committee—ostensibly to teach her a lesson in loyalty. She resented, among other things, being in an all-male committee whose members smoked cigars. She refused even to step in the room and proceeded to spend her two years sitting in her seat in the well of the House. (Remember, members in Vermont have no office or staff.) Morse let her sit there, but as time went on the incident proved embarrassing, initially to the woman and eventually to the Speaker. The message didn't go unnoticed by the other members. The recipient of this petty dose of House politics never cried "uncle," and we came to admire her resistance to arrogant power. She served out her term and left with her head high—but she never ran again for public office.

Other Committees

One notch below were the Municipal and Elections Committee and the Agriculture Committee. The former dealt with local municipal bills and was not a favorite of anyone but those holding down a town clerk's post. The Agriculture Committee, once one of the more coveted and prestigious committees when Vermont had more than eight thousand small farms, was reserved for those remnants of Vermont's past, farmers, or members not on the Speaker's valentine list.

The Fish and Wildlife Committee, with seven members, was dreaded by all but those few native-Vermonter members who appeared each snowy morning wearing their fishing license on their caps-with-earmuffs. For the rest of us, being assigned to this committee was equal to boarding a ship to Devil's Island.

General and Military was often referred to as the "landfill" committee, but Murphy presided over his nine members like the commander-in-chief he was. Obviously Vermont, like all other states, had long ago gotten out of the military business; thus the Speaker dumped here any bill for which he couldn't locate a proper committee. It became the repository of bills with labels like "A Bill to Legalize Firecrackers."

This landfill collected people too, as it was also often a dumping ground for members who hadn't quite mastered the unwritten political rule that to get along, one must go along. It was still some time before I was to learn this dictum, and the landfill committee was where I found myself on a cold winter morning in 1983.

Getting Dumped

The opening of the 1983 session had seen Speaker Morse chosen once again to preside over the House. This time he ran unopposed, a so-called free ride in political parlance (I ran five times and never managed a one). Edgar May, my protector and mentor, having decided he had no future in the House, had now become Senator May from Windsor County. I was the returning member from Bennington, but it was rumored that I was in line to take Edgar's post on Health and Welfare, so I hoped to become Chairman Wright.

Under the Vermont Constitution a new biennium begins on the first Wednesday following the first Monday in January. Tradition dictated that the three-day, first week be devoted to ceremony. This included the assignment, by lottery, of new members' seats.

Where you sat was a big deal for a lot of legislators, as your new legislative license plates corresponded with your seat number. Bigger egos vied for the lowest seat number possible. Veteran legislators were allowed to take seats left vacant by nonreturning members. The open seats remaining went to the newcomers, as determined by drawing numbers from a hat. Seat number 1 belonged to the Speaker, and though he never sat in it, since his duties were at the rostrum, it was the most coveted. But it could not be won in any lottery—no matter how lucky one might be, there was never a chit in the hat with the number *1* written on it.

I cared little about the number of my seat; it was more important to me to be where I had a view of the whole House chamber. That's why when I got the chance in my second term to move up from seat 23 to seat 132 I jumped at it. From there I could see all that was happening, and as an added amenity it afforded a ready exit that served as an escape hatch to the committee rooms, telephones, and cafeteria.

It also served the purpose of seating me beside my friend Paul Poirier, the member from Barre City, in seat 133. This closeness proved to be a distinct advantage when I became Democratic leader and Paul became assistant Democratic leader, or whip, later in 1983. It allowed us to converse at will and avoid the delay of communicating through notes carried by the pages.

Seating also created friendships. And it didn't matter whether a conservative Republican happened to be seated beside a liberal Democrat. They would be together for hundreds of hours over the two-year period, helping each other in a multitude of ways and usually becoming good friends. This often meant that the stronger personality just might influence the weaker. (Once in leadership, I made what effort I could to seat a new conservative Democrat next to a liberal Democrat. I hoped that the new guy would turn to the left, not the right.)

The big day for members is the Tuesday of the second week. This is when they learn their committee assignments—the sanctuary where they're going to spend a good part of the next two years of their life. The Speaker, having huddled with his lieutenants over the weekend, has finalized his assignments, and protocol dictates that they are read from the podium. The well of the House always seemed electric with nervous anticipation at this moment.

I, too, felt the excitement, as another rumor had begun to circulate that I might also be in line for the chairmanship of the Education Committee. "Wow!" I thought. Two horses in the same race. How could I lose?

I was about to find out.

The bang of the gavel quickly brought the excited members to a deathly quiet as the Speaker began reading the committee assignments; this was done alphabetically and by committee—Agriculture, Appropriations, Commerce, Education, Energy, Fish and Wildlife, General and Military Affairs, Government Operations, Health and Welfare, Judiciary, Municipal Corporations and Elections, Natural Resources, Transportation, and Ways and Means. I didn't have to start listening until he at least got to the Education Committee, and that was thirty or more names away.

"The member from Guilford, Mr. Hunt." He was reading the first name for the Commerce Committee. The first name read is chair, the second name read is the vice-chair, and the third name read is the so-called ranking member. The remaining members of the committee were simply recited in alphabetical order. "Get ready," I mused. Education would be next.

"Education," he continued in a monotone.

"The member from Charlotte, Mrs. Morse."

OK. No problem. Not my first choice anyway. I relaxed a bit. There were still a bunch of names to be read before he would get to the Health and Welfare Committee. I tuned out.

Then it happened. Or did it? Did I just hear my name? Can't be. Where the hell is he? I swung around to Poirier.

"Did I just hear him read my name, Paul?"

Paul, as stunned as I was, said, "Yeah! I think so."

"You sure?" Heads were turning.

"Yes, I'm positive. He said, 'The member from Bennington, Mr. Wright.' "

"Where the hell is he?"

I was about to find out.

"Health and Welfare," came the chant. Morse had started the Health and Welfare assignments.

And my name had already been read.

"Jesus H. Mahogany Christ, Paul," I gasped. "I'm on the goddamned General and Military Affairs Committee. And I'm the last member named."

So much for fame. I hadn't fallen off the bridge. I had been pushed.

My New Committee

It was a long walk to the General and Military Affairs Committee room, and though I knew where it was I had never been in it. I was about to meet the infamous Mr. John Francis Murphy, known to many as simply "the General." And though not in my wildest dreams would I have imagined it, I was about to embark on a friendship that I've never equaled, before or since.

I was in no hurry, as I was trying to gather my composure; consequently I was the last to enter the committee room and took the only remaining seat. I tried to show no emotion by maintaining a fixed stare at the bulletin board across from me. Time for whimpering would have to come later. Eventually, I turned my attention to my new chairman.

He sat, leaning back in his chair, at the head of the conference table that served as our desk. Though the session had hardly begun, the table was littered with junk—newspapers, bills (left over from the last session), law books, a couple of cheap paperbacks, and barely visible under the heap, a big old tape recorder with fishing line entwined that Murphy never could get to work. The General, knowing that his return as chair was certain no matter who assumed the speakership, never bothered to box his goods and take them home as all other members were required to do at the end of a session. He appeared relaxed and very much at home among this mess.

If I had ever visualized the humanization of "Paddy's Pig," Murphy was it. He seemed as wide as he was long, with short legs that didn't touch the floor even when he wasn't leaning back in his chair, hands that barely connected when across his belly, and a full head of beautiful hair. His face was the color of a perpetual blush.

I watched him as he went around the table asking everyone to introduce themselves. Since the General and Military Affairs Committee was reserved for unknowing freshmen and unruly members (like me), a majority of its members each biennium needed introduction. Each intro produced an intense stare from Murphy, as if he was sizing everyone up. (I later came to realize that that was exactly what he was doing.) After each member spoke his or her name and stated where they were from, Murphy would mumble, "Nice to have you."

Across from me was a man, perhaps in his late fifties, smoking a pipe. He had a 1950s crew cut and the huge, swollenlike hands of a farmer who had milked a lot of cows over a half-century. Somehow he seemed an appropriate symbol for how far I had regressed.

To my left sat Bob Harris, D-Windsor, one of the true characters in the legislature.[2] He was a returning veteran, having served with Murphy for two full terms before being defeated for reelection and thus forced into a two-year hiatus. Now he had won back his seat and found himself where he had started. Not very pleased with his assignment, he had referred to his previous tenure on the committee as his "four-year sentence on Elba."

To my right a cloud of cigar smoke, hid whoever was there.

After introductions, Murphy explained how pleased he was with his new committee:

"There's a lot of very capable people on this committee [though none more politically capable than he], and I want to make clear that each of you will be respected and utilized [by Murphy, of course] while you're a member on this committee. Everyone should feel that they are an integral part of this process, and if there's anything you want to bring up, or any bill in which you're interested and feel this committee should bring up, all you have to do is raise your hand and speak up. Nobody's suggestions are too insignificant to get a fair hearing as long as I'm your chair."

Harris's hand shot up.

"Ah! Mr. Harris"—a tint of sarcasm. "Nice to have you back. What can I do for you?"

"I move there be no smoking in this committee room."

The sudden tension in the air made me look up.

Murphy, glaring out of half-closed eyes, shot back, "Mr. Harris, I'll make like I never heard that motion."

"Well, then I'll say it a little louder, General." Harris then repeated the motion. Murphy's chair came crashing down on all four legs.

"Listen, Harris, you've been trouble since I inherited you from Speaker O'Connor. Why the good folks from your district keep sending you back here is beyond me, but you're here and I have to deal with you. I'm just warning you that we'll have none of your shenanigans in here for the next two years."

"Mr. Chairman, I believe I have a proper motion on the floor here. And let's make something perfectly clear before the other members get the wrong idea. I consider my reassignment to this committee as a sentence to be served. I didn't ask to be here, and I'm not too happy that I've been remanded here. Now, oh Commandant, I respectfully request that you call the roll."

"OK, Harris, that's it. I'm going to see the Speaker." And he got up and waddled out of the room, headed for the Speaker's office.

Well, I thought, this was certainly going to be different from Health and Welfare. I wondered if there was a back exit to this place.

Murphy's Law

"Listen, White." I didn't say anything. "I know what you're thinking—that you got dumped by the Speaker. But I don't look at it that way. The Speaker's made a big mistake." Murphy, who barely reached to my chest, confronted me outside the committee room, grabbing my arm. "He's only wounded ya," he added. "You're hurt, but you'll get over it."

I simply stared down at him in amazement.

He had more to say.

"I knew from the minute you came here two years ago [I had actually entered the House four years ago] that you were gonna amount to somethin'." He was looking up at me. "Ya wasted two years on May's committee [I had been there four years] thinkin' more about issues than a lot of other stuff. Well now it's time for the other stuff that makes this place run. Here's ya chance."

I hadn't a clue as to what the hell he was talking about, but I was to learn that Murphy had a lot of the Irish poet in him. He often talked in parables, and though I might walk away from a conversation with him without a clue as to what he had said, it never failed that at some later time, even months later, the lightbulb would flash on, and I would think, "That's what the little bastard was trying to tell me."

He wasn't going to let me interrupt.

"See, White [I was sure he didn't know my first name either], now you've got time to move around. Roam the hallways talking to people. Building relationships. You're no dummy. Members know that. Morse saw that before a lot of others. That's why he's Speaker. That's why you're here. But you can be that, too. He broke a big rule—'Keep your enemy close.' " Christ, now he was quoting Machiavelli. I had heard enough and I cut him off here.

"Murphy, you gotta have spaghetti for brains. I've just been thrown over the bridge, and you're talking all this nonsense. I'm really not in the mood for it."

"OK—you'll see. I just want you to know that as far as I'm concerned you're free to come and go from the committee any time you want. Actually, you don't even have to show up. When there's a vote I'll have somebody track you down. I just wanted to let you know that."

The irony of my appointment to the General and Military Affairs Committee was that this was going to be the most enjoyable two years of my legislative career. Johnny Murphy and his antics were worth the price of a ticket, and I looked forward to going to his committee. Even when I became Speaker two years later (he was right) and I occasionally found myself with a few moments to move about the building and visit with people or sit in committees that I normally would not have had time for, I always seemed to be drawn to Murphy's room.

The committee itself was filled with characters right out of "Li'l Abner." Bob Harris and Murphy were the stars of this off-Broadway comedy, as they never passed up an opportunity to torment one another, and when they weren't after each other they were fully capable of forming an alliance and going after some other poor soul. They always had their own secret agendas, and they both overflowed with political street-smarts. I often thought you could drop these two off at any city hall or statehouse in the country and they would end up doing exactly what they were doing here.

But Murph was one of a kind, and I was constantly impressed by his almost daily displays of a new instinct. Edgar May once explained that

Murphy had an ability to read the mood on the floor unlike anyone he had ever seen. This was an extremely valuable advantage during floor debate, and I was to witness it firsthand dozens of times over the years.

Murphy once, during a heated and angry debate on the floor, rose to speak and, when recognized by the Speaker, proceeded to place the mike next to his ear, and then attempted to speak into his earplugs. The confused act brought the House down with laughter and changed the entire mean tempo of the debate. He always professed that he never meant to do that, but I was never convinced.

Indeed, it was a careless foe who underestimated Murphy. I learned quickly never to try to guess what he might do in any given situation until he had made his intent obvious. That way, I might have ended up disappointed but never surprised.

Working with Your Committee

The committee room is the place where a legislator is going to spend the better part of his or her two-year term. Thus, it is imperative that you like the committee assigned to you and, equally important, that you have mastered the qualities of patience and tolerance. To be on a committee that you have no interest in or to be seated with other members with whom you don't get along is equivalent to serving a two-year sentence.

Perhaps the closest I ever came to finding myself sitting with a member that I didn't like was in Murphy's committee during my third term. And though my time there was limited because I was elected Democratic leader shortly after arriving in Murphy's committee, I was present long enough to come to a conclusion that the vice-chair, Francis Manning, R-Island Pond, was motivated by something other than a desire to help his fellow man. There was a negativity to the man that I, and most others, found less than attractive. His story has a note of humor as well as tragedy to it.

Manning was a retired railroad worker from way up in the Northeast Kingdom. The most rural part of Vermont, tucked away in its northeastern corner, it encompasses three thinly populated counties. He was from a decidedly conservative little village situated alongside the pastoral Clyde

River that consistently dispatched Republicans to Montpelier. Manning was something of an anomaly in that he was both a union man and a Republican. As vice-chair he seldom missed an opportunity to be aggressive, and sometimes even rude, to witnesses, who found themselves being attacked for stating their opinion on a bill. He also appeared to have little regard for their sometimes obvious nervousness in front of a committee, and on one occasion he brought tears to the eyes of a young woman who, he thought, was less than forthcoming. I don't think I ever heard him vote yes, as there was always something that he could dislike—be it witness or bill.

Being a union man was his only saving grace, because Murphy could control his vote on any labor issue that entered the committee. Labor was Murph's passion, and had it not been for John Murphy, union members in Vermont would have been assigned second-class citizenship. As it was, the labor movement had never quite taken hold in this staunchly Republican state, and it took all of Murphy's time, energy, and political talent to at least give them a seat at the table.

I was to learn that during his early years in the legislature Manning was an alcoholic who had seldom missed a last call. Much to his credit he had gone on the wagon, and when I arrived in the committee he had been sober for many years. Sobriety, with all its benefits, had brought out the worst in Manning's temperament, and we on the committee were daily witnesses to his often harsh nature. Murphy, as only he could, put in words what we all felt. Once, after a more than usually obstreperous confrontation with a witness by Manning, Murphy turned, after the room had cleared of witnesses, and stated with both disdain and empathy, "Ya know, Francis, I think I liked you a lot better when you were a drunk."

Whether Murphy's words brought on what was to unfold we'll never know, but they were followed by a terrible tumble off the wagon and the beginning of the end of Manning's career as a legislator.

The Annual Committee Party

Each year toward the conclusion of the session the committees arrange parties at a local club or restaurant. Coincidentally, General and Military had arranged its party for the very night that Murphy had spoken his words to Manning. Off they went (I, fortunately, didn't make it) to what was then the most exclusive restaurant in the Montpelier area—a four-star establishment, run by a meticulous and very disciplined German hostess, up on the prestigious Stowe Mountain Ski Road.

Well, Murphy; Bob Harris; Torrey Carpenter, R-Burlington; Mike Silver, R-Bennington; and the rest of the gala group arrived loaded for bear. They had already got themselves off to a good start with midafternoon cocktails in the committee room. (This, of course, was against all rules of decorum, but then, this was Murphy's committee, and in those days things were obviously more lax than they are now.) The evening went along with much good fellowship, and it wasn't long before the other patrons were being treated to the harmony of Irish songs and bawdy limericks. It was too much temptation, and sometime during the evening's festivities, unknown to the others, Francis Manning took his first drink in years. With each round the laughter grew and the hostess's short supply of patience waned. The finale came when the committee members gathered the ornate metal salad plates from the waiter's prep table and began marching between tables, singing and banging to the tune of "McNamara's Band." It was the end for the aghast hostess: She ordered them all to pay the bill and vacate her establishment immediately.

When Manning, who had devoured the specially prepared salmon and was in the best of moods, expressed his displeasure at the hostess's less-than-cordial decision to throw them all out on their ears, she was mortified to hear him say with his finest Irish lilt, "Madam, I've eaten better sucker out of the Clyde River." Manning's lame attempt at culinary comparison proved to be the last straw. She called the cops.

The night didn't end there, as they proceeded back to their motel and carried on until the wee hours of the morning. The climax came when Torrey Carpenter dared Mike Silver, on a mission to fetch more ice from the machine below, to lower himself over the second-floor railing of the motel's balcony, as Harris rushed down the stairs with outstretched arms, promising to catch all 280 pounds of Mike should he take up the dare. He did, Harris didn't, and off they went to the hospital.

The next morning the sergeant-at-arms was officially notified by the still very angry hostess that never again would a legislator be welcome at her four-star restaurant. The message was received cordially and with understanding and relayed to all the members of Murphy's committee as they arrived, somewhat late and the worse for wear, for the day's session—all, that is, but Francis Manning, who disappeared for four days. Of course, everyone was worried, but a search for the missing member proved futile until the following week, when we learned that he had shown up at his home. He came back, eventually, to the legislature, but it would prove to be his last term. A decision had been made, not by the voters in his district but by his wife.

Things Miss Cheney Never Mentioned[3]

Paul Poirier and I became close friends over the next two years, a friendship that grew even stronger in the next decade. From our seats next to each other, in the top row to one side of the horseshoe-shaped well of the House, we could see every member and had a side view of the podium. This meant little before both of us became leaders, but once that happened it proved to be bad news for the opposition. Now two minds not only could witness all that was happening on the floor but also could communicate instantly with one another. We were political junkies and people watchers, and little went on that we weren't able to watch silently from our seats. This was important, because all the floor action in the Vermont General Assembly takes place with nearly full attendance of the members. The floor is where the action is, and I've always felt the members of Congress were missing out on the vitality and knowledge that assembling each day as a group would afford.[4]

Assembling regularly as a group also provides an opportunity to rub elbows with members one is otherwise unlikely to see during the day. The Vermont State House is a crowded place, with 150 House members, 30 senators located in committee rooms a floor below, scores of lobbyists hanging around in the hallways and crammed into twenty-five various committee rooms, the sergeant-at-arms's staff, government officials, gaping tourists, interested citizens, and on most days a half-dozen school groups running excitedly through the building. One could go through an entire session recognizing members' faces but being unaware which committee they served on, the district they represented, or how long they had been in the legislature, let alone having the slightest knowledge of their personal lives. Floor debate, which toward the end of the session could consume the entire day, provided a glimpse into their lives and personalities. As a leader I focused my attention not only on the debate but also on those members participating in the debate. So often I would turn to the legislative "Biographical Sketches" handout when someone I knew little about rose to speak, hoping to gain some insight into where he or she was coming from.

In addition, having the full membership on the floor meant that the leader had to be extra vigilant in regard to the rules of the House. To get caught napping on rules of procedure or points of order was something the leader's fellow party members had every right to look upon with disapproval. Alertness was indispensable to doing the job. It meant that when Paul and I became party leaders our unwritten rule of having one leader on the floor at all times seldom was broken.

As just another member, with no designated responsibility to the party as a whole or to the success or failure of the bill being debated on the floor, one could settle back, chat with one's seatmate, read or answer mail, peruse one's hometown newspaper (out of sight of the Speaker who, if his attention were brought to it, would remind the transgressor, privately if one was lucky, of the rule against reading "frivolous" material on the floor while the House was in session), or simply lean back and enjoy the greatest show on earth.

What can I compare it to? That's tough, but if forced, I would ask you to imagine the buzz of the standing-room-only crowd on the opening night of a hit Broadway show. The excitement comes from the anticipation that the next few hours hold in store the possibility of an array of emotions from joy to sadness, rejoicing to lamenting, derision to respect, triumph to defeat.

Personally I was fascinated from the very first day by all the action that enveloped me. At first the rapidity of the Speaker's recital confused me. But Edgar May early on stressed the importance of learning the different motions that were a constant with all bills, and these, once learned, could translate the Speaker's almost indecipherable intonations. It was sound advice and paid dividends for all the years I spent there.

I also paid close attention to who was sending notes and who was receiving them. Sometimes sports fans divert their attention from the game on the field to watch the crowd, finding as much to catch their interest there as in the game. I did the same in the legislature. The difference was that in the legislature, the crowd *was* the game.

Middle-school-aged pages responding to the raising of a hand or the often-subtle tapping of a pencil on a wooden desk would catch my eye. I would follow the page as he or she would rush over, seize a note, and then dart off to deliver the message to the proper recipient. Most of the notes would be personal and trivial: "Where we going to lunch?" "How's your bill doing in the Senate?" "Nice tie on the member from Manchester." "Member from St. Albans looks like he had a rough night." But not all were frivolous, and it paid to watch the so-called players. If the chair of a committee reporting a bill sent off a note to another member of the committee, it often signaled that he or she would soon be standing up to join the debate. If a member involved in the floor action sent a note to a lobbyist in the gallery, that was a sure sign that the lobbyist had a special interest in the bill on the floor. Particular attention would be paid to notes going to and from the Speaker. Nowhere was the communication traffic more noticeable than at the Speaker's podium.

Murphy understood this as well as anyone.

The "Landfill" Boss Collects the Trash

I was sitting up in my back row seat one early evening, and I was alone except for Murphy, who sat almost directly across the well of the House from me in seat 150. I had slipped in quietly through the side door, and he, preoccupied with something at his desk, didn't notice my presence.

Busy writing a note to a constituent, I hardly noticed Murphy getting up and waddling along the raised platform that was situated on each side of the Speaker's podium. Momentarily distracted, I followed his movements. He turned at the rostrum to exit down the ramp that led to where the Speaker's office was located. He didn't just turn and exit but halted prior to pushing through the red curtains. He was looking around. I could see him, but because of his short stature, the podium blocked me from his view. He then moved back, approaching the podium. He reached down under the podium, grabbed something, and in one quick motion stuffed whatever he had taken into his coat pocket and left abruptly through the curtains.

Hmmm! Curious! I certainly was.

I waited a moment and then got up and headed for Murphy's committee room, which was just a few yards down a hallway in the west wing of the building. He was sitting facing me as I entered the room, riffling through a small pile of crumpled notes. I put two and two together quickly.

"Murphy," I cried, "I saw what you just did. Let me see what you got there."

Murphy grabbed the notes and made a futile attempt to stuff them in his pocket.

"What are you talking about?"

"Never mind the bullshit, Murphy. I saw you take those notes out of the Speaker's wastebasket." I had him cold and he knew it.

"Listen, Wright, keep your mouth shut." He had finally gotten my name right. "Close the door. C'mere. I'll show you what I got." The devil was in his smile.

I spent a minute reading. "What the hell ya doin' going through people's trash? These are all the crap notes that Morse gets from his ass kissers while we're on the floor."

Murphy responded with the air of excitement that came over him every time he was into his mischief. "Wright, if you're goin' to amount to anything in this place, then you better learn how things work around here." He was lecturing to his student, again.

"The Speaker knows everything," he said. "That's why he's powerful. That podium is like the great communications system in the sky. Nothing happens without it going through the Speaker. If they're dumb enough to put things in writing, and he's dumb enough to throw them in the basket, then I'm smart enough to gather them up. That's what he does every day, and that's what I do every day. I know everything he knows, and he doesn't know anything I know. I know who's sending him dumb stuff, sending love notes [Morse was a bachelor at that time], who's asking when they should get up to speak, what the arguments are going to be, and so on. Information is knowledge; knowledge is power. You better get that through your head, Wright." A big Cheshire cat grin exploded across that perpetually red face.

I was Speaker for ten years, and though I never went through other people's wastebaskets, I never threw a note from a member in mine. Over ten years I accumulated thousands of notes. They now rest, forlornly, in a dark and dank cellar, surrounded by old skis, hockey sticks, and other once relevant memorabilia.

Women in the Legislature

In 1978 when I first went to the legislature it was very much a man's world. But things were changing, and by the time I left in 1994 women had made some pretty giant strides toward equality.

Men had been in control of the legislature since the very first day Vermont had been admitted to the Union in 1791. Things hadn't changed a whole lot in nearly two centuries, but by 1978 women were accepted as members, if not leaders. The good ol' boys were very much in control, and it didn't matter which party caucus you belonged to: men held the reins. By 1983 (two years prior to my becoming Speaker) the session opened with a total of 29 women taking seats (13 Republicans, 16 Democrats). A decade later, as the 1993 session dawned, there were 53 women, the largest membership of that sex, I believe, in a 150-member house in the nation. Democrats, once again, outnumbered Republicans, 38 to 15.

During the twelve years that I participated in House candidate recruitment I eagerly sought out women to run, which may have accounted for the party discrepancy. It wasn't that I was all wrapped up in the women's movement, though I did work hard to get Vermont to endorse the Equal Rights Amendment. My motive was more selfish than that; I was

Source: State of Vermont Legislative Council.

Note: Total House membership was 246 from 1921 to 1965 and then 150 from 1996 to 2004.

convinced that, pound for political pound, women made the better candidates—and often the better lawmakers.

They were better candidates because they never agreed to run with the notion that too many of my male friends had—a sense of entitlement. Though it was not openly talked about, they were, from the get-go, well aware that they faced obstacles. There were the obvious ones that encompassed all we know about male chauvinism. I don't have to jog anyone's brain to understand the unfairness of that. But there also existed the reality that many of the women candidates, though knowing they had to give all the time that campaigning requires, had the added responsibility of children still at home. And even if they were fortunate enough to have a liberated partner, their minds were always wired to other schedules. To be sure, men had other schedules, but they didn't usually involve the main responsibility for the kids' daily demands (read: food, clothing, shelter, and the bulk of the nurturing). It was something that always had to be considered when we were trying to assist them in their campaigns.

In addition—and I can't give you any scientific evidence to verify this—I always felt that there was more pressure on them to win, simply because they were women and were often the first to attempt to win a seat in their district.

Other, less-obvious things handcuffed them to some degree. For instance, I had always advised candidates that, when campaigning, they should arrive at the door without a gang following them. They were the ones who wanted the vote of the guy answering the door, and it was their burden to get up the courage to ask for that vote. This presented no risks at the great majority of the doors, at least for men. But Vermont is filled with lonely dirt roads that even I sometimes felt a little edgy traveling up—and "up" it always seemed to be in the aptly named Green Mountain State. It could be scary after nightfall, and my constant advice to the women was to "get home before the street lights come on." I would also caution them to not enter a home unless they could see a child or another woman from the doorway.

But in spite of these things I still fall on the side that women, in general, make better candidates. Most of those I worked with were novices. They had never run for or held office. We didn't have to deal with the know-it-all attitude that a lot of my male candidates displayed. Nor did I have to cajole women candidates (as I did men) into accepting that the fact that they could stand for election to some local board was probably not going to be enough to get them elected to the state legislature. Consequently, most women candidates took nothing for granted, listened to what other Democratic officeholders and I had to say, and carried out their political chores with unusual promptness and sincerity.

Moreover, I am certain that they made better lawmakers. At least they cared about the issues that I discerned were most important. You didn't have to explain to them issues that dealt with education, family, choice (whichever side they fell on), mental health, aid to dependent children, or the environment. They may not have been up on the meaning of "suspension of the rules," but I never met one who couldn't explain the intricacies of *Roe vs. Wade.* These were all issues dealing with the quality of life, and they knew a whole lot more about that than most men—myself included.

So once they were elected they were a lot easier for leadership to deal with on the "people" issues. But in 1979, my freshman term, those were not issues that the Democratic caucus had decided were priorities. And though I quietly disagreed with this, as a new member I wasn't looking for an opportunity to stand alone for any lost cause, especially against the good ol' boys.

Sometimes "Dancing with the Gal Who Brung Ya" Makes for a Long Night

In the political arena loyalty is another word for love. It is, perhaps, the most admired attribute that an elected official can display. Loyalty is also the quality in every politician's repertoire that gets tested constantly and becomes the measure that underlies the very soul of his or her reputation. To be known as someone who will "hang tough" under pressure or ridicule is a badge of honor every novice strives for. But it also can get one in a whole peck of trouble.

It didn't take long for me to be put to the test. It came at the end of my first session, when the last-minute scrambling reached a crescendo and the women in the House discovered they had lost funding for their Women's Caucus. It was a relatively small amount, perhaps $30,000, but it was at a time when the women were fighting for the smallest advance on the long road to equality. The funding had been a little-noticed line item buried in the appropriations bill. Speaker O'Connor, as a small gesture of appease-ment, and perhaps fairness, had seen to it that it stayed in the Big Bill as it passed on over to the Senate. The Senate, being more conservative and perhaps less enamored of the march toward equal rights, had simply cut it out. The only hope the women in the House had was to unite as a group.

This was one of those curious times the women showed that they would forgo party allegiance to come together for a cause by refusing *rules suspension*[5] on the entire appropriations bill and forcing it back into a conference committee[6] to have the funds restored. This was no small matter, as the Big Bill, containing the billion-plus dollars that enabled the state to operate in the coming year, was always the very last bill passed in any session. Passage meant we were going home.

Speaker O'Connor may have believed in the women's cause, but he didn't believe in it enough to hold up adjournment. In an effort to move the bill forward without the funding for the Women's Caucus he had tried rules suspension the first time on a *voice vote,* in which individual votes are not recorded but simply shouted aloud by the members from their seats. This presented no problem to me, as I could sit in my seat and keep the commitment I had made earlier to the female members to vote no on suspension. When I did this, in as low a voice as possible, my friend and seatmate, Ray Poor, who was hard of hearing, gave me a surprised look. He was too much a gentleman to say anything, but he realized I was heading down a treacherous path with the leadership. The Speaker, attempting to ram through what he hoped was a yes vote allowing suspension, was poised to declare, "The ayes have it," when he was interrupted by one of the women members, who rose to her feet and demanded a *division.*

Now this was getting serious. A division means the Speaker calls for the ayes and nays by having the members stand and be counted. Only Rusty Sachs, a decorated Vietnam Marine veteran, and I, and maybe a few other men (I couldn't tell, as I kept my head down) rose and stood with the women.

It took the longest time for the clerks to count the thirty of us standing. As I felt the eyes of the Neanderthals surrounding me, I was hoping we'd fail and not have to do this again. It was a telling moment in my new life as a legislator. Hang tough, Ralphie, babe. It'll all soon be over. Damn. "The nays have it," echoed down from the podium. "You have refused to suspend the rules."

No sooner had O'Connor abided by the rules and brought up another bill, than the request came to try once again to suspend the rules. Sachs and I got up again. If not losing our masculinity, we were at the very least rapidly relinquishing the right to borrow the power tools or sit in on the Friday night poker game.

It seemed as though they tried the rules suspension another half-dozen times during the course of the day, each time with the same results. Finally, leadership realized that the women were going to stand their ground for as long as it took and had the conference committee put the money back in the budget—amid an outbreak of feminine cheers. I received a note: "Congratulations. A victory well deserved by 30 women and a handful of Queers." Of course, it wasn't signed.

Women in Leadership

By the time the 1983 legislature opened, the casual observer might have been fooled into believing that women had indeed found their place in the Vermont General Assembly. It would not have been an impression connected to reality.

Judy Stephany, from Burlington, had emerged from caucus as the minority leader in 1981, and amazingly, the representative from Essex Junction, Althea Kroger, had managed to become the assistant minority leader. Both Democratic leaders were women. Both were exceptionally bright, filled with energy, and as it turned out, naively determined to make a difference.

One couldn't help believing that Vermont was ahead of the pack in women's drive to become equal partners in the American democratic process. From outward appearances, it appeared so. But if one looked more closely, it was at best a marginal partnership.

What had happened was that our male-dominated caucus looked upon its leaders as just the cheerleaders for the Republican leadership's agenda. Tom Candon, D-Rutland, the ultimate good ol' boy, had held the post for many years prior to my arrival in 1979 and used the caucus as a rubber stamp for whatever the majority Republican leadership put forth as an agenda. In fact, I don't recall a Democratic agenda even existing. For whatever nebulous reason, Candon had decided to step aside, and Stephany and Kroger had gotten themselves elected. Perhaps this was simply a polite gesture—what "gentlemen do to keep the ladies happy." Perhaps he saw no need for a Democratic caucus and agenda.

Judy and Althea didn't see it the same way. They immediately began formulating a Democratic agenda and, to the incredulity of the Old Guard, pushing it in caucus. Well, the reception was, to say the least, cold. This wouldn't do. It jeopardized the comfort level of those who lived by the political code of never rocking the boat.

We had a cozy arrangement with the ruling party: as long as Democrats cooperated, they would be allowed to pass a small number of their bills, provided they didn't collide with Republican priorities, and as a reward for good behavior they would receive perhaps two or three chairmanships (May and Murphy) and a respectable number of seats on the money committees. Under no circumstances would the latter equal a sufficient number to control a committee. This, it was hoped, sent a quaint message that signaled the bipartisan nature of the citizen legislature.

To be sure, O'Connor had served as a Democratic Speaker for six years, but he was never—nor was anyone else—under the impression it was because the minority Democrats had put him there. Consequently the attitude hung heavy that because Democrats had never, in the entire modern history of Vermont, held majority status in either house, rocking the boat would guarantee the withdrawal of what few benevolently granted perks the Republican majority allowed us. It was, "Remember your place or suffer the political consequences."

For two years Stephany and Kroger were allowed to present ideas and issues in caucus, but with little result. They would be listened to with the appropriate amount of courtesy and some show of deference, only to be ignored. Both parties showed growing frustration and intolerance. Candon, who still controlled the caucus behind the scenes, eventually manipulated the solution to the problem.

It was simple and blatant. When Speaker Morse took the podium in 1983 to begin his second term, he presented Althea with an offer she couldn't refuse. She, perhaps tired of "rolling the rock up the hill," reluctantly accepted a seat on the Appropriations Committee. In return she was forced to give up her leadership position.

One down, one to go.

The next move had no connection to anyone, at least directly. Stephany, seeing an opportunity, or perhaps seeing the fruitlessness of carrying on as leader, announced that she was leaving the legislature to run for mayor of Vermont's largest city, Burlington (38,000). The deed was done. The old guard could once again rest easy. Or so they thought.

Notes

1. Republican Consuelo Bailey served as Speaker from 1953 to 1955. (The speakership was once subject to the "Mountain Rule," an informal agreement that rotated the Speaker's post east and west of the Green Mountains, which essentially divide the state. Bailey came from South Burlington, west of the mountain.) Democrat Gaye Symington, Jericho, was elected Speaker in January 2005.

2. Harris once held a winning Tri-State Megabucks lottery ticket worth $4.8 million, which he shared with three other winners. He was a college graduate who painted houses for a living and held an auctioneer's license. He died six years later, in 1998, of a brain tumor at the age of forty-eight. I miss him a whole lot.

3. Miss Cheney was my seventh-grade civics teacher, my first connection to government, and my first crush. Nearly fifty years later, while being inducted into Boston University's Distinguished Alumni Society, she showed up looking as pretty and proud as ever.

4. This is one of the vital ingredients that makes up one of America's last citizen legislatures, as compared with professional lawmakers in other states and Congress. Floor debate provides the same eyeball-to-eyeball impact as any other meaningful communications between people. Not debating on the floor of the House is like buying a car on eBay. You never get that distinctive enticement that the "new car smell" brings, and you don't get to kick the tires.

5. Our Founders set out to make democracy an extremely deliberative process. There were to be no "hunch bets." All legislative proposals (bills) have a series of three readings that normally take three legislative days to move from one house to the other. It is based on the logical concept that all decisions should be slept on. To "suspend the rules" simply allows the entire process to be hastened forward and accomplished in one sitting. It is an infrequently used tactic, generally called for in the waning days of the session when the assembly is driving toward adjournment. It takes a three-quarters vote of those present to pass instead of a simple majority.

6. A conference committee is necessitated when a bill, having passed both houses, has been altered in any way by the receiving body. As few bills work their way through the process without change, a committee is established to work out the differences for each bill. The Speaker of the House and the president pro tem of the Senate each assign three members to the committee of conference. Once they resolve the points of difference the compromise is returned to the house of origin. Since the compromise cannot be amended, in any form or manner, the members must then vote to accept or reject it in its entirety.

4

Gaining Leadership

The Cork Comes to the Rescue

"You can win this," Corcoran said, throwing his clothes in the back seat and then jumping in front.

"Win what?"

"The leadership post." He opened the morning *Bennington Banner* and proceeded to ignore me.

And that's exactly what happened. I won the caucus election that afternoon and became Democratic leader of the House.

A lot of politics is luck. That's a fact. Being in the right place at the right time makes up for a lot of deficiencies. I had to be made aware of it, but I was in the right place at the right time on this cold January morning in 1983. It took Corcoran's uncanny political instinct to push me toward the mountaintop.

Timothy Corcoran was as raw a political animal as you'll ever come across. Born into an Irish Catholic family in 1950, a block from the soon-to-depart old cotton mill, he was a Democrat because the family lineage didn't permit any other choice. Grandma Hogan had helped raise her children by changing bedsheets for the Republican aristocrats atop the hill in Old Bennington fifty years earlier, and Corcoran had never forgiven them. He seldom spoke of his family, but I learned enough over the years that we rode together to Montpelier to decipher that his roots over the generations were what would be considered "shanty Irish." At the age when kids were lining their bedroom walls with Mickey Mantle posters, the Cork's room was lined with political banners and pictures of Jack Kennedy. He was elected a Bennington selectman at the same age he became eligible to buy a beer—twenty-one. And though he spent a couple of years attending the local junior college, his real education came from the streets. He once told me that he never read anything that didn't have his name in it, but you could be certain that whatever little he read he would remember, as he was one of those rare human beings who had a photographic memory—a God-given gift in the political world. Now approaching forty, his life had been one political battle after another.

The departure of Althea Kroger to the Appropriations Committee the first week of the session had opened up the Democratic whip slot. My friend and new seatmate Paul Poirier had jumped in that caucus race and emerged the winner. Now, just three weeks into the session, another surprise was unloaded on the membership: Judy Stephany, the Democratic leader, announced in a tearful address on the floor of the House, that she, too, was leaving—to run for mayor of Burlington.

The few weeks I had spent under Murphy's wing had proved a tonic, and I was feeling better about my future in the legislature. As the door to the chairmanship of Health and Welfare had barely slammed shut, another door swung open. Corcoran and I went back and forth the entire three hours it took to get to Montpelier, and by the time we pulled into the parking lot, Corcoran had convinced me I just might win the leadership post. I was the sixth and final one to declare my candidacy.

Poirier was my biggest obstacle to the prize; shucking aside the fact that he had only been assistant leader for three weeks, he now was an announced candidate for Democratic leader.

I scurried around the statehouse all morning and worked the cafeteria at noon, doing what I could to line up support for the weekly caucus scheduled at one o'clock.

The Democrats, sixty-five strong, filed into the tiny caucus room and listened to the six of us give brief speeches saying why we should be their choice for leader. No one had any questions.

Except Cork.

He rose and asked Paul why, if he was running for leader, wouldn't he resign his whip's position in fairness to others and let those of us who wanted to, run for that vacated post.

"Take one or the other," Corcoran said, "but make up your mind."

Paul was surprised, and for a moment you could see he was weighing what to do. He had done his count and couldn't be sure that he had the votes to win the leadership. It was a quick and unexpected move by Corcoran—one even I had no idea was coming—and it placed Paul in a very tough spot. He knew that I had been in the House two years longer and that I had probably reached more of our Democrats than he. For both of us it had been a spur-of-the-moment decision only hours earlier.

"If that's how this works I guess I'll stay where I am."

I emerged that day the new leader of the Democratic Party in the House, but it was no Roman legion that I now inherited. It more resembled a discouraged and disparaged ragtag army that ran the gamut from despairing to uncaring. As for taking on my friend Paul, he recognized it as one of those political defeats that seasoned politicians learn to put behind them.

And it was no unanimous victory; not everyone thought I had leadership qualities. Though many of my fellow Democrats saw me as a fighter for causes I believed in, a large proportion of the caucus, which had been controlled by the good ol' boy network for as long as anyone could remember, had grave worries as to my reliability. I wasn't someone that they could trust to do the expedient thing. To add to their worries I had, throughout my first four years, shown a propensity to push my own ideas, and my willingness to make politics a partisan war at every opportunity left many with a feeling of apprehension. The Republicans saw me as, plain and simple, a troublemaker. That's why Murphy inherited me. This, of course, was of my own doing. I had made no secret that not only was I a Democrat through and through but I was a liberal Democrat, who believed that government had no purpose other than to help those in need. This, to many conservatives in my caucus, amounted at best to tilting at windmills and at worst to stupidity.

Defining Our Problems

Paul and I didn't win much of anything over the next few months, but we were learning a great deal. Most important, we came to recognize that we had two major problems.

The most serious was the numbers. Democrats had always been the minority in the Vermont legislature, and the fact that they couldn't simply unite and win the day on an issue forced them to go into what I called survival mode. They had long ago learned through harsh experience that "rolling over" went far in maintaining the majority's patronizing demeanor. I had this driven home to me shortly after becoming minority leader.

The Republicans had made no secret that the bill on the floor was a high priority of theirs. I, in return, had publicly stated that I thought it was just another giveaway to the electric power companies and that the consumer would end up paying the cost. I had done my homework and felt I had a good grasp of a very complex, thirty-page bill. I was ready to do battle on the floor.

A battle it was; the debate went on for the better part of an hour. Back and forth we went, with the two Republican leaders receiving notes from lobbyists strategically seated nearby in the gallery, their cannon aimed directly at me. When it was all over I slumped in my seat convinced that I had taken them apart piece by piece. I was certain this was going to be the first significant victory of our young regime.

When they called the roll we found that we had been trounced 91 to 55. Give me a break. We had sixty-five damned Democrats out there. Obviously, some had put on their survival suits and left me out to dry. I was devastated. I was also mad as hell.

After any fight such as this, the normal procedure is to accept the "good try; better luck next time" compliments and go off and lick your wounds. On the way out of the well, Carmel Babcock, a Democrat from Burlington, came by and gave me a hug.

"Ralph, you were great. I wish I could express myself with such eloquence. You really put them in their place, and I was almost moved to tears when you pointed out the plight of the seniors under this bill."

"Thanks, Carmel. I appreciate you saying that."

Then it struck me.

"Hey! Wait a minute, Carmel. You voted against me. What's the deal?"

The answer was brief and brutally honest.

"Ralph, you were going to lose anyway, I thought I'd go with the winner."

Welcome to the real world, Ralphie. I might have had sixty-five Democrats in body, but there were only fifty-five in spirit. I didn't have to know higher math to realize we had more than a numbers problem—I could safely add the undeniable and unpleasant fact that we had an attitude problem to go with it. It became very clear that we had to win something—anything—and quick.

Winning One

Victory came at the most inconceivable time and in the most unsuspected situation—amid the rush to adjournment through another rules suspension. That was a subject I knew a little something about, as I was never allowed to forget my stand beside the women two sessions earlier.

We were scheduled to adjourn Saturday night, April 14, 1984. All that remained on the docket was a half-dozen "small bills" and, of course, the appropriations bill. At this late date in the session, if someone had a pet bill he or she had to take heed to beat the Big Bill to passage, or suffer the consequences. It was understood that once the appropriations bill was passed the next motion would be to adjourn, leaving the remaining work either to await the second year of the session or, if in the final year, to die. Buried in the small pile of so-called unimportant legislation was a consumer credit bill that lifted the ceiling on the interest that credit card companies could charge consumers. If taxes made Republicans break out in a rash, then a bill such as this threatened to send liberal Democrats into cardiac arrest. This was a bill the Republicans and the banking interests swarming the hallways wanted badly. I gathered my Democrats in a quick caucus and persuaded them to kill the bill by refusing rules suspension. Up on the floor a few minutes later that's exactly what we did. Then all hell broke loose.

I've already described how rules suspension is necessary when things need to be speeded up. In some cases, when there is low attendance, thirty people well organized can bring the speeding train of adjournment to a screeching halt. And like the women two years earlier, we had done that now.

Our action didn't just frustrate the Republicans—it infuriated the Republican governor, Dick Snelling. He had already announced that he and his wife were scheduled to set sail on a cruise on Monday, and our action that evening threatened to push the session into the following week. Once into a new week there was no telling how long the session would be extended, as some members would look on the extra time as a reprieve for causes once thought of as lost.

I tried to explain to the press that we were aware that we were playing a dangerous political game but that we felt our cause was just. But even the governor, with prepaid, nonrefundable tickets for a cruise on a "Love Boat," couldn't just call the captain and explain that he was tied up "here in Vermont by a Machiavellian demagogue named Ralph Wright." The ship was going to sail with or without our governor.

Instead he called a press conference and did the next best thing. He called me a "tyrant and a bully." I heard he really got nasty in private.

Like the rest of the members, I went home for the weekend.

I was as scared as I had ever been. Prior to entering politics my name had been in the papers perhaps a half-dozen times, never for anything negative. But this was different. Our failure to allow suspension of the rules not only had made a lot of folks very angry, but now that the entire legislature had to return for another week it was costing the taxpayers an additional $100,000, which the press mentioned at every opportunity. I did plenty of soul searching that weekend. Having second thoughts as to the repercussions of our drastic action, I fully realized that we didn't have the votes to do anything but delay the inevitable. All I had done was guarantee that it was going to cost the taxpayers an additional $100,000 to do on Tuesday what could have been done on Saturday night. I couldn't figure a way out of what I was coming to think was close to a felony. Since then I have been called a lot worse and have been through episodes of derision and name calling that put it all in perspective, but for that moment in time, I was sure I had committed a crime that, if it didn't put me in the clink, was certainly going to bring a halt to what I had hoped would be a promising political career. I did what any smart con would do: I called my lawyer first thing Monday morning.

In this case my lawyer happened to be Bill Russell, chief of the Legislative Council. Beyond drafting bills and assisting members in legislative matters, the lawyers in the council on rare occasions are asked to assist members who find themselves in a legal bind deriving from their legislative responsibilities.

I took a shot in the dark and asked Bill if he would mind thumbing through the old journals to see if any leader, or anyone for that matter, had "abused" the rules suspension in the same manner as the governor was now publicly accusing me of doing. I didn't think there was a chance he would be successful in finding it.

To my amazement, it wasn't fifteen minutes later when he called back and said he thought he had found something.

"It's been done before," he exclaimed, sounding incredulous.

"You're kidding," I responded with excitement.

"Yeah! Back in 1975, the Republican leader held a group together and they refused to suspend. And just like now the entire assembly had to adjourn and return the following week to finish business." I could hardly restrain my glee.

"Actually," he went on, "this was a worse scenario in that the same leader who made the motion to suspend then turned around and voted against his own motion."

"Who the hell was arrogant enough to do that?" I asked.

"You won't believe this, Ralph. It was then-Republican floor leader Richard Snelling."

Well! Well! Even a blind squirrel finds an acorn once in a while.

Here's what Bob Sherman wrote the following Tuesday in the *Rutland Herald*: "House Democrats gave Ralph Wright a standing ovation when he appeared at the afternoon caucus. Most had signed a card, commemorating his Saturday night clash with Snelling and advising him to 'grin and ignore it.' Democrats view Wright as a conquering hero for standing up to Snelling."

Snelling and the Republicans in the House eventually won the issue because our returning the following week caused the bill lifting the ceiling on credit card interest to move automatically onto the Calendar, so that it required no rules suspension. But my Democrats had hung tough and stood up for what we believed. The Democrats had finally tasted victory. We were becoming believers, and it appeared that we had left our "bad attitude" behind us.

Now we had to do something about the numbers problem.

Becoming Speaker of the House

Paul and I stumbled through the next year and a half picking our fights carefully and, when the rare occasion arose, joining with the opposition. Vermont, like the rest of the nation, was experiencing some rough economic times. Revenues were down, and that meant either raising taxes or cutting programs—sometimes both.

We were fortunate in that our governor possessed both a caring attitude and the courage to do the right thing in this fiscal crunch. In his State of the State address Snelling announced that he had no intention of laying on poor Vermonters the burden the state now faced with the Reagan recession. He would introduce a bill that cut some programs in a peripheral way but had found a source for the additional revenues that were needed to meet his goal of a balanced budget. He would raise taxes.

House Republicans met this announcement with cold stares, none colder or more intense than that of the Republican leader, Bob Kinsey (of Craftsbury).

Kinsey was all that one might imagine if one were to draw an image of the prototypical Vermont legislator. A dairy farmer who could trace his heritage back five or six generations, he possessed the stoic independence that being his own boss provided. He could be a very stubborn man. And though he was not one to philosophize at length, no one ever walked away from Bob Kinsey wondering where he stood.

So it didn't take long for the Republican leader to tell his Republican governor, "We have no intention of supporting any tax increase, whatso-ever"—"we" being a major segment of his Republican caucus.

Not having the support of a majority of his party in the House, Snelling was forced to turn to his only other option—the Democrats.

We weren't exactly enamored with raising taxes in an election year either, but we weren't going to sit back and watch the programs we cared about get hacked to pieces up in the Appropriations Committee or down on the floor—both still decidedly controlled by the Republicans led by Speaker Morse and Kinsey. We drew up an alliance and set out to help the governor and his small number of remaining Republican faithful do what both we and they thought was the fair and right thing to do.

Snelling did the heavy lifting throughout the long and contentious struggle to get his tax package through both the House and the Republican-led Senate, and it became law as the 1984 session drew to a close. I'd be less than honest if I failed to admit that we enjoyed the schism now plaguing the majority party. It was also refreshing to know that the Snelling dominance of his party was going to allow us to be players in another successful effort. For three months the governor treated us with special care, and even Speaker Morse talked to us from time to time. Kinsey, though he still had a following of seventy or so of his caucus, ceased to communicate with both his governor and his Speaker. Morse had perhaps a dual reason for siding with his governor and cold-shouldering his floor leader. He had decided it was time for a change. He was not going to run for reelection to the House. We were going to have a new Speaker come 1985, and I decided, Why not me?

Narrowing the Gap

Politics in the Green Mountain State is a rather laid-back endeavor. At least it was at the time that I was entering into it. People didn't campaign for office. They "stood" for office. Paul and I set out to change all that in our effort to find Democratic candidates to run for the House. And much the same way we struggled through the 1984 session, we planned for the general election in the fall—by the seat of our pants. Oh! We were very much cognizant of the problem. You didn't have to be a neurosurgeon to realize I wasn't going to win much of anything, let alone the speakership, with an 84–65 minority (there was one independent), but what to do about it was another matter.

There was no background material we could turn to, so it became a simple choice for us to set about hacking a way in a political wilderness. Paul would recruit and train and, we hoped, help get elected all our Democratic candidates north of Montpelier; I would handle all those south of the capital.

Actually, it became more complicated than that, but not much. The first problem was how to find candidates. Vermont, as I noted, was filling up with a lot of bright, young activists from "down country," who were making their impact felt at local school board meetings and in town affairs. But attending meetings and voting at the local town hall wasn't the same as putting one's name on an election ballot.

We must have put fifty thousand miles on our cars that summer and fall, made somewhat easier by the fact that we were both teachers and had the summer free to roam the byways of rural Vermont. Although I was to do this every two years for the next decade, it was never the same as this first effort in 1984. I enjoyed every minute of it. We rumbled through towns and villages that we had never heard of before, searching for candidates for the House. It was a difficult task, for we often found ourselves in backwaters where we didn't know a soul. That wouldn't stop us though. More than once while grabbing lunch or wandering around the village we would strike up a conversation with one of the locals, hoping to come across a person we could run down and persuade to join our team and run for the district's seat. It wasn't the best method of recruitment, but it was all our inexperience allowed. The quality of the candidate was foremost on our minds, but the political nature of the district ran a close second.

That was a subject that we could research back ten or twelve years to project a picture of five or six past elections. So we spent time going over those trying to configure a master map of the entire 150 House districts and whether they had voted Democratic or Republican. The trick was not just to find a candidate but to find one in a district we could win. There are districts in Vermont so solidly Republican that we could have run a John F. Kennedy clone and taken a bad beating. We concluded that it served little purpose to have a Democratic candidate in all 150 districts and that we were better off targeting districts that we felt we could win.

Recruiting was just the first phase of our intended quest. The July filing date pushed us into our second stage, the training of candidates. Most of our efforts at training took the form of one-to-one counseling, but we did something else no one had done before: we ran training sessions. We would bring all the candidates to a central meeting place, usually Montpelier, and always on a Saturday, and spend the day teaching the rudiments of political campaigning. We encouraged them to do everything in their power to recruit and bring with them a campaign manager. We held two training sessions focusing on the normal things, such as leaflets, advertising, phone banks, and door-to-door canvassing. But we also included the little things that could decide a close election: absentee ballots, registering voters, compiling as many names on a petition as possible before filing deadlines, bullet votes, and the consequences of not having a running mate if in a two-member district. Knocking on doors was our focal point, and we reenacted actual presentations by having some of our fellow Democrats role play the different types of situations a candidate might run into.

Though our time became limited, Poirier and I kept at it through the fall, hitting the road on weekends and spending hours on the phone weekday evenings with our 135 candidates (new and old). We were going to accomplish something the Democrats had never seriously attempted, let alone brought to fruition. We would win the House and then conquer the podium. We believed that we could do it as sure as we knew we existed. I never remember being tired, and I can't recall Paul ever complaining of being tired either. We were wired.

Election day came all too fast. We had the feeling that we hadn't done all that was possible, but that's always the way it is. You're happy it's over but nervous that you haven't done quite enough. Now it was up to the people. Our fate was in their hands.

We won seven additional seats that election day. And though we were a little disappointed that we didn't reach the majority we had sought, it

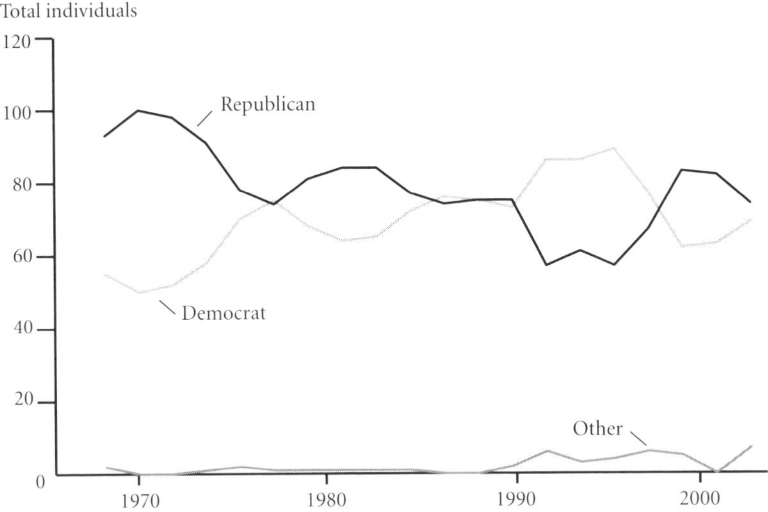

Source: State of Vermont Legislative Council.

was a giant step in the right direction. Our numbers were now at seventy-two, and we had narrowed the gap significantly (see Figure 4.1). The Republicans had lost seven seats to stand at seventy-seven (the one independent returned). Encouraging as this was we still were well aware that we were going to have to get a little help from our friends across the aisle if we were going to capture the podium.

Getting the Democratic Nomination for Speaker

We surprised a lot of unsuspecting people on that election day in 1984. We had moved from sixty-five House Democrats to seventy-two, placing the speakership within striking distance. With the Republicans' 77–72 advantage there was no guarantee that we could pull it off, and the Democrat chosen in caucus to vie for the speakership had to face the raw fact that there was not a minority Speaker in power in the entire nation. Still, we were convinced that we could woo a handful of Republicans to cross over and give us the seventy-six votes we needed to claim the crown. Before any of that, however, we had to decide who our candidate for Speaker would be. Corcoran had no doubt, and Poirier quickly agreed, that I, as Democratic leader, should be the one.

Once again it was back in the car as I hit the road intending to see every Democrat on his or her turf. There were approximately four weeks between election day and the first Saturday in December, when our caucus met to select its leaders and a candidate for Speaker. This was going to prove difficult, as my announced opponent was John Zampieri, a conservative Democrat from Ryegate in the Northeast Kingdom, the mostly rural northeast section of the state. He was a twenty-year veteran who had chaired the Transportation Committee for the last four years. A cozy enough member of the inner circle, Zampieri had befriended Speaker Morse sufficiently (I assumed, as did everyone else, that meant he had crossed party lines and voted for him) to be appointed a Democratic chair in a Republican regime. I didn't take him lightly.

My strategy was simple. Hold my liberals and work hard to win the trust of the moderates who made up the middle third of the caucus. The new members were going to support me; I had been their lifeline during the campaign and could take some credit in their being where they were.

I campaigned with the same energy that had carried us through election day, with Paul or Corcoran riding shotgun at each stop. At caucus time I felt I had the votes, but secret ballots are a scary experience, and the nervousness that accompanies one into these frays doesn't leave much in the way of pleasant memories.

When the votes were tallied I won the nomination 45 to 27.

The Republicans, who nominated Bob Kinsey to be my opponent in their own caucus a week later, had to suppress their joy at what had occurred in our caucus. To their aristocratic eyes, Zampieri, as a conservative, held out what little hope the Democrats had of enticing some of their Republican members to cross over and vote Democratic. John, after all, had been a congenial fellow and was a welcome member of the good ol' boys club. Kinsey presented a few flaws in that he had created a rift in his party over the deficit issue during the past session, but that small breach in the Republican dike had been sealed with the unity of the caucus nominating procedure. More subtle but potentially lethal to his party's unity were three flaws: (1) Kinsey was not a very good speaker on the floor; (2) he had gained a reputation within his caucus as being somewhat obstinate (his refusal to cooperate with Governor Snelling on the previous deficit problem); and (3) he had a reputation of "being a good dancer." None of these flaws would have amounted to anything had his ambition never risen above a committee chairmanship, or being leader.

Being Speaker was another matter. The members, no matter the party, set a higher bar for their Speaker. This was a post that required a level of polish and respect that other members did not have to meet. I served with chairpersons who drank too much and others who flitted around the clubs after dark.[1] And though they might have risen to a committee chair, these character flaws left them little hope of being Speaker. Their agenda after dark was not a matter of concern for most of their colleagues, but it was for some, and I would meet one a couple of weeks later who belonged to the Republican side of the aisle. He never accused Kinsey of anything, nor do I, but he committed his vote to me.

Regardless, my nomination allayed all the Republicans' fears of party-jumping, as for Republicans, it bordered on the incredible to think of a liberal Democrat with a funny Boston accent presiding over the Vermont House. This, coupled with their five-seat majority, broadened their comfort zone. If you were Jimmy the Greek, you were probably hedging your bets on me. It appeared the Democrats had self-destructed by choosing the least strong of their two candidates—me.

Winning Republican Support

At the time, the Republicans' prognosis looked to be right on. Even if I held all seventy-two Democrats together I still needed four Republicans to come over to get to seventy-six. And it was no sure bet that all my Democrats would stay loyal. Murphy had been quoted in the *Rutland Herald* the day after our caucus as saying after the tally was read, "There goes the speakership." Of course, he denied it. But if Murphy was uttering such things aloud, what in good heavens could the likes of Tom Candon be thinking and saying behind my back? But that concern would have to come later. I had to round up some Republicans who were willing to jump party and vote for me.

I immediately set out for the Rutland area, for it was in this blue-collar working community that I could test my support on both sides of the aisle. My first stop was "Ab" Wilson's Barber Shop in Fair Haven. Ab, a Republican representative, had a mind of his own and the courage to do what he thought was right. I had been out to dinner with this real Vermonter and his wife several times while in session and had got to know him quite well. I had also taken advantage of Ab's largesse by visiting his makeshift barbershop in the Transportation Committee room after hours. Now I found him at home and got right to the point.

"Ab, I'm here to ask you for your support in my run for the speakership. I think we're close enough friends for you, hopefully, to agree I would be the better Speaker to represent us all." I waited, fearfully anticipating his answer.

And the simple response nearly floored me.

"I'll vote for you."

That was it?

Then he added, "But I don't want to read about it in the papers. They'll get mean if they find out. They won't even talk to Harold Weidman."[2] He went on, "I saw poor Harold the other day. Ever since his announcement on the radio that he was going to support you he's got a flood of calls trying to get him back on board. I don't need the hassle."

"I hope you won't change your mind, Ab. They know we're friends and they're not stupid. They'll put two and two together and you'll be hearing from them."

"That's fine. I can deal with that. I gave you my word, and you don't have to worry about me changing my mind."

Coming from Ab, I didn't spend any time worrying about it. The next person I sought out wasn't going to be quite as easy.

Dealing with the Godfather

Tom Candon was a poker-faced veteran of over twenty years in the legislature. He had for years been the behind-the-scenes Democratic leader in the House. Even when the women held that brief tenure in leadership it was Candon who had allowed it to happen, and when they gave it all up for their different reasons, it was Candon who engineered their departure, indirectly and quietly. He was the epitome of the good ol' boy gang and its uncontested leader. It was no secret that he looked at my rise to leadership as a mistake; he considered me a young upstart who was rocking the boat his Democrats had steered in calm waters for nearly twenty years.

But I desperately needed his support now, and I had to do whatever it took to get it. Not his vote, just his support.

My problem, not to seem abrupt, was that he didn't like me. And he didn't much care for my stand on the issues, either. He may have given up the reins of the Democratic leadership just after my first term, but he still had a firm grip on the other conservative Democrats, and he was the best Democratic friend the Republicans had. I wasn't imagining this; the grapevine had made it very clear that he thought the caucus had made a huge mistake by nominating me as their Speaker candidate, and I wasn't planning on his vote.

I hoped to survive his not voting for me, but I was certain I wouldn't survive without his outward support. I knew I would lose a small number of Democratic votes, but I hoped I could keep it at just that: a small number, very small. His lieutenants were the ones I was after, and I was certain they would take their cue from Tom. They didn't call him the Godfather for nothing.

I straightened my shoulders, took a deep breath, and began the long walk up the four flights of stairs to his office. This was a scene right out of a Sam Spade movie. It was not the cleanest of hallways I walked down, trying to read the writing on the smoked glass windows in the doors. The forty-watt bulb overhead didn't help. I tapped gently on the door labeled "Thomas Candon, Appraiser" and was beckoned in. He certainly wasn't expecting me.

We exchanged hellos and I got right to the point,

"Tom, I know I probably didn't have to drop by," I stammered, "but I don't want you to think I'm taking anything for granted. . . . Well I want you to know I care enough to ask you for your support. You know—not taking anything for granted."

He interrupted, "Well, you didn't have to waste your time stopping by here, Ralph. You can count on my vote. How's it going?"

"Great. I've got enough Republicans," I lied. "If I can hold the seventy-two Dems, I'm pretty certain I can beat Kinsey." He never rose from his chair but sat motionless. I continued nervously, "I need you to talk to a few of the members for me. A word from you will go a long way. Guys like Keefer [Bud Keefe, R-Rutland], and Walter [Moore, D-Rutland], and maybe Jack [Candon, D-Norwich, his son—newly elected], though I think I'm OK with Walter, as we get along pretty well. Vote a lot alike. But Keefer will feel more comfortable if you tell him it's OK. You could help me with Danny [DeBonis] and Joe Reed [D-White River Junction], too."

"No problem," he returned the lie. "I'd be happy to help. Of course, you're gonna take care of them. Not going to move them around to other committees, or anything, are you?"

"No. No, of course not. They should stay right where they are, unless they want to go to other committees. Where do you think Jack would be happy? Then there's the chair of your committee; that's yours if you want it."

He totally ignored my solicitous offer of the chair of the powerful Ways and Means Committee, on which he had been a long-serving vice-chair, and moved instead to his son Jack's situation. "Just don't put Jack in with me. He'd start bossing me around in front of everybody."

"No problem, I just want to make sure I don't put anyone where they don't want to be." I got up to go and walked past the ceiling-high, dirt-stained window. All that was visible was another brick building next-door and pigeons huddled on the ledge.

"Quite a scenic view," I joked sarcastically, as I opened the door. He hadn't moved from behind his desk. Suddenly I turned as if I had forgotten something. Looking straight at him, "Oh, by the way, Tom, no big deal, but I'd like you to nominate me from the floor."

I thought his teeth would fall out.

"I, uh, I can't do that." And then he caught himself. "I mean I'm not the best one to, uh . . ." He struggled to find the right excuse. "You should get someone else. I'm not that great a speaker on the floor."

"You'll do just fine, Tom. Just fine."

"Really. I'm no good at speech writing. Get somebody who can do you more good than I can."

"Don't worry a bit about that, Tom. I'll write it for you. You just deliver it."

"OK, I guess so." The pain was almost visible.

I skipped down the same stairs that I had trudged up just minutes earlier. Candon might hide behind the secrecy of the ballot and vote against me, but his followers would see him on his feet singing my praises, and that would be all the signal necessary for them to follow and vote for the liberal Democrat with the funny Boston accent. As for Tom, I knew him well enough to know that if he sinned against me on the secret ballot with his own vote, it would be something not even his priest would ever be told. He would outwardly play the good soldier with his lieutenants.

I worked hard the next four weeks, and if I did slack off, Poirier and Corcoran were right there to make sure I made that extra effort to meet and speak to members personally. They, just as I did, felt the real possibility of pulling this thing off. No call went unmade, as we divided the list and kept counting. Paul and Tim would follow up calls I had made. Both were uncanny in reading people's voices, and Corcoran, especially, wouldn't hesitate to tell me when he thought someone was lying. If that happened I would have to make a special effort. More than likely that meant a second visit. Inevitably, there was something they wanted, and more than likely, Kinsey had already promised it to them. Often I couldn't top Kinsey's offer, but I could at least attempt to match it and put myself back on a level playing field. Amazingly, I never had to make a whole lot of promises concerning committee assignments. This was especially true with the Republicans who had committed to me. Harold and Ab had made it clear that they were offering their support for reasons other than a promise of a plum appointment. They wanted nothing. They had their own reasons for standing with me. The same held true for the other half-dozen Republicans that I had gotten commitments from. My Democrats proved less shy, but even they did not have an unreasonable number of demands.

The session opened on a bitter cold January day. Everyone showed up, 150 strong, as was to be the case in all my races for Speaker over the next ten years. I must have entered the State House just minutes after the janitor unlocked the doors. It was still dark outside. It seemed like an eternity waiting for the gavel to fall at ten o'clock.

I don't remember a whole lot of the four-hour period, but I shook the hands of a lot of people.

Vermont is unlike most states and Congress in that the legislators choose their Speaker by secret ballot right on the floor of the House, with all 150 members present. In Congress, and in all states as far as I am aware, the Speaker candidate is chosen in each party's caucus, sometimes by secret ballot, and then the members go to the floor for the ceremonial duty of making it official. The floor vote is a very public affair; members' votes are there for the world to see. Any member breaking ranks on the floor would be ostracized and drummed out of the party, his or her political life over. The procedure guarantees that the party in the majority always wins. Not so in Vermont.

The Vermont Constitution mandates that the vote for Speaker occur on the floor, *by secret ballot.* Astonishingly, it does not require that the candidates nominated be members of the House. Technically, a tourist from Kansas could drop by, be nominated, and become Speaker of the House. Only in Vermont.

Rumors had been flying back and forth that each side had been twisting arms and threatening members who were showing an air of independence. The press took advantage of the backbiting and name-calling and never seemed to have any trouble getting a quote from one side or the other and stirring up the pot. Word had spread that the Democrats had designed a secret coding system to reveal just how members had voted. The problem with that was that neither Kinsey nor I had any access to a ballot other than our own. Jim Douglas, then secretary of state and the future governor of Vermont (R; elected 2002), presided over the House election, and he was the only one who actually would have the ballots in his hands after the vote was counted and announced. What he did with them we will never know. The best I could do was to peek at the ballot of someone who was seated next to me. That was Poirier and I wasn't concerned about his vote.

Bang! Bang! Bang!

"The House will come to order."

Bang! Bang! Bang!

"The House will *please* come to order," Douglas implored the members, who began the scramble to their seats.

All I remember going through my mind was, If you lose, remember— no tears; no show of anger. Then it dawned on me, Christ, you haven't even prepared a concession speech. What'll you say? Do you walk out to meet Kinsey on his way to the podium to accept the gavel from Douglas? It'll look so clumsy, so stupid.

Now the clerks were calling the attendance roll. Then, like a ton of bricks, What if I win? I haven't even prepared an acceptance speech. What do you do, Wright, just stand up there looking like a jerk? I turned to Paul.

"Paul, we didn't prepare a speech. What am I going to say?"

Paul was little consolation, as his sage advice came back, "No problem; just wing it."

"Just *wing* it?" Thanks, Paul.

"Wright of Bennington," came the monotone of the clerk as he neared the end of the roll. Here goes, and I swear my mind passed into a semiconscious state for the next thirty or so minutes while nominating speeches were given for both Kinsey and me. I don't remember much of what was said, except for Candon delivering the speech of his life, presumably written by himself. His voice rang out in his praises for me, and he had members believing that we were witnesses to a historic moment. I never felt certain Tom voted for me that day, though Harris, who sat right in back of him, swears he saw Tom mark an *X* next to my name, but that didn't matter any more. I will say this: he was at his best.

It seemed like a thousand years we sat and waited, while the eight members selected to be counters by the secretary of state, supervised by the clerks, counted and recounted the 150 paper ballots. I couldn't tell anything by their movement or actions as they huddled around the conference table situated in the very center of the House. Then the word passed up the rows, and I turned anxiously to Paul.

"What's going on?" I asked, my voice nearly breaking with both alarm and anxiety.

"They're counting them a third time," he hurriedly responded. "It's tied up."

"Tied up?" I said in a loud voice. "How can it be tied up? All this and it ends in a tie?"

"I don't know. Maybe somebody didn't vote, or voted for somebody else."

And then with a tremble in my voice, "Paul, I'm dead if this is tied up and we have to revote." We had talked about this before, and we both agreed that if anything like this happened the Republicans would surely call for a recess, go into caucus, and that would be the end of us. They'd have beaten the truth into the handful of "traitors" and then harangued them into coming back up on the floor and voting for Kinsey.

The rumor of a tie was wrong. But it was a very close race. That's why the recount. Another two lifetimes passed and I still couldn't read a thing from the group on the floor. Finally, a single piece of paper was handed by the head clerk to Secretary Douglas. And words came from the seat next to me.

"I think we're OK." It was Paul's comforting voice. "Douglas doesn't look too happy."

"Christ, he's smiling, Paul."

"He wasn't a second ago when he first saw the results."

And then the gavel banged again.

"The House will please come to order." Instant silence swept down from the huge, overflowing crowd in the gallery.

"Please listen to the results of your vote."

"The member from Craftsbury, Mr. Kinsey, seventy-four.

"The member from Bennington, Mr. Wright, seventy-six. The member from Bennington having obtained a majority of the votes of those present, *the Chair now declares Ralph Wright your new Speaker of the Vermont House.*"

I went totally numb.

We had done it.

Leadership

It may seem strange, but I never gave leadership much thought. I spent twelve years of my sixteen-year legislative career as a leader and never went much beyond a somewhat trite explanation of how I approached leadership, by quipping, when asked, "Just do what's right and be prepared to fight." The simplicity and nonchalance of this statement, some would say the arrogance, amazes me to this day.

Leaders come in all shapes and forms. There are no set rules for a new Speaker to follow, and thus they tend to adhere to the attributes that got them there. These would include intellect, energy, self-confidence, and a driving need to achieve. But surprisingly, at least in my opinion, the successful leader in a democratic legislature has to find someone to follow. I've been up close to, and known well, four Speakers, who either preceded or followed me. In many ways they were different, but all were captive to what others wanted: one to a forceful governor; another to the majority of an opposing party; a third to events of the time; and a fourth to maintaining the status quo. Each led, some farther than others. Two were re-elected once; two twice.

I was captive to my caucus, and that, I believe, is a major reason why I managed to serve five terms. As the majority of my caucus throughout my tenure was either liberal or moderate, I had few second thoughts as to the direction they wanted me to take them. They decided their agenda, and I rarely was in disagreement. I seldom attended the caucus because I felt that my leaders had a tough enough job finding a true consensus without the Speaker's presence intimidating free discussion. But I always was well informed about where they wanted to go. The members who participated felt free to speak without fear or favor, and this allowed the leaders to trust their final decisions as to which issues they wanted to push and hang tough with, and which they didn't. From the very first meeting when they stood and applauded my victory over Governor Snelling back in 1985 they maintained a high energy and enthusiastic temperament. Not until my last term, 1992–1994, when we finally captured a big majority, did I experience a break in the cohesiveness of the members.

After my initial win of the speakership in 1985, I was fortunate to win reelection to the post four more times. Each election was hotly contested. As I shake hands with Ed Zuccaro, my Republican opponent, after my 1987 victory, many Republicans (over my right shoulder) don't mask their disappointment.

Then it seemed that success had presented the nonchalance that comes with safety in numbers, and our relationship began coming apart. For my part I had grown weary and less daring or caring, and that is a sure sign that the leader can no longer lead.

I served with three governors, but served under none. I did have to deal with being a minority Speaker for four of those terms, but I survived because I had created and nurtured as friends a small cadre of Republican supporters that became known as my "hockey team." As for events that might alter one's course, we took those lemons and made lemonade.

But none of this explains the rudiments of leadership. After all, times and events might have placed me at the podium with a majority of Democrats in control, weak governors, and nothing much happening to alter a sedate agenda. That I served as a minority Speaker, with three pretty strong governors and in fairly turbulent times, meant that I was forced to draw whatever leadership qualities I had from other sources. I can name five.

Having the Energy

I took my job seriously. It was a full-time endeavor, and I was willing to spend whatever time it took to achieve my goals. Only Mike Obuchowski (who would become the Speaker after I left) ever arrived at the State House before I did. I remember many a cold winter morning that I would arrive before the sun and use my key to gain entry to an empty cafeteria to make the first pot of coffee. This would prove to be the only quiet time in what became a routine fourteen hours at the State House. My day ended only after the vast majority of members had left for home or dinner. Because I stayed in the capital during the week, I was usually in bed no later than ten o'clock, only to have anxiety and nerves awaken me six hours later, ready to start all over again.

Leadership is not for sissies.

Doing Your Homework

There were a lot of issues that the members understood a whole lot better than I, but no one ever spent more time trying to understand the people behind those issues.

I did more listening during my sixteen years in the legislature than I had done in my previous forty-three years on the planet. No matter how minor the problem, everybody had a story, a viewpoint, or a better mousetrap. And I heard them out, always probing, and not infrequently using humor and sarcasm to force them to reveal where they were truly coming from. Conversations lasted longer than either participant might have liked, but I sometimes came away a lot smarter on the issue than I had entered and, more important, knowing a ton more about the person than he or she ever meant to reveal.

It was through these numberless one-on-one conversations that I accumulated knowledge that I don't believe I ever could have obtained in formal meetings. Not that there was any lack of those, but I found too many of them constraining as to forthrightness and purpose. Meetings that encompassed more than two people often ended in petty squabbles or, worse, having to listen to too many who had nothing to say but felt compelled to say it anyway. The drone that permeated this type of meeting could be overbearing, and I avoided them whenever possible. As a leader I was always cognizant of whom I was leading.

Using People

I mentioned earlier that I was very fortunate in that I served with a whole lot of very capable people, and I used them. Poirier, Campbell, and Brooks were great leaders themselves, and I was as close to them then, and am to this day, as I have ever been to any colleagues. We worked together, ate together, and drank together for better than a decade. I spent more time with them than I did with my wife. They knew things I didn't, saw people I couldn't, and did things I wouldn't. We built a trust among us that allowed us to venture into places we might not have gone alone. And often they saved me from disaster.

But no state legislature is successful if it is dominated by a handful of leaders, and I take both pleasure and some pride in having been surrounded by dozens of members who knew how to organize and control a committee, report and defend a bill, work with their counterparts in the Senate, and stay true to the cause. These members were my orchestra, extraordinarily talented in their own right, playing instruments I had little knowledge of, waiting for the maestro to tap the baton. I had come to know them, their strengths, their creativity, their moods, and their fervent desire to create great music, and we sometimes produced a symphony to the ears.

Anticipating the Opposition

All my life I have been a reader. Once when I was a youngster I stole a book. Not a bike, nor a hubcap—a book. I still remember the title: *Andy Jackson Goes to War*. The memory of that crabby old librarian shooing me from the counter, after I had nervously asked how I might take a book out, is as vivid in my mind today as it was over sixty years ago. She admonished me for not being old enough to borrow a book (eight years of age) and ordered me to place the book back on the shelf. I dragged myself red-faced back to the children's reading room and, determined not to be denied, slipped up to the window and dropped *Andy* out. I then took the long march past her desk, exited in disgrace, and ran around the back of the building and retrieved the book. I still have the damn book, and the fines have to be in the thousands of dollars. The librarian, I'm sure, is long gone, but not the knowledge she once tried to deny me. As Murphy said, "Knowledge is power." The difference is that Murph only stole notes from a wastebasket—I stole a whole book.

As a leader I always tried to see the viewpoint of the opposition; actually I often made it a study—to know what they knew and, if possible, keep them from knowing what I knew. If I could anticipate not just their arguments but, more important, their motives, I could then act accordingly. If this meant endless hours of preparation, I was willing to do the work. I always banked on the opponent on any issue being a whole lot more careless than my side would be, and usually this proved out. I don't ever remember losing an issue on the floor of the House over ten years, and that wasn't due to luck. Nor was it due to our being "right," as it's not enough in a legislature just to be right. You've got to be good first, and then pray to the baby Jesus that you were also right.

Being a Leader

Perhaps I've convinced you that a leader has to have energy, do the homework, use the surrounding talent, and anticipate every possible avenue of opposition to the goal. But when does the leader step forward and lead?

The short answer is, when nobody else can.

In the perfect world of the leader, he or she would magically awaken in a legislature filled with members who all have the same agenda he does and can't wait to help achieve it. This legislature would obviously be made up of the best and brightest, who cared not a diddle whether they ever were reelected and would never aspire to the governor's office. In this "Wally-World" (it was in one of those great "family vacation" movies, with Chevy Chase) the leader could merely point the way and bask in the astounding accomplishments his or her flock delivered, obviously without raising a penny in taxes, adding a single new program to the bureaucracy, or regulating anyone or anything.

But that's not how I remember it.

A leader has to lead, and that means placing himself or herself in harm's way—politically speaking. The members expect it and would quickly refuse to follow any leader not willing to step to the front. I have boxes of old press clippings that are testimony to the dangers of leadership.

The leader, by the very title, becomes the target, not just for the opposition party but for a press that needs to be fed daily; for a caucus that always has a contingent that wants more or less than can be delivered; for the pettiness of too many individuals; for a Senate that has its own goals in mind; for a veto-wielding governor; and for a public that expects us all to get moving on what we're intent on doing and get the hell out of there.

I was never confused as to my role as leader.

I led. Sometimes successfully, sometimes not—but I led. When things got hot I was in little doubt as to how my members understood my job description—"You're the Man; you take the heat." Others saw it much the same way. When the press aimed their pens, it was seldom at the sponsor of a bill, the chairperson who muscled it out of committee, or the leader who helped push it through on the floor. The bull's eye was right where it had to be—on the chest of the leader. I might have had next to nothing to do with creating the bill; the truth of the matter is that the vast majority of the legislation a legislature pushes through originates in the governor's office, party caucuses, or the minds of individual members. But the machinations of pushing a bill through a legislature nearly always involve the leader and consequently distort what might really be happening. It is here that the press and public often see a very different picture. And it is here on the bill's journey through the legislative maze that the focus becomes re-centered on leadership.

Don't get me wrong, I received more than my share of "puff pieces" from the press that too often gave me credit for things I had absolutely nothing to do with. But there was another side to that coin: I also took some blame for things I had little or no participation in. That was the nature of things, and in my case, as a leader, I was very proactive and consequently out front and an easy target. I didn't especially like it, but I learned to deal with it. I came to grasp the very real meaning behind the old advice that if one wants to lead he or she had better develop a tough hide.

A leader, knowing all these consequences, can avoid discredit and eventual loss of support, but he or she would have to possess the allure of a snake charmer or the patience of a fence sitter. I had neither. What I did have was a pretty clear understanding of the trust and power that I inherited when I was handed the gavel. They asked me to lead and I set out to do it. It wasn't easy. It required that I overcome my innate fear of failure and also required a never-ending search for talents I wasn't sure I possessed. I take some small pride that I found those qualities when I most needed them, and in this way I think I was able to comprehend and care about my members and their shared values, as well as display a willingness, whatever the cost, to lead them to their goals.

Notes

1. There are "watering holes" located near every state capitol that cater to legislators and lobbyists. The favorite at this time was a tavern six miles south of the capitol called the Little Red Roadhouse. It was isolated and became a regular gathering place on Wednesday nights for those who liked to dance, not always with their wives.

2. Republican Harold Weidman was the third member of the "odd trio" that made up my condo conclave. Weidman and I were both freshmen in 1979, and we roomed across from the State House at the Tavern Inn. We became close friends while kibitzing night after night in the Tavern's lobby. When Corcoran and I decided to rent a condominium we asked Harold to join us. Harold, politically unsophisticated, had received a call from his local radio station asking him how he was going to vote in the Speaker's race. Harold being Harold, he answered, "I'm going to do the old-fashioned thing. I'm going to vote for the best man. Ralph Wright." The Republicans had been hounding him since.

5

The View from the Podium

Conducting the Symphony

I WOULD ENVISION the House chamber as a symphony hall. Where the representatives sat was where the 150 members of the orchestra sat. As the Speaker at the podium, I was merely the conductor. The talent was arrayed in front of me. They were the strings and horns, and it was my job as the conductor to know who the various musicians were and when to bring them in. If I did it right, and anticipated timing and talent, this orchestra produced a symphony of sound, music to the ears, so to speak. If, on the other hand, I brought in the wrong players at the wrong time, all that occurred was noise. It was no different with the people's legislature.

I don't believe anyone comes to the Speaker's job prepared, because I don't know where one would go to gain the insight or gather the knowledge required just to stay on top of things. It doesn't matter whether we're talking about California with its full-time professionals or tiny Vermont with its part-time citizen legislature. The same ingredients are required. Survival necessitates that the person in charge has to deal with the opposition party, members of his or her own party who have different agendas, an executive branch, the press, special interest groups, lobbyists, and a ritual of process that must be followed. I recognized early that a new suit and a ready smile weren't going to be enough.

Right from the time a Speaker is announced the winner, sworn in by the secretary of state, and handed the gavel, they are on their own. The press rushes out, the galleries empty, and there one is—on top of the world and seemingly all alone.

Of all the images that have stayed with me over the years, none give me more joy and satisfaction than the view from the podium. I am still honored to have had the privilege to preside over the House for ten years.

Only the members' understanding and the historical knowledge of the clerks seated below the dais got me through my acceptance speech and the motion to adjourn for the morning. The clerks had prepared for a new Speaker and did their usual efficient duty. The acceptance speech was something else. When I got to the part (remember, I was winging it) where I pledged "to lead this great state of Vermont," it didn't come out exactly as I wanted. For some unknown reason I didn't say that. Instead, what the members heard was "to lead this great Commonwealth of Massachusetts." My friends roared in laughter; the Republicans, realizing their darkest nightmare, groaned in despair, convinced that "this guy doesn't even know what state he's in."

Getting On with Being Speaker

As I mentioned earlier, there's no IQ test for admission to the legislature. The place would not be full if there were. Still, I worked with some absolutely brilliant people during my tenure. There were others who struggled with the complex. Perhaps not surprisingly, it is the bright who run the risk of going bust. The legislature, like most other entities, works best on the premise, Keep it simple, stupid. The members who complicated their effort to the point that nobody could understand what they were talking about ran the risk that the rest of the members would invoke the rule, When in doubt vote no.

Maintaining any semblance of control in the House took all the personal and political skills I possessed and then some. A Speaker, no matter who it is, or which party he or she belongs to, is ultimately and fatally at the mercy of the membership. It was a significant enough trick to become a minority Speaker in the first place; it was a miracle of sorts to maintain that high post. There were times when it seemed everyone had a gripe or was on a mission with or against the Speaker. The trick was to be able to see trouble as it entered the building—and if you were really lucky, *before* it entered.

I broke the membership into several loosely defined categories, which made it easier for me to generalize about what motivated them. I soon earned a reputation, only somewhat deserved, for being able to read people. What I really had developed was the patience to take the time to learn all I could about what was important to them. Then it was a matter of delivering the goods.

Category 1: The Issues People

Mostly liberals, but also a number of fiscal conservatives, the issues people came to the legislature with an agenda, and they were, to a person, legislators who knew what they were after and worked hard to achieve their goals. They read their bills, got involved in the minutiae of committee, and took life a whole lot more seriously than the normal Joe or Jane. And though I felt the Democrats had the greater number of this type, Republicans had their share of conscientious conservatives, who might be reactionary on fiscal matters but liberal on social issues. Because membership in this group crossed party lines, at times they joined forces to achieve a common goal, as when the women of both parties hung together and created a force such as the women's caucus mentioned earlier, or when Republicans and Democrats in a district or county had the possibility of bringing services or funds home to their constituents ("pork") and would forget their differences and fight as a team.

When issues of the soul and of deep importance, such as abortion or gay rights, arose the "conscience members" could be relied on to break party ranks and do what they felt was right. This is what occurred under the Snelling administration in 1984, in the case of the deficit, when Democrats and Republicans put aside their party differences and followed their consciences to bail the state out. This cross-party unity was to emerge many times over the years—for example, in 2000, when the civil unions bill became law (see chap. 8).

Issues people couldn't be bought, if I may use the common political vernacular. Or at least their price would be considerably higher than normal. A promise of a junket or financial help in their reelection would be curtly dismissed as an insult to their integrity. They hadn't put their finger to the wind in arriving at their beliefs. These were people who had evolved a philosophy over a lifetime of learning and knew who they were and what they believed. Consequently I never insulted them in this manner. My approach to redirecting them might be a stab at explaining to them that perhaps their cause was just one battle in a long war to change society, and that a different choice of when to fight that battle held out more promise for success. Becoming arbitrary, talking down to them, or in any way questioning their commitment or intelligence put a stop to the conversation.

To a Speaker with a liberal agenda of his own they were a godsend. Seldom did the leadership have to spend inordinate time trying to persuade them to vote a certain way on an issue. When we did the count on issues that we knew would bring opposition they served as a base for the building to the magic number seventy-six. The base might be thirty or forty strong. Getting the remaining thirty-five-odd votes would be something else. I often said that one could get forty votes for the craziest of ideas. Getting the last thirty-six took heavy lifting.

I don't want the reader to think that the what's-in-it-for-me folks lacked intelligence or a moral code. Both are, like art, often in the eyes of the beholder. It's just that this group seldom had an agenda. Or if they did, it was ever-changing. In many ways they understood better than others the lifeblood of the legislature, or any deliberative body for that matter, the art of compromise. And compromise frequently was interpreted by these smiling souls as, "You get something, and I get something, right?" Though they were not without ambition, and nobody goes to the legislature without at least a tad of that, they never seemed to overreach. An appointment to a House committee that afforded comfort or expediency to them or their constituents—a farmer to Agriculture, a former town clerk to Municipal Corporations and Elections, a small business owner to Commerce; assignment on one of the hundred or so regional or national legislative committees that provided them with the opportunity to see the country and at times the world; or just a plain old junket to Las Vegas or Disney World was enough to bring them around. Even special events entered the picture from time to time; I once used special invitations I received to the Ryder Cup Tournament to persuade a foursome to come on over. They came back and presented me with an umbrella emblazoned with the Prudential Insurance Company logo. It may still be stashed in the back of the closet in the Speaker's office.

The what's-in-it-for-me contingent also crossed party lines, for, as mentioned earlier, some Republican friends had supported me for Speaker. The core of these supporters were decidedly "conscience" members, but a few were what's-in-it-for-me supporters. The press referred to them as the Speaker's "hockey team" because a very persistent *Rutland Herald* reporter once caught us trying to sneak down to Boston to attend a Bruins game as the guests of a corporate friend. Of the eight of us who made the trip, six were Republicans. It proved embarrassing, and though no violation of the Ethics Rules (of which there were few at that time), it was wrong and we shouldn't have done it.

Though I never could dispel the criticism that my hockey team was being bought and paid for by the Speaker, this was only a half-truth. Of the ten or twelve Republicans from whom I would get commitments prior to each Speaker's race, six were die-hard supporters, and not for any superfluous reasons. They were close friends, roommates, or just simply believers that I was the best man for the job. Never did one of these six ask me for anything. What shored up the critics' case was that I gave without the asking. The others in my so-called dirty dozen weren't shy about letting me know their wishes, and I did my best to accommodate them.

I don't want the reader to think the what's-in-it-for-me group were money in the bank. They weren't. The group knew the game and always looked forward to playing it. Too often, even if they agreed on the issue at hand, they would send word through one of the leaders that they didn't think they could support it. Then it was just a matter of finding out what they wanted. Sometimes it was simply an audience with the Speaker, to air a gripe or reestablish themselves as players; other times it might be a commitment for some help in getting their pet bill out of a committee or on the calendar. If the bill had a comfortable majority and I knew we didn't need their vote, I simply wouldn't show up to play their compromise game. If we needed their vote I'd have to suit up.

Category 3: The Backbenchers

There they sat like cows in their stalls, and almost without exception, all members of the Grand Old Party. The "loyal opposition," it seemed, knew only one word—no. It didn't matter the issue—taxes, aid to dependent children, mandatory kindergarten, immunization for children. They saw no reason to change the way the world worked. As far as they were concerned everything was fine just the way it was, and I often wondered what they were doing in the legislature. They would probably tell you, "Protecting the people from the likes of Ralph Wright."

Many in this group saw the State House as a pleasant place to spend their final years in retirement. The pay, though miserly, was a nice supplement to whatever they had stashed away during their working years, and the hours weren't bad either. Some of the backbenchers were remnants from the old days when each of the 262 Vermont towns got to send a representative to the assembly. And though the "one man, one vote" Supreme

Here in 1987, I listen to debate while leaning on member Walter Pyle's (R-Shoreham) legislative office. From time to time I handed over the Speaker's gavel to a Democratic leader or sometimes a Republican and moved around the floor. It was an exercise to remember where I came from and that I was still one of them.

Court decision in 1962 had almost totally revamped that archaic idea of democracy there were still more than a few towns in the more rural districts that remained little fiefdoms of conservatism and continued the tradition of sending their own version of the ayatollah to Montpelier. They tended to group together in one section of the well of the House, I suppose so that they could better appreciate the snide remarks and constant criticism of some of their more bitter members. My election as Speaker did little to lighten their mood.

My daily routine included a walk-around of the House floor prior to the opening gavel just saying hello and recognizing the more reserved and less-extroverted members' existence. Walking through the naysayers' section was like a stroll through a giant freezer. They'd say "Good morning," but I was never sure they meant it.

Of all the different enclaves in the House, this group required the least time and trouble. It would have been futile to solicit their support on the vast majority of our issues, and I seldom did so. Their numbers almost equaled those of my surefire liberals, though their energy, willingness to do their homework, and consequently their debating ability fell far short. (Thus the Democrats' success or failure often was in the hands of the what's-in-it-for-me group.) Exceptions to the negativity of the back-benchers occurred about as often as Halley's Comet. But I did get a yes out of one of them on an issue close to their hearts, a pay raise.

Virginio "Maxie" Perrotta was a Bennington Democrat who enjoyed their company. He was several years short of spending his winters in Florida when he got himself elected to the House. A World War II veteran who was discharged with the rank of captain—I often wondered how that happened—he settled into a long life as a character on the town stage. In his earlier years he had gotten himself arrested for running cockfights, and he was elected as a selectman, in that order. But everyone makes mis-takes, and besides, Maxie was a most lovable character. All was forgiven by the time he was ready to become an "Honorable." I liked Maxie because he would give you the shirt off his back and, more important, his vote for Speaker. The fact that I had never heard him speak out "yes" on a roll call vote made him one of those few Democrats welcomed in the back rows that some called "the barn." The pay raise bill was the exception.

We were on our way home for the weekend and just coming off the ramp of Interstate 89, when I turned to Maxie at the wheel. "Maxie! Can I ask you something?"

"Sure."

"Today, when we were voting on our pay raises—you voted aye. You shocked the hell out of me."

"You wanted me to, didn't you, Mr. Speaker?" he answered with some confusion.

"Yeah! Sure! It's just that, Maxie, I've never heard you vote yes. You've voted against every conceivable social program since you've been here. Today your aye brought the House down, Max."

Still searching for the answer, "I wasn't trying to be funny, Mr. Speaker."

"Then, you mind telling me why?"

"Look, Mr. Speaker. I'm no dummy. The people who vote for me aren't, either. Imagine if I had voted no on my own pay raise. Why they would have thought, 'Here we send ol' Maxie all the way to Montpelier and he ain't even smart enough to help himself. How can we expect him to help us?' That'd be the end of ol' Maxie."

It was my first hint at just how Maxie rose to the rank of captain.

Finding Common Ground with the Republican Leader

The Vermont State House is a very old structure that offered little in the way of comfort or convenience. The Speaker's office in 1985 had to be the smallest and most squalid in the country. The committee rooms were crowded with just the members present. When they filled with witnesses and lobbyists they became unbearable with the heat and the stench. It was time to do something about it, and I proposed that we put a two million dollar addition onto the existing structure by cutting into the hill behind the building. It would lend us two floors of extra space for staff, a new and expanded cafeteria, and a new Speaker's office with secretary's alcove and reception area. The last raised the hackles of the Republican leadership. Sara Gear, a bright and energetic Republican from Burlington, had worked her way up the ladder to become Republican leader. She would hear none of it.

When I first took occupancy of the Speaker's office I was so taken aback by its wretchedness that I set out to buy a couple of gallons of paint and spruce it up a little over a weekend—my labor, my dollar. The Republicans put up a hissy fit, and to stop me from carrying out my "renovation" they invoked the State House Preservation rules that said nothing could be done without an act of the legislature. So that's what I did—I proposed that two million dollars be added to the capital construction bill.

The proposal was well on its way to falling on its face, as the Republican majority vehemently opposed it, and even some of my Democrats were reluctant to stick their necks out for what appeared to the public to be a project solely for the comfort of the already "pampered legislature."

The breakthrough came when I learned from one of my Democrats, Barbara Grimes, Burlington, who was a close friend of Sara's, that the plans for the addition did not include access for the handicapped, including restroom facilities, ramps, and elevators.

"Yeah! I know. But the Buildings and Grounds commissioner says they're not required by law," I answered in a justified tone.

"That's not the point, Mr. Speaker," she shot back. "If you want help in passing the project you better put those things in there."

"You're right, Barb. It's not fair that only the able-bodied can enjoy the new building. I'll see that it's done." And then I added, "Unfortunately, it won't matter. The damn thing isn't going anywhere, anyway."

"It will if it has those added." She was now steering the conversation.

"What do you mean? How will this get us the votes?"

Then out of the blue she said, "Sara's husband has been in a wheelchair for twenty years. He's proud of his wife and would like to come see her here in the State House. He's never been able to do that."

Vermont's State House is a work of architectural artistry, arguably the most beautiful in the nation, and I'm proud that the legislature has added to its luster. I'm also puffed-up proud of my backbench Republicans for supplying the deciding votes.

And, oh, by the way, I may have failed to say it: Thank you, Sara Gear. You showed me what adversaries can accomplish when they can find common ground for common good.

Assigning Committees

A Speaker's obvious duty is to preside over debate on the floor of the House. He does not serve on any of the fourteen standing committees, though he could assign himself to one if he so chose. Except for chairing the House Rules Committee and sitting on the Joint House-Senate Rules Committee, his time is consumed in a host of other functions that make it possible to enact laws. The first of these is making committee assignments.

I really disliked making committee assignments. It seemed no matter what I did, I couldn't avoid having thirty or more members furious at me because they had been "dumped" into committees on which they didn't want to serve.

The Republicans realized, of course, that to the victors go the spoils, and they resigned themselves in the hopes that my election was just a two-year aberration in the normal scheme of things. The eight Republicans who had supported me on the secret ballot (the number who quietly claimed they had voted for me doubled right after the results were read) all received their first choice on the committee request form.

The committee request forms had been distributed on a Thursday morning, and I had the lot of them to take home for the weekend, to begin the process of not just satisfying all 149 members but taking care to create committees that would actually function—function in accordance with a Democratic agenda.

Keeping a Sense of Humor

The following Monday evening the Democratic leadership (Paul Poirier and our new whip, Dr. Howard Dean, who went on to become governor and presidential candidate), a few trusted lieutenants, and the uninvited Corcoran (he assumed he was to go wherever went the Speaker) sat to finalize the assignments to be announced the following morning. We found ourselves with an almost impossible task.

There were more than fifty requests for the Appropriations Committee alone, and we had but two actual vacancies. True, we were going to remove some Republican members to create a committee of at least seven Democrats, in order to control the committee's agenda. This was important because vital bills had to pass through these "stacked" committees. But we didn't see any way to avoid having a whole lot of disgruntled Democrats who felt passed over.

The number of seats in each committee was set by rule, and making the assignments required being selective. I already had decided that I would retain the competent Republican chairman, John Hise, and it was important that I quarter him with my most trusted and loyal supporters, who would not fall victim to his grandfatherly manner but would carry out our agenda. I had also decided to return Bob Kinsey to the committee. Being dumped right after losing a Speaker's race was more than Bob deserved. But a problem arose because to maintain Kinsey on Appropriations I had to dump another conservative Republican, Wally Russell, who had served on the Appropriations Committee for two terms. Russell, who ran a farm not fifteen miles from Kinsey's, had sat beside him in the well for a decade, and they were close friends. Of course, Wally had very much wanted to return as a member of the prestigious money committee, but one of them had to go, and I was resolute it wouldn't be Kinsey. Wally Russell, though no friend of mine, was still a hard-working member with a good deal of respect. I just couldn't see a way out of having to shoulder the blame for demoting him. Corcoran's diabolic mind solved the dilemma. He suggested that I let them decide.

"Call Wally and tell him you want to keep him on Appropriations, but you can't have both him and Kinsey. Tell him that if he can persuade Kinsey to give up his seat that it's fine with you. He can keep his seat." I called Wally and explained the problem.

Wally called back fifteen minutes later. His angry answer came as no surprise.

"The bastard said no."

That was the end of a lifelong friendship. Kinsey remained in the legislature another fourteen years, his last effort, as a Democratic candidate, failing. Wally passed away several years ago. I don't know if Bob was at the funeral.

We ended up giving the committee a seven to four Democratic majority.

Smith, Smith, and Smith

The small group huddled in the Speaker's office in an empty State House that evening were well aware that they were playing with at least two years of people's lives; sporadic arguments would break out as one of us would argue the case of a friend or, infrequently, against a political enemy.

Methodically we worked our way through the maze of committees until finally all was in place. It had taken until nearly midnight, we were all tired, and no one was satisfied fully with the results. But enough was enough and the lists were final. I asked that they listen to my rundown of the fourteen committees, which I would read on the floor of the House in just ten hours. All went well until I began to read the eight members on the Fish and Wildlife Committee. After reading the names of the chair, vice-chair, ranking member, and the next two alphabetically, I heard myself say, "Smith, Smith, and Smith." We looked at each other, startled. Every House member named Smith was on this committee. We all broke up in tired and silly laughter.

"I can't do this," I said, my eyes watering.

There was just no way, at that hour, that we were going to begin the process anew. Consequently anyone who had an interest in fish and wildlife matters during the next two years found it was smart to get their Smiths straight before entering that committee room.

Crossover Day and Committee Bills

During the first month or so of the House session the amount of time the members are on the floor is brief; the bulk of what is going on is bills working their way through the committees. There would be a reverse once we reached what was referred to as *crossover day*. This was an arbitrary date, usually during the first week in March, that the Joint Rules Committee established in the first week of the session designating the session's halfway point. Crossover day was the day by which the respective chambers had to make sure that their bills moved over from House to Senate, or Senate to House. Any bill not meeting the deadline could be ignored by the receiving chamber. It didn't mean they couldn't deal with a bill arriving late; it simply meant that they had a handy excuse to ignore a tardy bill that they didn't like. The exceptions would necessitate the drafting of a *committee bill*. This was a bill introduced by a committee rather than an individual member. The number of committee bills was not high because their use was reserved for emergency legislation or overlooked ideas that were suddenly discovered to be "critical." Any bill, individual or committee, proposed after the deadline would have to have the approval of the House Rules Committee.

Assigning Bills to Committee

Each year the legislature would have up to 800 or 900 bills—perhaps 1,600 to 1,800 for the biennium. They would be numbered and introduced as they were drawn up. It was the Speaker's responsibility to decide which committee received them, and sponsors often lobbied me to ensure that their bill went to a receptive and friendly committee. If the leadership frowned on a bill, the Speaker could send it to a *black hole committee,* never to be seen again. The clerk could present his tradition-bred list of proper committees for any given bill, but the final decision lay in the hands of the Speaker, and I sent my share of bills off to death row during my tenure. Often the choice was Murphy's committee, as he always seemed happy to prepare a last meal for these doomed creatures.

Just Another Day in Paradise

I never had a day in the legislature that was the same as any other. Making law, no matter where, is a fascinating experience. I don't believe there's a similar setting anywhere, or a better group of people to be surrounded by. The legislature reflects society as a whole; it contains the very best of what America has to offer and, in fairness, the very worst—a perfect cast for the creation of days one might want to forget.

But even the worst days eventually ended. Members have to accept the inevitable certainty that today's pressing problem will be tomorrow's memory. Things happen fast and issues line up so incessantly that one soon learns to move from one to the other with a fluidity that often looked callous to an outsider. It's like working in a big-city emergency room without the benefit of miracle medicine. Putting the past behind us and getting on with what was in front of us at any given moment not only made life bearable but pushed the sound and sane always to look to the task at hand (as Poirier was able to do after defeat in the caucus for leader).

It could be hard on sensitive and more reflective souls, those who couldn't shoulder defeat. But once this operational mode was understood and mastered, it made for an exciting way of life. I marveled at the way alliances came and went among the members and how easily most of us adjusted to victory and defeat. Woe to those who never "got it." A few, unable to understand the seeming callousness of the many, refused to seek re-election.

Seasons of the Legislature

The kind of day I was going to have could seldom be predicted. It would depend what year we were in, what month we were in, what day we were in, or even the hour of the day. These things mattered, as there were seasons in the legislature: planting seasons (January and February), when the seeds of ideas took the form of bills being worked on in the committees, and harvesting seasons (March and April), when the seed came to full bloom. There were moods that coincided with these seasons and they were recognizable. Early in the session, people would be upbeat and friendly. Midway through, they would be connected to their work in committee—showing faint signs of wear and tear. Then would come a period when the contents of the issues worked on so long and so hard would be connected with the politics of getting their work through to final passage. Here one would witness thoughts of renewing acquaintance with long-ignored "stepbrothers and stepsisters" in other committees and the Senate, in hopes of enlisting aid in the passage of a bill. In the final days tempers would grow short and fierce battles would begin.

If it was early in the session, my days would be consumed with housekeeping or management rituals. Sessions were scheduled to begin promptly at 9:30 a.m. (I confess I wasn't the best at this.) Opening Prayer would be offered by an invited minister, rabbi, or priest. The latter two participated for the first time when I became Speaker. We would then have Announcements. Members would announce any special social function or birthdays and take the opportunity to introduce any guests that they might have sitting in the gallery.

Next would come any Resolutions that might be ready for introduction, such as ones commemorating a local selectman back home, congratulating the University of Vermont's women's basketball team, or applauding a local Boy Scout for earning his Eagle badge. Nothing was too insignificant to warrant a resolution. Through all this, which never took more than fifteen minutes, the floor might be occupied by no more than fifteen or twenty diligent souls, the rest sauntering in from their commute or the cafeteria at their leisure, aware that there existed no time clock to punch in a legislature.

First Reading of a Bill

The bang of the gavel and the call by the Speaker for Orders of the Day, meant the session had officially begun. Here the first order of business would be to introduce bills and announce the committee to which each would be assigned. Members would have had these new bills to be introduced placed on their desks by pages before they arrived. This was called the *first reading* of the bill. Upon completion of this long and mundane chore, which I often had the clerk perform by reading only the title of the bill and its number, we would then turn to whatever second and third readings were ready to go.

Second Reading of a Bill

The *second reading* would require the assigned reporter of the bill to stand and explain to the members its general nature and the significant changes that the committee assigned had made to present statute. The reporter might take only a few minutes to finish his or her report if it was a "simple housekeeping bill," though one learned quickly that there was very little that was simple in lawmaking. Here, once again, it was important for the members to be able to judge whom they could trust to report a bill clearly and honestly and whom they couldn't.

If the bill was more complex or of heavier import (the appropriations bill would be several hundred pages), the reporter was always wise to take the members through it section by section, or even paragraph by paragraph. If the bill had been, under the rule, shuffled off to a second or even a third committee, those designated reporters would give their report as to the changes, if any.[1] At the end of each report the reporter would have to inform the members how that committee had voted.

It was at the conclusion of the report, or reports, that the members at large would be able to *interrogate* the reporter. Most often that didn't mean that anyone was confused but that the member asking the questions had begun his or her attack. (Mason's Rules dictated that both parties, the reporter and the interrogator, address their questions and the answers to the Speaker. This served the purpose of directing debate at a neutral third party, with the hope of keeping the give-and-take from getting personal.)

It became extremely important that the reporter assigned the bill had mastered it—and believed in it. All the work done in committee could be cut to shreds by a reporter who stumbled and mumbled on the floor. He or she might not have given a lot of thought to the bill, but the odds were pretty good that of the other 149 members, someone had.

Give-and-take might go something like this:

"Mr. Speaker!"

"Member from Middlesex."

"Mr. Speaker, I wonder if the reporter of the bill might clear up some confusion I have as to the third sentence in section 22; subsection 4, line 8. I know it says '*shall* meet the requirements in sections 19, 20, and 21.' Mr. Speaker, is that what the member from Burlington intended? Shouldn't it have read '*may* meet all the requirements in sections 19, 20, and 21'?"

"Member from White River."

"No, Mr. Speaker. That was the intent of the committee."

At the conclusion of the report, any member can rise and offer an amendment to the committee report.

"Mr. Speaker, I have an amendment that I have given to the clerk."

The Speaker would then receive the previously drafted amendment from the clerk.

"Listen to the amendment. The member from White River proposes to substitute in section 22, subsection 4, line 8, the word *shall* with the word *may*."

This usually is followed by a great deal of laughter from the other members.

Bills on the floor can be amended, as I say, and even amendments can be amended. (I know it's getting complicated, but hang with me here.) But amendments to the amendments can't be further amended. In other words, under Mason's Rules, a bill can only be amended twice. If someone offers an amendment to the proposed amendment to the amendment, that's three, and the Speaker would rule the person out of order. Actually if things got this screwed up, most probably a diligent and compassionate chairman would rise and take the beleaguered reporter off the hook by asking that the bill be *recommitted to committee.*

A bill properly amended twice would have a question similar to the following posed to the body: "Shall the House amend the report of the Committee on Commerce, as amended by the member from Rutland, as offered by the member from Brattleboro?"

Easy, huh?

Once all questions have been answered, debate exhausted, and amendments voted up and down, the question becomes, "Shall the bill, as amended, be read the third time?"

Now we vote. It can be done in one of three ways.

1. *Voice vote.* The Speaker, hearing no call for a *division* or *roll call,* will simply ask for the yeas and nays. Here is an example of one of the numerous little edges the Speaker has: he can decide what he hears. Some Speakers have better hearing than others. Prior to his announcing, "Listen to the result of your vote," any member doubting the Speaker's hearing ability can stand and call for a division or a roll call.

2. *Division.* In this case the Speaker will ask, "All those in favor, please stand while the clerks count your vote." Then, after they are counted and seated, "All those opposed." The clerks, each counting one side of the House, will then inform the Speaker of their individual tallies.

3. *Roll call.* Neither of the above is a recorded vote, but this one's for posterity as it is a recorded vote. Your name is called alphabetically, and if you are in your seat you must vote—no "ifs," no "I'm confused," no "maybes." It's yes or no. If your nerves get the better of you and you decide you don't want to vote—you can withstand the

glares of your fellow members and rise and leave the House. This is called *taking a walk.* You cannot return, once having left the chamber, and vote. Assuming the bill passes after all this, it is then put on the calendar for a *third reading* the next day.

Third Reading of a Bill

After the members have heard the third reading by the clerk, the question put by the Speaker is, "Shall the bill pass?" This is usually a formality, but it does give a member who has had second thoughts overnight (or who has had his arm twisted) the option to "reconsider his vote" of the previous day. To do this the member must assure the Speaker that he or she voted with the majority during the second reading. It's already known what the nays think about the bill.

A vote is then taken to see if a majority want to reconsider. This is seldom done, but in the small chance that a majority of members have shown up with their arms in slings, the Speaker will bring the question back to "Shall the bill be read a third time?" Assuming no reconsideration, then it's off to the Senate and the same ring of fire.

Now you know what Mary Evelti was talking about when she compared passing laws to having babies. The only difference, I might add, is that sometimes it can take longer to pass a bill.

The Routine

There were things that occurred every day no matter the season. I always arrived at the State House before seven in the morning, and I seldom left before six in the evening. I used to joke with members who would chide me over my late hours that I once left the State House before the last Republican and got beaten the next day on a tough issue. Neither part of that story is true, but it reflected what I believed in putting in whatever hours necessary. The fact of the matter was that these were my hours, the hours that fit my metabolism, and I just maintained the routine.

I would settle in at the cafeteria, drinking coffee and reading the morning newspapers, to be joined by fellow early risers. Murphy was usually one of the first to join me after making his morning call to his wife, Flora Belle. Murphy liked to eat, and I could always tell what Murphy had for breakfast by observing the remnants decorating his tie. I kidded him often about his midsection, but he always professed to be adhering to his diet; this in spite of the fact that with each new session and renewed commitment to his diet, he always appeared to grow larger from January to adjournment.

By seven forty-five the "lieutenants' table," so labeled by those who would sit alone, would grow crowded, and whoever sat with us could expect a lot of teasing and general bantering that seldom got heavy. It was the most relaxing and fun time of the day for most of the members and at times bordered on the hilarious—or sadistic, depending on how you view the following incident.

We were all assembled around our table in a cafeteria that had reached its normal, overflowing capacity one noontime when Sen. Vince Illuzzi came off the line carrying his tray to the adjacent table. On it were a hamburger and a Coke. The senator, realizing he was without a straw, quickly set down his tray and returned to the mess line to get one. It was then that I silently witnessed Bob Harris spring into action. He rose, nonchalantly walked over to Senator Illuzzi's tray, picked up the hamburger, and proceeded to dump it, not the bun, in the trash can. He then casually returned the now-empty bun to Illuzzi's tray, went back to his table, and indifferently continued on with his lunch.

Illuzzi returned, sat, and picking up the ketchup squirted a measure on the hamburgerless hamburger. Too embarrassed to comment, he sat there staring at the bun for what seemed the longest moment. Finally, he rose once again and made his way back to the mess line, where he informed the lady at the cash register that his hamburger sandwich was missing the hamburger. Of course, she, not believing Illuzzi's claim for a minute, called on the chef to come listen to this incredible tale. The chef, having the temperament of a Parisian connoisseur and having seen all too much of legislators and their off-camera eating habits, quickly accused poor Illuzzi of trying to pull off some sort of scam. Voices rose, tempers flared, and Illuzzi stormed out of the cafeteria, vowing never to return. Startled by the uproar, members began to clamor among themselves.

All except Harris. He quietly finished his lunch, got up, and as he passed our table on the way out remarked with a great deal of indignation, "Can't even have a peaceful meal around here without someone causing an uproar."

Early morning was also the time when I could be in the company of members whom I might not see on a day-to-day basis, and it afforded me the opportunity to say hello and ask how they were, or was there anything I could help them with. This contact was important; it was risky business to go weeks without seeing and chatting with a member. To avoid this I kept a brief list of members who, for whatever reason, didn't make it a ritual to drop into the Speaker's office to bring up a problem, complain, or simply say hello. If a week or ten days went by without my noting I had seen them, I would make a point to search them out and ask how things were going.

I would be back in my office usually by eight and would go through the day's schedule with my secretary, sort through mail that she could answer—usually simple requests for information—and set aside those letters that I wanted to answer personally. No letter went unanswered.

In addition, there would always be a pile of "While you were out" phone messages, and I would take these out into the reception room and begin returning the calls. This was the "sick call" hour, and I would have to vacate my office and let the MASH unit, led by Doc Shea, have the privacy necessary to see patients.

Legislatures are not for the very young. Everybody seems to have a bottle of pills. If you have high blood pressure, it's sure to rise. An "eating-out diet" is not the best for those with high cholesterol. As we had no doctor or nurse on duty in the State House (remember, this is a citizen legislature), Dr. Jim Shea, another representative from Bennington County, had been drafted to listen to the members' daily aches and pains. The only room that provided the privacy necessary happened to be my office. By eight o'clock the patients would be lined up.

Even the outer office served a purpose. Members, lobbyists, and visitors from the Senate were aware that this was where I'd be at this hour, and they would stroll by. It was also the only warm room in the building that allowed smoking. Needless to say, it was always crowded. Even Dr. Shea, after treating his patients, would stop by for a smoke.

Once the sick and wounded left our little MASH unit, the office would be mine again. I would take fifteen minutes to go over the day's work with the clerk, Bob Picher.[2] If it was during the period in which bills were flooding the floor, I would go through the ones up for second or third reading, noting in the calendar who was reporting the bill, the complexity or impact it might have with the members (fight or easy passage), and the vote in committee. This last simply gave an additional hint as to the level of argument that I could expect. If it came out of committee with an 11–0, or 10–1 vote, then I could conclude at the very least that the committee was in agreement with the contents of the bill. An 8–3 or 7–4 vote sent warning signals. A 6–5 vote might be a signal to get everybody off the beach.

At 9:25 sharp, Barbara Grimes would introduce me to that morning's guest cleric and it would be off to the podium for another day in paradise.

I don't want to lead the reader to think that a Speaker's day was lived out in an arena that included just duly elected members. Far from it. At any given time the building is crowded with people who have interests not only in the business being conducted but simply in visiting. Some, such as tourists, curious citizens, and school groups, are there for the day and add to the aura of hustle and bustle in a positive way. I always tried to accommodate these groups; I never came to believe, as some others did, that the building was the legislators' own private domain. As the sergeant-at-arms had fairly strict rules that I was constantly violating, we often clashed. Of course, I got away with taking these guests to places that were off limits and into committee and hearing rooms because the Speaker and the president pro tempore of the Senate had direct jurisdiction over the building and all that was in it. The Vermont state capitol had always been a most open place, and I had every intention of keeping it that way.

I recall with fondness visiting my office one day in the middle of the summer, when the building was pretty much empty and the ropes had been put up to keep the occasional tourist a good distance from any working area that they might have traveled a whole lot of miles to view.

Dressed in dungarees, an old T-shirt, and my Red Sox cap, I came through the well of the House to find a father and mother with their early teenaged son and daughter peering through the glass doors trying to catch a peek at the chamber. I came through the doors carrying an old empty box that I was going to drop in the dumpster on the way out, looking for all the world like the custodian. The foursome was the reincarnation of *Ozzie and Harriet,* and I stopped to chat. I couldn't resist and proceeded to take them on an hour's tour of the entire building. The fact that I had a key to the Speaker's office didn't seem to faze them—what janitor wouldn't? But when I proceeded to unlock the Speaker's cabinet and give each of the kids a little Vermont state flag Dad finally spoke up.

"Perhaps we shouldn't." He was certain they had run into a janitor without a conscience. "I mean the Speaker may have these for special people."

"Oh! No problem. I assure you, I know the Speaker pretty well. He won't mind. Besides, you and your family are special people."

We finished the tour and I left. My new friends from Kentucky, still feeling some discomfort, went to the sergeant-at-arms's office to thank somebody for the great personal tour, and perhaps to turn in "stolen goods." When asked where they got the flags they answered, "The janitor."

The sergeant-at-arms assured them that all was fine and they didn't have to hand over the flags, and when they asked the janitor's name in anticipation of sending a thank you note, the reply came back, "That wasn't the janitor, that was the Speaker."

When the legislature reconvened in January, there was a box beside my desk. I opened it and found several bottles of bourbon specially labeled "From the liquor cabinet of Speaker Ralph Wright." How could I know my long-forgotten friends had owned a bourbon distillery?

I don't drink bourbon, but some of my trusted lieutenants saw to it that it didn't get sent back. Amazing what human kindness can bring.

But not everybody who roamed those corridors turned out to be as warm and friendly; for instance, there was the press corps. There would be no boxes of finely distilled bourbon left by them.

Notes

1. I once sent a property tax reform bill to eight committees, which meant that when it finally worked its way onto the floor it had already garnered eighty-two votes in committee, assuring its passage.

2. Bob Picher was a twenty-year-plus veteran clerk of the House. He was perhaps the most efficient and competent man I ever met and undoubtedly the finest gentleman I had the pleasure of working with over my sixteen years at the State House. My life would have been immeasurably more complicated without Mr. Picher, especially in the early weeks of my speakership.

6

The Press

The Speaker and the Press

DEALING WITH THE press is a lot like dealing with prospective in-laws. You have to be careful what you say and extremely mindful how you say it.

I never really "got it" when it came to understanding the relationship between the press and myself. Perhaps it was because Vermont is different from other places in that it is a small state and does big things in a small way. Our smallness did not exempt us from dealing with controversial issues, however, and the advance of media attention forced both the legislature and the press front stage.

The evolution of the press appeared to me to be much like the evolution of the legislature; prior to the 1980s it was a congenial affiliation of two or three reporters who spent the entire session with us. When reporters from smaller dailies or weeklies showed up, it was such a special occasion that we would put on the dog and treat them like very special guests. As far as television coverage went, in the early days of the eighties there was only one station—which covered perhaps half the state— Channel 3 in Burlington. My local newspaper, the *Bennington Banner,* could never afford to station a reporter in the capital for the entire session. This was not unique, as most of the small-town dailies lacked such funds. So members like myself felt pretty safe in whatever we were doing, or not doing, in that the only news my constituents might get about our conduct or performance would be what they got off the wire from the Associated Press, and even that was infrequent.

The change to expanded coverage was gradual and took a sharp eye to discern as it happened. What I did notice was a change in style. The two statewide papers (the *Rutland Herald* and the *Burlington Free Press*) added a reporter or two. The new reporters weren't just young, eager, naive cubs, though, but ones sent to the capital with a different attitude. And the attitude was not the collegial "Let's talk about this over a beer" style of the past. It was no longer "Give me a quote and I'll return a 'puff' piece."

My experience with the press was much like war—long periods of boredom interrupted by moments of terror. At times, often for long periods, I seemed to be of no interest to the press, but if calamity broke out, the scene took on the drama of a Hollywood movie.

The press were in attendance during the ho-hum periods, but they weren't circling around me. The occasional early riser would be up and about at the fall of the gavel at nine-thirty and take a seat adjacent to where I stood at the podium. The reporters had their own separate section in the balcony, but I always allowed them to sit in these now-empty seats reserved for the Senate when we had call for a joint session. As they afforded the best view of the members seated in the well and any debate, I was never sure whether they positioned themselves there to be close to the Speaker or simply to taste the panorama that I enjoyed every day. Maybe they just enjoyed being visible to the members. When the session ended I always stayed as long as they asked, but it never seemed to amount to more than a question or two on the proceedings that had just transpired. Boring stuff indeed.

So it wasn't that I didn't give open access to the press. Actually I made efforts to encourage more interaction. Early in my second term I decided it was a good idea to hold a weekly press conference. I set it up for Friday at noon in the Speaker's office. The first week they all showed up; the second, but a handful. The third week I found myself holding a press conference alone with the Democratic leader.

Moose Invade Vermont

Sometimes the press got their teeth into an issue by accident. Several years into my speakership I was confronted with a seemingly innocuous issue, which I could not in my wildest dreams have anticipated. Vermonters had discovered that there were moose (that's right, *moose*) aimlessly wandering over hill and dale, mostly minding their own business. My only awareness that moose even existed in Vermont came from the occasional reports that one or two of these hapless creatures had wandered into the path of incredulous drivers navigating the back roads in Vermont's most rural northern sections, obviously with serious results for both driver and wanderer. Now, being a city kid who had never seen so much as a cow until moving to Vermont, I paid less than scant attention to the ruckus then stirring in the backcountry. But into the issue I was dragged.

It had been a routine day, and needless to say I was totally surprised when reporters popped into my office and asked me what I thought of a proposal circulating that called for a season on moose. It was like a bolt out of the blue, and all that rushed into my frontal lobe was the image of the cartoon moose Bullwinkle. My only thought was, "Why would anyone want to shoot this lovable, if dimwitted, beast?"

"Mr. Speaker, there's a bill being introduced to have a moose hunting season. Will you support such a proposal?"

"Well, er, I haven't heard of this proposal. I, ah, haven't, quite frankly given it any thought, but now that you ask, I, ah, . . . My instant thought is, Why? Why would we want to do that?" I was fumbling, fruitlessly searching for something intelligent to say, while at the same time desperately trying to harness this vision of big, stupid Bullwinkle creeping slowly but inexorably forward in my mind. I couldn't find an intelligent answer, and I couldn't stop the vision, and I heard my voice, as if far away, utter, "Hell, shooting a moose is like shooting a parked car."

As in old Hollywood movies, several reporters rushed out of my office, while the others roared with laughter. Well, the bill was introduced and proved popular with a whole lot of my "sportsmen" members. It took a whole lot of arm-twisting for me to finally get it killed on the floor of the House.

Over the next six months I was threatened by "sportsmen," answered calls from as far away as Australia, and received an award from an animal lovers' group whose name now escapes me.

Twelve years later, while casually thumbing through a copy of the March 29, 2004, edition of *Sports Illustrated,* I came across the magazine's series called "Great Athletes and Great Sports Moments in the 50 States of America." This particular week's coverage happened to be highlighting Vermont. Guess what? There it was, under the category of "most memorable quotes" in the history of Vermont sports:

"Shooting a moose is like shooting a parked car."

Then Speaker of the House Ralph Wright, in 1992, arguing against the State Wildlife Commission's decision to reintroduce moose hunting in Vermont after a 96-year hiatus.

Of all the things I did or said during my career, this is my legacy—not exactly what I could have predicted, but then it just might point out that my destiny wasn't always in my hands. There's a message here somewhere. There's also a new visual.

The message is, Be careful what you say, or at least remain silent if you don't know what to say. The power of the press is immeasurable.

The visual—one I have never been able to shuck—is that of Elmer Fudd firing a shotgun blast into the trunk of someone's car.

Learning to Deal with the Press

Obviously I have an immense amount of respect for what the press does, and I am convinced that without it to keep a constant watch over our shoulders we politicians might actually be the scoundrels that far too many Americans have come to perceive us to be.

However, members of the press are not without human traits and faults. To begin with, they are by training, and perhaps nature, a suspicious lot. Consequently they assume that whatever they are hearing has more to it than the words spoken. They almost always think that at best, we are not telling them the whole story, and at worst, we are just flat-out lying. The polite political jargon for all this verbal dancing is "spin." Your mother would call it "fibbing." God knows it as "not telling the whole truth." More than I like to confess, the latter two judgments are closer to the truth than the former.

I offer no defense for lying but simply a rather inept explanation. Politicians spend a good deal of time trying to present themselves in the best light. Looking good to the public and supporting their quest for re-election are always at the top of any agenda. Novice legislators have an easier time telling the truth, and therefore are better able to maintain their high ideals and integrity, for the simple reason that because they are newcomers nobody cares very much what they think. They are asked little or nothing and thus find few opportunities to read their name in print. But as one ascends the ladder of power in any legislature, one's thoughts and actions become of greater interest to all wandering the halls of the statehouse—especially the press.

Should one climb to the top of the power structure, the Speaker's dais, one's every action becomes a point of interest to the fourth estate. The humblest of personalities may find it difficult not to bask in the fame and glory of "good press," but therein lies the dilemma: Leaders' words matter. Bad things can happen when a leader runs off at the mouth without giving thought to the repercussions of the words. And woe to the leader who disregards the unwritten rule that I'm sure is applicable no matter which statehouse one works in: Don't say anything that you might find unpleasant to read on tomorrow morning's front page.

As true as this rule was, I often violated it. There were nights I lay awake trying to imagine how what I had done or said the previous day would be depicted in the soon-to-arrive morning newspaper. It was usually as bad as I imagined, and I never got used to it. A tough skin takes a lifetime of hard labor to develop.

Of course, over the years I got somewhat better at controlling the conversation, for as a leader I learned to always keep in mind that others often become victims of your careless responses. Does a legislative leader, when asked a question, deliver an unsullied answer that might reveal a future strategy to the opposition and thereby jeopardize the goal of the party? Or on a more personal level, should a leader reveal information he or she has that would embarrass a fellow legislator? Sometimes these things have to be learned the hard way.

I once responded callously to a reporter who inquired why I had removed a less-than-sterling member from a money committee, "Well, I can't believe that the former Speaker appointed him there because of his brains." The member and his family read it in the next day's newspaper and I spent the next ten years apologizing in every way possible to the member for my thoughtless remark.

I experienced this quandary a multitude of times, but none proved more frustrating than an incident during our effort to pass a bill dealing with abortion and parental notification. In this case, it wasn't the truth that got me in trouble but a blatant effort to keep the truth from becoming public.

Sometimes You Just Have to Find a Way around the Truth

We had narrowly defeated, on third reading, an attempt to push through a parental notification bill and felt confident that that was the end of the effort by its supporters. Lobbying had been heavy in support of the bill, and I received lots of mail and calls trying to persuade me to "see the light." Some of the more zealous took the time to inform me that they and their congregation were praying for my soul. It was a nail-biter to say the least. When the vote for passage was tallied, the clerks handed me a slip of paper signifying that supporters had won—by one vote. I immediately used my prerogative as Speaker to vote to break a tie, or in this case create a tie. I voted no, tied up the count (in politics, ties don't go to the runner), and consequently the bill died. Or so I thought.

Early the next morning a rumor began to circulate that one of our Democrats who had voted against the bill and with the majority was going to rise on the floor and use his prerogative to request a vote for *reconsideration*. The rule on this seldom-used motion was that the wavering member would rise during Announcements and, before the full body took up Orders of the Day, inform the House that "assuring the Speaker that I voted with the majority on third reading the previous day, I would now request permission to change my vote." This would be an unusual move on even the most innocuous of bills and jolting on one so controversial. If true, the single vote switch would mean passage, turning our hard-fought victory into agonizing defeat. The vote on the floor would now become, "Shall the House agree to allow the member to change his vote?"

Leadership immediately began inquiring as to who the Democrat was. Within thirty minutes Sean Campbell, D-Rockingham, rushed into my office and revealed the culprit. Trying to avoid the scrutiny of the press and pressure from those of us who were certain to try to change his decision, he had tried to lie low in one of the more obscure committee rooms. I immediately set out to haul him back into the Speaker's office, where I knew we could have some privacy and where I hoped to persuade him not to do what was now common knowledge throughout the building. We didn't speak a word on the trip back from the committee room, but as we fast-paced through the crowded cafeteria everyone went silent, all eyes on the perpetrator and the arresting officer. Only minutes had passed since I had left the office, but word had raced through the State House that the would-be sinner had been found. Of course, the first to respond was the ever-vigilant press corps; awaiting us in my reception room were several television reporters, with their glowing klieg lights and running TV cameras, as well as a crowd of print reporters standing poised, pencil in hand, ready to pounce. The crowd was swelled, much as at the scene of an accident, by other overzealous parties. We managed to run the gauntlet and with some less-than-polite pushing and shoving reached the sanctity of my all-but-barricaded office. There occurred a most extraordinary conversation between Jeff (years have passed and I still can't reveal his real name) and me.

"Why are you doing this, Jeff?"

"I have to, Mr. Speaker."

"Why?" I persisted.

"I can't tell you why."

His discomfort set me back, as he was not a wishy-washy type of guy. In fact, he was one of the more stalwart members of the caucus, highly thought of as an extremely capable lawmaker and a die-hard loyalist who could always be depended on to be there when the party needed him. We had entered the legislature together back in 1979, had grown close over the years, and our friendship had been hardened by the many political wars we had endured together. He was someone I had come to depend on for his ability to take heat and never buckle. I was totally befuddled by his intended action now.

"Look, Jeff, all hell is going to break loose if you go out on the floor fifteen minutes from now and change your vote." I then spent the next five minutes attempting to convince him that this was not something he should be doing. He listened but seemed not to hear a word I said. He made a few lame attempts to justify his dramatic turnaround, but it was clear they were just that—lame. His extreme discomfort with our conversation was obvious, and I reached the end of my rope.

"OK, cut the bullshit, Jeff. There's something going on here, and the least you can do is be truthful about it. I'm through trying to change your mind. You are obviously going to do what you are going to do, but I really resent, after all we've been through together, your not being able to at least tell me why."

The longest time passed as he sat in silence, avoiding eye contact. Tears welled up in his eyes, and in a voice that he could barely find, the truth slowly bubbled forth.

"They're blackmailing me." His chin almost resting on his chest.

"What do you mean they're blackmailing you? Who's blackmailing you?"

"My minister. I got a call in my room last night. It was my minister. He told me if I didn't change my vote he was going to go to my wife and tell her about Sally. My family's more important. It'll not only end my political career; it'll end my marriage. I've got no choice."

So there it was, the underbelly of politics—sinners sinning against sinners. The story now would be not the changing of a vote, but the scandal of infidelity, and blackmail—the juiciest of stories, with all the ingredients to bring a smile to the publisher of a supermarket tabloid.

Jeff did what he had to do and changed his vote. I did what I had to do and delayed Orders of the Day long enough to twist a few arms to vote against the request by Jeff to change his vote. The arm-twisting did not take a lot of effort. A legislature is a lot of things, but it is not an institution that, once a game is lost, likes to replay it or overturn the result. Jeff's request was denied by a comfortable margin, and the bill gasped its last.

The press, of course, wanted to know the truth. I flat-out lied and told them that the member simply had had a change of heart.

"Why?" they badgered.

"I never asked. It was a conscience issue and I never question a man's conscience."

Nor, since, have I questioned my own.

The Press Corps

Reporters come in all shapes and forms and it is difficult to categorize them. I've known a lot of reporters who are fair and accurate. The vast majority are decent and hardworking and feel genuinely out of sorts when they nail us in a story, but I've never known one to fail to write the worst of stories if they got the opportunity. Their retort to running a negative story would be, "We're not in the business of making the news—we simply report it."

Then there are some (thankfully, few) who opt to take the easiest route to meeting a deadline. Scoffers are not especially enamored of hard work and consequently end up writing things that are not in tune with all the facts or representative of the whole story. These shortcutters represent a small minority, but they exist and unfortunately have done a lot of damage to the innocent. Such behavior can be tolerated as long as it doesn't represent a lifestyle but just a bad day.

Journalists are very much aware of what catches the public's attention. That's why we don't get to read in our morning newspaper about all the planes that landed safely the day before, only about the one that didn't. The story isn't focused on the black box but rather on the last words of the desperate pilot. It then becomes very personal, and when the person is you, for better or worse the words and deeds become defining. Fair enough. But when the story gets twisted, whether by the reporting of only half the story, or even by unsubstantiated details, a line has been crossed, and the reporter has become part of the story. Not good.

Good reporters manage to walk that fine line between reporting the story and becoming the story. The few who venture over have now entered the realm of "gotcha" journalism. This becomes dangerous to both the individual victim and the reading public as a whole. It's one thing to have a lazy, or even a corrupt, politician; he or she, once exposed, can be voted out of office. But members of the press come close to being untouchable, as they never have to place their names on a ballot. The public finds it nearly impossible to get at them. The press, like the rich, "never complain; never explain." The several recourses available to politicians have their pitfalls and drawbacks and may not prove effective.

The first recourse is one we are all too familiar with. I call it the "What'd he say?" approach. Always presented in a monotone, it is the drone of a politician speaking at length, often saying nothing of substance, and frequently not even answering the question posed. It can literally send reporters fleeing and is almost guaranteed to lessen the crowd at the politician's next press conference. If they take this approach, leaders risk relinquishing their ability to communicate and may find that when they need to communicate a message through the press, the press is not interested. If you won't answer reporters' questions or provide them with a quote, they'll find someone who will. Reporters have to produce on a daily basis—that's their job. If you won't help them with their job, you certainly can't fault them for not helping you with yours. A leader without an avenue of communication is a leader with a short tenure.

A second way to deal with reporters is to develop a thick skin. Someone once advised me to just ignore them. This meant that one would have never to read the newspapers or watch the news on TV. I found this advice impossible to follow; as painful as it was at times, I couldn't shut myself away from devouring every word printed in the morning paper, especially, if the story had me in it. That was motivated by something very personal and perhaps reflected a dark side. But more important was that the media provided me with a ton of information that I might otherwise not have been aware of. As John Murphy said, "Information is knowledge, and knowledge is power." I don't want to exaggerate the point here, but heck, there were times when I found myself reading a recap of some complex legislation that we had passed the day before and finding a more complete and understandable explanation of it than my leaders, chairpeople, or House members had been able to convey while we were in the process of ramming it through.

And finally, the most potent weapon a leader has against being mugged by the press is access. I tried to look at the press as I would a family with a lot of kids. All must be loved (even if they sometimes wrote less-than-loving things); all must be treated with respect and a sense of individuality; all must be treated fairly; and all must get quality time with you. The latter didn't mean, at least for the vast majority, picking up the tab at the local tavern, but access.

Obviously, it was much easier to be with some reporters than others, but to show overt partiality to one only served to raise the wrath of the others. A leader could, through leaks, gain favor with a reporter, but then he or she would have to spend great energy in keeping the fact from the rest. I made the mistake of leaking a story to a reporter from the *Burlington Free Press* early in my second term as Speaker, and I never recovered my credibility with the *Rutland Herald.* He had something I wanted (the results of a secret *Free Press* poll taken the week before the vote for Speaker), and I had something he wanted (future committee assignments). We made the deal. When *Herald* reporters learned they had been scooped it obviously embarrassed them. They never mentioned it, but the incident was put in their memory bank. I never could shake their displeasure and animosity. But that was just another example of how naive I was and how unprepared to deal in such crucial personal matters

One of the most shocking revelations for those who find themselves in a seat of power is how different their world has become. This is obvious to me, now that I have had the luxury of time and introspection, but I didn't have a clue when the mantle of power dropped on me. I also didn't have the time or the insight to realize that a Speaker, perched high atop the floor of the House is, as far as the press is concerned, no more than a lightning rod during a thunderstorm.

Most of the press's time is spent with eyes on the towering thunderclouds looming on the horizon. The title of "Mr. Speaker" may get doors opened and telephones answered, but these perquisites aren't accompanied by a sudden rise in one's IQ. I struggled constantly, day after day, never getting the hang of it all. Once my public image was defined by the press, I had to live with it. Of course, I supplied all the ingredients for the molding of the image. But what was acceptable private conduct, with people who knew and loved me, was something else with a public that was getting its first glimpse of this new public power holder. For those who didn't especially like me, negative press simply served as ammunition. In this respect, my critics soon learned the hot-button epithets—some of the more frequent were "Boston Irish pol," "arm-twister," and "most powerful man in the statehouse." None too endearing.

I regretted not being able to gain admittance to the inner circle of reporters so that I might get to know them better and consequently protect myself better. Almost without exception, they avoid this level of association with legislators. They want access, not a relationship. The old days of partying or hoisting a tall one with your friendly knight of the round table were long gone, at least in Montpelier.

Most reporters are fair and honest. But there are exceptions. Over time I figured out what separated the fair from the unfair. The answer seems simple to me now, but I struggled to get the picture clear while I served as Speaker. A reporter, like so many others who have to make difficult decisions every day, must stick to the issues. Once a story moves from the event to the individual, it becomes personal. Like a couple in the midst of divorce, who stop negotiating for an amiable separation and begin the war to hurt one another, so it is with a reporter and a leader who move from the event to the person. I'm describing here, "gotcha" journalism.

And into my life walked *Rutland Herald* reporter Nancy Wright (no relation).

Gotcha Journalism

Nancy Wright was a Speaker's worst nightmare—one of those small moments of terror. She was bright, tenacious, and cared little what others thought of her. She had little compassion for other people's feelings. A lone wolf, separated from her own pack of colleagues, she appeared happiest navigating the catacombs of the State House in the evening, long after the building had emptied of legislators, fellow press corps members, and lobbyists. The image, to some, was the hunter looking for prey.

I was my own worst enemy, as I constantly provided her with ammunition for her elephant gun. First, there was the hockey game, mentioned earlier, that a bunch of us (soon labeled my "hockey team") ran off to in Boston. The tickets were provided by an old friend who happened to be a lobbyist for a major insurance company in Boston, but one that did no business in Vermont. Nancy got wind of it and wrote scathing article after scathing article in her newspaper. Each time she made a call to Boston in search of details or tried to browbeat one of my newfound hockey fans, another story would appear on the front page of the *Herald.*

The rule is that once a story breaks, the embarrassed politician is almost always better off to rush immediately into *damage control.* Simply stated, get the whole story out as soon as possible, take the hit, and, assuming there's no more to the story, hope that's the end of it. It becomes a one-day story. But this advice was mere words to me, and I shuddered to think of reading that we had not only gone to Boston with seven free tickets to a Bruins game but also had a meal on someone else's tab. It didn't matter that we had broken no laws, went on our own time after the session had ended, and returned in time for the morning session. We had taken something for nothing, and that merited exposure. It was wrong, and we should have been smart enough, if not ethical enough, not to have fallen into the trap. The fact that we tried to hide it was proof enough that we shouldn't have done it. (I later learned that one of my Republican "friends" had leaked the story to Nancy.) But still, a week's worth of scandal" in the *Herald* did appear to be overkill. It became apparent that we had broken the cardinal rule once defined by Alan Rosenthal, of the Eagleton Institute of Politics at Rutgers University—we "had dared have a good time."

Nancy went after that as though she were on the trail of a deadbeat dad. She couldn't get one of us to answer the simplest of inquiries from her without its ringing with contradiction of what one of the others had said. This only made matters worse, as the discrepancies simply provided the meager basis for another story in the next morning's *Rutland Herald.* As the *Herald* had a pretty significant circulation in my district, it wasn't helping my political career. As for Nancy, she was quickly becoming the star of the Montpelier press bureau.

Join the Legislature and See the World

Being stung had made me more cautious, but not much more. Leaders who want to stay leaders learn fast to deal with the constant pressure to satisfy, or make happy, their members. House members' requests for help, often in trivial matters, are never-ending. A Speaker's power afforded me almost daily opportunities to come to their aid, and I spent a good deal of any given day listening sympathetically to their problems and assuring them that I would see what I could do to help them. It mattered not what their problem was: moving, or sometimes not moving, a bill; raising money for reelection; providing photo opportunities; helping to resolve personal squabbles; or simply giving a colleague publicity by appearing to confide in them in public view. This was part of the job description, as all these perks meant something to folks who decide a Speaker's fate every two years. It usually proved not so difficult a chore, except for the time involved; I found that most problems tended to solve themselves. Countless times I would make note of the member's gripe, only to have it slip my mind during the day. I always managed a humble smile when that same member might come to me a day or two later thanking me for settling his or her problem. I called this my "common cold theory." Pay no attention and most of the time the little aches and pains disappear all by themselves.

For many members the biggest perk is the opportunity to travel to pleasant places. Thus when it came time to distribute junkets I was well aware that travel not only expands one's experience, but it also often expands one's love for his or her leader. I, too, enjoyed travel for the same reasons they did, but it afforded me a second luxury—the opportunity to get up close and personal to a member in a social and personal setting.

One year the meeting of the National Conference of State Legislatures (NCSL) was held in Nashville, Tennessee (home of the Grand Ole Opry—they don't hold these things in unpleasant places). This was the biggest annual event held for legislators, and more than five thousand from all over the country would be in attendance. Vermont (under all Speakers) was accustomed to send fifteen or twenty members each year. They included not just my lieutenants and best Republican friends (my growing hockey team); protocol dictated that all leaders, Democratic or Republican, would be offered the opportunity to go.

As the crowd from around the country would quickly fill all available rooms close to the convention, it was NCSL rules that we make reservations for our members months before the actual conference. Late registration meant a decrease in the number of members allowed to attend or the levying of a late fee on the sending state.

By the end of March I would have to supply the names of the members who were planning to attend in July. But some members, often being caught up in the session's agenda, would not be willing to commit that far in advance. Others would hold out in order to measure what the fallout might be if they were reported to be on another junket. If the session went well and the public maintained a high opinion of its legislature, or if the economy was up and we weren't spending time cutting people's programs, it might be that attending wouldn't raise the public's eyebrows.

Others simply preferred to wait until the last minute because the later your name went on the list of junketeers, the fewer times it would appear in print. And you could be sure that it would appear.

None of this helped my predicament. I had to have the list of fifteen or twenty or whatever number I was going to send by April 1. After the Boston fiasco, I was not anxious to travel. I also realized that if the "big guy" wasn't going, it would be less likely to be much of a story—perhaps a list of the participants and the total cost to the taxpayers in the two major daily newspapers. Members living in the far corners of the state didn't have to worry about their constituents' reading their names in the paper, as the two statewide papers often never reached the more rural and distant districts. Those lucky travelers worried not a whit. But if I went, well, that would make it a different story indeed. Then there would be the agenda—not the convention's myriad daytime meetings but the side events—meals and enjoyable times financed, for the most part, by the corporate interests attending. They included family outings, golf, fishing trips, and the Opry itself—in other words, anything that a legislator and his or her family might have a good time doing.

The list went in as scheduled on April 1, and in keeping with House tradition it included the name of the House Republican leader, Sara Gear. My name didn't appear on the list.

Come June, Sara informed the Legislative Council that she would not be attending. I braved the risk and informed the council that I would go in her place. As it was too late to reserve a room in my name, I would simply use the one reserved for Sara. We had never canceled her room, knowing someone would make a last-minute decision to attend and would need it. I didn't know it then, but this was going to be another of my stupid mistakes.

Nashville, Here We Come

So off I flew with my good friend Rep. "Doc" Shea. I hadn't flown for more than twenty years, and somewhere over New York my terror forced me to ask Shea if he had something I could take to relieve my anxiety. I expected him to reach into his bag for a tranquilizer when he quickly responded, "Sure."

"Miss, would you kindly bring us a drink. Make that a double for my friend." And then with the thoroughness that only the best medical education provides to future practitioners, he added, "What the heck. Make that a double for both of us."

So much for modern medicine.

The flight did end, though my hangover hung on much longer.

I checked into my room, but not without a hassle. The desk clerk insisted that I could not occupy the room that was not going to be utilized by Representative Gear. I pulled rank as Speaker, and after some heated words with the desk manager, I got my way.

Back home, Sara, either convinced that I was in some convoluted way trying to use her to cover my decision to join the rest in Nashville, or seeing an opportunity to make some political hay out of all this, ran to the press claiming I was trying to make her look like a common junketeer. She reinforced her indignation by accusing me of putting her name on the list without her knowledge. She knew well that this wasn't true, but as emphasis she also argued that I was attempting to make it look as though she, in fact, was actually in attendance by leaving her name on the reserved room and then checking into it. I, of course, had left a pretty negative impression on the desk manager by insisting he turn the room over to Ralph Wright. That change had been made and was a matter of record. Actually, all she had to do, when asked if she had attended, was to simply reply no. The normally motivated reporter would have raised an eyebrow to the complaining Gear. But Nancy Wright wasn't a typical reporter. She jumped at this as if it were a winning lottery ticket.

Nancy hadn't lost any of her tenaciousness. She kept up daily attacks on my assumed misconduct, on the front page. And once again, I didn't know how to respond and fell back on my long-standing defense of remaining silent, hoping the story would be a one-day item and fade. I underestimated Nancy once again. She kept at it, and with each story managed to raise the false indignation of Gear. And Sara could do the indignation thing.

Sometimes It Is Better to Be Lucky than Good

And then I got lucky.

Nancy and Sara were trying to make the case that somehow I had managed to check in without ever revealing that I was not Sara (quite a physical leap of imagination). I tried to make the case to Nancy that that was a rather remote hypothesis, as I would not have used my own credit card if I had done such a thing. Even the dumbest of desk clerks could have surmised that I was not Sara Gear.

In this Nancy saw only another perverted angle to my chicanery. In a new article she claimed that all the rooms were prepaid by the Legislative Council, therefore, my alibi, as she implied it to be, didn't hold water because I would never have had to use my credit card. To confirm this, she got Sen. Dick Mazza, a Democrat from Grand Isle County, to go on record that he never had to use his credit card to check in, and to make it worse for me, she quoted him as saying that in fact his room had been prepaid by the Legislative Council.

Once again, my guardian angel arrived from the sky and landed in my lap. His name was Paul Teetor, a reporter rather notorious for his hard-hitting style and his ad-libbing methods of digging after a story. I don't know why Teetor entered the fray, but perhaps it was simply a competitive spirit, since he wrote for the *Herald*'s rival, the *Burlington Free Press.* Or perhaps he just saw a juicy story. Somehow Teetor got a quote from Senator Mazza angrily refuting the Nancy Wright story. Mazza was now denying that he had ever told Nancy that his room was prepaid. Nor, he explained, had he been allowed to check in without paying up front with his own credit card, as I and all the others had had to do. (This is a routine requirement in hotels; I assume they want financial assurance in case one runs off with the mattress.) A simple call, which Nancy had conveniently failed to make earlier to the Legislative Council, confirmed all this.

The next twist came when Nancy assured her editors that she had made every effort to contact me prior to running the story, so as to give me the opportunity to try to explain my side. Her problem was that she had been pretty specific as to the exact time she had made the attempt, failed to reach me, and, she then assured them, left a message for a return call. Fortunately, I could produce a telephone tape that contained messages just prior to and shortly after her claimed call. There was no call from Nancy or anyone else during that block of time. I headed for the *Herald*'s editorial office in Rutland.

I might as well have been Richard Nixon pleading, "I am not a crook."

I got steely-eyed stares as I nervously and laboriously went through my story. It soon became obvious that the editors weren't going to abandon one of their own and take up with the likes of me—another revelation from the dark side of the world of journalism. Only minutes into my plea for understanding, and realizing I wasn't getting very far, I asked to confront Nancy with the differences in our stories. A conference call was made to the press bureau in Montpelier, and it wasn't long before we were in an argument of some intensity and duration. A few minutes into this debate, I sensed someone else was in Nancy's company, on a separate telephone. I was a little upset when political columnist Jack Hoffman, Nancy's boss at the bureau, showed no embarrassment at what I perceived to be eavesdropping. The picture was becoming clearer that I was getting nowhere, and I left feeling I only had made matters worse by attempting to explain. The paper now had material for another story and perhaps a blistering editorial.

But those in charge must have had some doubts about Nancy because they pulled her off the story. An unusual move, it was probably instigated by Teetor's refutation of Nancy's tale about Senator Mazza and his credit card and to some degree by our differing stories about her effort, or lack thereof, to reach me. But nobody was about to pull Sara off the story, and she quickly called a press conference at the State House. The story was now well into its second week, and many in the competing press were showing signs of tiring. It was running out of legs.

It was Stu Seidel, another *Free Press* reporter, who finally declared an end to this war of words by asking Sara to explain how she could justify taking a trip to Germany at the expense of Pfizer Pharmaceutical while she was pretending she had no conflicts concerning the health care issues presently in front of the Vermont legislature. Now it was Sara's turn in the hot seat. As she futilely attempted to explain her own travel experiences, it became clear that the Nashville adventure had run its course.

The story died, and I had survived another battle, but not without a few more lifelong scars.

Never Get into a Fight with People Who Buy Ink by the Barrel

When people asked me why I didn't make more of an effort to respond to the amount of bad press I got, I always answered that if I reacted to bad press, then I had an obligation to do the same with good press. And I got my share of good press.

I'm talking here not simply about complimentary personal pieces but about the press's willingness to allow me to use them to advance a cause. The reporters had stories to write almost daily, and to be able to include the Speaker in their piece, especially if I could provide a good quote, added to the readability of their articles. They were always available when I searched them out to put a positive spin on an issue that I hoped to see passed, and I did this pretty regularly. This congeniality was not naiveté on their part; they well knew that it was in return for my willingness to help them. It was a tit-for-tat arrangement that an effective leader has to learn to use but not abuse.

And finally there is the quest for power. Like moths to the flame, the press can't resist being attracted to power. Leaders have what reporters want—access to the powerful. To the press, access and power are synonymous. Power, like wealth, is in limited supply in any well-defined environment. The statehouse is no exception. As I stated earlier, no one wants to interview freshman legislators. Leaders have power, sometimes of enormous proportions, and it's coveted, admired, and oftentimes feared by others. The press is a major part of that equation. But therein lies the quandary: The more access you give, the more risk you run of saying or doing the wrong thing, or worse, appearing strident. As long as you are doing things right it's a wonderful world. But God help the sinner. The only thing the sinner can be assured of is that the press will see to it that he or she gets a public trial.

And Then There Was Corcoran's Way

Having said all this and confessed my total ineptness in dealing with the press, I have often reflected on how my roommate Tim Corcoran managed to deal with it. As I've mentioned, Corcoran was a true character who seemed to have no higher purpose than the task in front of him. If he ever had an agenda I was unaware of it. It was the thrill of the battle that energized him, not the result. A political animal to his very soul, Cork was like the movie serial character who always seemed to escape from the most harrowing situations, I think because he was smarter than those who dared take him on.

I recall one pickle he seemed hopelessly entrapped in. A television crew out of Burlington made a special trip to the State House in anticipation of confronting him with the evidence to wrench a confession out of him. It concerned monies he had raised, in some cases pressured, out of lobbyists and local businessmen to finance field trips for sixth-grade students in Bennington to visit their state government in Montpelier. The students (future voters) numbered in the hundreds each year, and of course they were accompanied by a nearly equal number of teachers and parents (present voters). This all cost a lot of money, and Cork, an exemplary tour guide, treated his guests like royalty. Traveling in comfy buses and staying at hotels that had indoor swimming pools was, to say the least, an exciting and educational experience for these young future voters. For the rest of us it was like a two-day storm, as Cork, looking like the Pied Piper, would traipse the sixty or so members of the group in and out of the well of the House, committee rooms, and of course the governor's office.

All this demanded a considerable amount of planning and money, and as Cork preferred his own company he seldom included anyone else in his ventures. He managed it all, including raising the funds and writing the checks. This is what the reporter now camped outside my office with her camera people wanted to ask him a few questions about. Cork, aware of what was in store for him, lingered in my office. He hung tough for as long as possible, hoping they would grow tired of waiting, but it soon became evident that they weren't going anywhere until the reporter asked him about his accounting procedures. I kept myself busy, captivated by the dilemma he had gotten himself into and attempting to picture just how he was going to escape.

Finally, out he went, and of course was immediately accosted by the reporter.

"Representative Corcoran, can we have a moment of your time? We have a few questions we'd like to ask you."

Amazingly, on came the Cork's Irish charm. "No problem. Happy to answer anything you want. Is this going to be on camera or off?" Of course he knew full well that they hadn't lugged the camera fifty miles to just do an audio.

"Well, we'd like to get you on camera if you don't mind."

"No, of course not, but would you mind if I freshened up a little? I've just come back from working out." (Let me assure you that Corcoran's idea of working out was going to lunch.)

"Ah! I guess we can do that."

"Thanks! I'll be right back." And he disappeared down the hall in the direction of the men's room on the right. The reporter, unfamiliar with the layout of the State House, was totally unaware that just across from the men's room was an exit out into the back alley of the building. Cork, familiar with every nook and cranny of the building, took a left, bounded down the stairs, hopped into his car, and was fifteen miles closer to home by the time the press people realized that their victim was not coming back.

Of course this was something that a leader would never have gotten away with, but I have to be honest and tell you I never, in my wildest thoughts, would have even been able to conceive of it.

7

Lobbyists

The Morphing of the Lobbyist in Vermont

VERMONT IS A small state and I'm sure can't compete with other states as to the amount of money spent by lobbying interests to affect legislation. But still, lots of dollars come into play.

It wasn't always that way. When I first arrived at the legislature, in 1979, lobbying was a laid-back affair, more collegial and social than high powered. To be sure, there were lobbying interests that were a part of the State House fraternity, but in greatly smaller numbers than today. Most lobbyists, in fact, were part time, and more than a few worked for nothing. There were several reasons for this, but the overriding one was that business interests didn't have to perform heavy lifting to steer legislation in those days. The conservative, and very decidedly Republican, legislature did it for them.

Times have changed, and so has the life of the lobbyist. Today one would find dozens of lobbyists filtering in and out of the State House, and should a high-impact issue be up for debate, the number wandering the hallways and crowding the committee rooms might triple. Where there's money involved you can be sure you'll find a horde of well-dressed lobbyists.

As a newcomer to the legislature I paid little heed to lobbyists, and of course they didn't spend much time thinking about me. As time went on I did get to recognize certain characters who showed up at the local watering holes, but even then I was background material for whatever clandestine discussions were taking place in darkened corners. What became obvious rather quickly was that lobbyists gravitated to the members who had positions of power, including committee chairs, caucus leaders, members who were known as wheeler-dealers, and of course the Speaker. I was far from being any of these, and my first real encounter with the species didn't happen until the process of discussing bills got under way in the Health and Welfare Committee. Here lobbyists took on a very different character because they became conveyors of information that was vital as we tried to decipher a bill's merit. Most often they were appreciated for their knowledge. They seemed very professional and always very well informed.

What Makes an Effective Lobbyist?

Lobbying, unlike legislating, comes much closer to being a science than an art. Good lobbyists—and you can oftentimes identify them by their fees, which are a matter of public information through the secretary of state's office—understand certain rules and violate them at grave risk to their reputation and consequently their livelihood.

The first rule in being an effective lobbyist is the same as it is for the press. Gain access to people who have the power to help you achieve your goals.

The obvious seat of power is at the top—the governor's office. Lobbyists with close connections to a governor have a decided advantage over those who do not. These would include someone who has worked for the governor, perhaps in an administrative role, in earlier times; someone who worked to help him or her get elected by donating money or time in a campaign; or just someone (usually someone very wealthy) who has spent a career hobnobbing with people who happen to become governor or have the potential to rise to the governor's office. The latter may be someone far off in the background, known only in small circles of intimate colleagues, and only infrequently actually registered as a lobbyist. All these folks, unless they push their self-importance or in some way have a falling-out, find their telephone calls returned. Most have money; all have access.

I remember that at one point Gov. Madeleine Kunin had made a courtesy call to inform me that she was ready to announce the appointment to the state Board of Realtors of a real estate agent in Bennington whom I knew to be a staunch Republican and certainly no supporter of mine. I couldn't convince her of my doubts about the depth of support this person had afforded her in the just concluded governor's race, and Governor Kunin ended the conversation by informing me, "Mr. Speaker, she contributed $500 to my campaign." After hanging up I made a quick call to the secretary of state's office and got a little more information.

I got the governor on the line once again. "Governor, I'm not calling to try to dissuade you from appointing your new friend to the Realtors Board, but I just wanted you to be aware that though she gave $500 to your campaign, she gave $1,000 to your opponent."

Even governors can sometimes be duped.

But really good lobbyists don't put all their eggs in one basket. Effectiveness can be achieved in all parts of the statehouse by those smart enough to befriend the Speaker, the president pro tem, the lieutenant governor (after all, he or she is next in line), party leaders, committee chairs, or members of important committees (read here: the money committees, for the corporate lobbyists). Even individual legislators on a committee to which a bill of interest will be assigned can be useful to a lobbyist.

All this really points out is that lobbyists learn to be extremely friendly people endowed with a generosity not often found even in one's church. Surprisingly, the same personal characteristics that make a highly respected legislator are those that make a good lobbyist. Be diligent; know what you are talking about; never mislead a committee or individual in one's testimony or conversation; and be available to assist upon request. Conversely, a lobbyist who badgers, floods a member with unwanted mail or calls, or gets a reputation for trickery is doomed to the refuse pile of humanity.

Good lobbyists are never absentee agents for their clients. They work long hours. Lobbyists who hope to be effective have to have a constant presence in the statehouse. It is in the endless hours of standing in hallways or sitting in committee that lobbyists become familiar faces and, they hope, begin the process of building personal relationships.

That's the personal side of lobbying. There is a tactical aspect.

The Rhythm of the Legislature

Successful lobbyists, without exception, know the bill under discussion in any committee as well or better than most of the members. They have dissected every sentence and phrase and know what a difference the words "will" and "shall" can make. They also are well aware that the lobbying process is long and often convoluted, calling for patience and often cunning.

There's a rhythm to the legislative dance, and lobbyists have to become masters of the steps. Like the seasons, the ebb-and-flow of legislation changes and occupies different venues.

Early in the legislative session the center of power is brought into view by the governor and his proposals, now resting in the committee rooms of both the House and Senate. Several months into the session, the power shifts onto the floor of each house with the ensuing debate. Then the power transfers back again to the committee rooms, as the Senate and House deal with each other's wants and hopes in bills that have managed to navigate successfully through their respective houses. Finally, in the closing days, the power is in the multitude of conference committees, themselves in the control of a few leaders and committee members—the governor now but a nervous expectant father, hoping for a healthy child but prepared to accept whatever the outcome.

Lobbyists, through all this, have taken on the confidence of the tortoise seemingly unworried at the apparent swiftness of the hare. The obstacle course that a bill has to wend its way through becomes second nature to them. What they can't achieve in one committee they can attempt to achieve in another. What the House can't get done for them, the Senate can. When all else fails there's always the corner office, where the governor sits with the power of the veto.

Perhaps the greatest advantage business lobbyists have is that they often are working not to change things. Their cause is different from that of activist legislators or fellow lobbyists who are trying to bring about social or environmental change in that they have human nature on their side—the primordial urge that rests in most souls to leave things as they are. Change brings discomfort to the comfortable and the satisfied and, more important, puts those who fight to preserve the status quo at a distinct advantage. It is so much easier to kill a bill than to pass one. This was driven home to me early in my political career.

My Baptism under Fire

Though I seldom introduced bills, I did sponsor one in the second year of my first term. It would provide a great lesson in understanding the intricate path a bill must take on its way to becoming a law. It seemed as simple a bill as one could imagine; all it did was change a single word in an existing statute.

Vermont, having been in the vanguard of protecting the environment, had passed a bottle redemption law several years earlier. This had put a nickel deposit on all beer and soft drink containers and had worked miracles in cleaning our roadsides of litter, to say nothing of advancing our recycling efforts. As a reward to grocers and redemption centers that collected the returns, the law had specified that they receive a penny per can or bottle for their efforts. My bill, recognizing inflation, would change the "one" in front of the word "penny," to "two." What could be simpler?

In the legislature there is no such thing as a "simple little bill." And as I was still very much of a novice, I was not prepared for all the hidden forces that lay in wait on the road to success.

Off I went tending to my little bill every step of the way, and after much beseeching, conniving, and hand-wringing I finally managed to get it out of four different committees and onto the floor of the House.

Up to this point I had barely uttered a word on the floor, and in effect this would be my baptism under fire, my maiden speech. I felt pretty confident that I had support for the bill, as I had made an effort to speak to my fellow Democrats, as well as those Republicans who cared enough about the environment to recognize that the penny was necessary to give the army of grocers collecting the tens of millions of containers each year their just reward.

Unnoticed at the time was the lack of volunteers who might rise and assist me in debate on the floor. I had been aware of the cost of a penny increase, but I had not given a whole lot of thought to whose pocket it would come out of, or how much it would amount to for the various distributors of soft drinks and beer.

Vermonters drink their share of beer and soda, and the distributors are more than happy to ship them all they can guzzle down. But they're not too enamored of accepting the empties back, especially if they have to pay the redeemers a penny or two. The cost to Coca-Cola, Pepsi, 7-Up, Miller, Budweiser, and other companies was in the hundreds of thousands of dollars. They didn't much like the idea of recycling to begin with and had hoped that it would be such a mess that the bottle redemption law itself would be overturned.

Now, my bill was doubling the cost to them to collect the containers, which only made it more likely that the law they had little desire to live with would gain a foothold. Had I known how vociferous the attack would be I would have been a whole lot more frightened than I was. It came from all sides, and the beating I took on the floor probably had some members, who supported me if not my bill, beginning to feel sorry for the beleaguered freshman trying to stay on his feet. I couldn't answer a whole lot of what seemed to me trivial questions dealing with numbers, and those I could answer I fumbled and stumbled through.

The beer and soda companies had hired an assortment of lobbyists to see that my bill did not get through the House, and those lobbyists had done their jobs, as each had their designated members prepped to argue against me on the floor. The debate was lengthy, and I was relieved when the Speaker decided to break for lunch. I left the building and took in the cold wind that represents Montpelier in February. For the first time I realized my suit jacket was soaked through with sweat.

A Fatal Mistake

Though I was too consumed by the debate to truly understand how I might be faring, someone must have been worried that my bill would go through because, during lunch, a lobbyist for one of the beer distributors had, in violation of the specific House rule that no material or propaganda may be distributed on members' desks without express permission of the Speaker, placed on each member's desk a quickly photocopied letter. That was the first bit of sloppy disregard by someone for House protocol. Their second mistake would prove even more ill-advised, for in the memo, whoever wrote it (it was unsigned, another House no-no) got personal. He questioned the integrity of a member—me.

The writer pointed out to the members that I ran a bottle and can redemption center and that with the increase in the "handling charge" my profits would obviously double. In other words I was pushing a bill for my own personal gain.

In fact, nothing could have been farther from the truth. I ran a redemption center—that was true—but I didn't own it. Actually it was the only nonprofit collection center in the state and was a work classroom for the dropout program that I had originated and directed for my school district. The school district owned it.

At the center, kids in the program spent fifteen hours a week learning work skills; it was hoped that the program would make them see some merit in achieving gainful employment sometime in life. The alternative program was a combined work-study program, and we had kids working in various jobs all over town. But some were simply not employable, and we had created the redemption center to begin the process of their "learning to work." We paid them through a federal work program for low-income teenagers. The redemption center did manage to make a profit, but every penny of that was turned over to the local school board to help defray the expenses of operating the program. In other words, the kids were working, not just to learn rudimentary work skills, but to actually help pay for their own program.

Two other staff members and I had to supervise it beyond our responsibilities of teaching. Thankfully, they were dedicated. The three of us put up with running an operation that was open ten hours a day, six days a week, twelve months a year.

And we didn't receive a nickel for these added responsibilities.

The lobbyist had made a fatal mistake, and he must have realized it as members returning to their desks in anticipation of the continuing debate began chattering among themselves. I was more than chattering; I was livid. My Irish boiled over, and I wanted to know where I could find the sonofabitch who had questioned my integrity. I looked up to see standing in front of me none other than Tom Candon, my Democratic leader. Beside him was another man I recognized from the hallways but didn't know.

"Ralph, I have somebody who wants to apologize to you. He realizes . . ." I no longer heard what Tom, the mediator, was trying to explain. Fortunately, I was immediately restrained by little Mary Evelti and several others as I tried to climb over the desk after Tom's friend. Tom hustled him off the floor of the House and out the door.

It took time and some sympathetic words from Speaker O'Connor to calm me down, but it was Mary who talked some sense into me. She said this was a "lemon that we could make lemonade out of."

"Ralph, listen to me. This is an opportunity. You were probably going to lose this bill. They're smart and know all the catchphrases to make your bill unpalatable to a lot of members who would tend to side with them anyway. Frankly, you're losing the debate because they know a lot more about the subject than you. But now you've got an opportunity to explain to the members just who you are and just what you do for kids whom nobody else wants. Don't you see? Get up and tell your story."

God bless Mary Evelti.

Not exactly the recommended way to pass a bill, but amazingly it passed, by the smallest of margins. I thought I had won the championship, when in actuality I had barely eked out victory in the quarterfinals. It represented just the first hurdle in what was to be a long, cross-country race.

Discovering the Lowest Common Denominator

As I emerged from the floor of the House I was accosted by an irate Jim Finneran. I knew who he was; his reputation as the guru of lobbyists was legendary in the capital. He was the hired gun whom the big money turned to when they had a cause. He also was the owner of the Brown Derby, a motel-restaurant that was the favorite watering hole for the movers and shakers among the House members. And he was a generous innkeeper, making sure that the bar stayed open as long as anyone was still standing, running tabs that sometimes got misplaced for legislators a little short on cash, and in general playing the friendly and generous host to those who gathered there every night after the day's session ended. He was also the headline lobbyist for the guys whom I had just stuck for hundreds of thousands of dollars. Now this tightly wired little bantam-cock was in my face.

"You know, Wright," no honorary title here, "you think you've just won a big victory, don't you?" Not wanting an answer he continued, "But you haven't won shit. And you're not going to win shit. I know how this place works, and I don't think you have a clue." I stood there, not sure what to make of it all, more aware of the small crowd gathering and his face growing redder.

"Now I may not be able to control that gang of crazies in there," pointing to the glass doors leading into the House, "as anytime they get together any damned thing is likely to happen, but I can have more than my say in the Senate, where sixteen votes makes you a loser."

He hesitated long enough to catch his breath and for me to interject, "What the hell are you talking about?"

"I'll tell you what I'm talking about. The lowest common denominator, that's what I'm talking about. You don't have a clue, do you?" Taking some measure of himself he lowered his voice a decibel or two and continued. "Listen, kid," he said, now almost counseling. "You haven't won anything, yet. Anyone can pass any cockamamie idea in that place." I presumed he was still referring to the 150-member House. "But it gets a lot tougher over there," now gesturing toward the 30-member Senate. "There, reasonable people reside, and I have to convince but sixteen to do the right thing. You did a good job. Actually, I admire what you do." Wow! I assumed he was referring to my other job. "But it was my fault, as I should have dissuaded you from even introducing this thing when it was just a thought in your head. That was my mistake, but I won't make it again." And off he went in the direction of the Senate.

So there it was—the lobbyist's secret to success: Kill it when it's still in the womb. Legislative abortion. The lowest common denominator.

The bill did have some support in the Senate, but I didn't know how to help my cause, as I had never ventured over into that rather austere and to me mystical body. Hell, I still hadn't figured out how the House worked, let alone the Senate. I had no friends among the senators and few acquaintances. I didn't have the foggiest notion how the place functioned. I'm not sure, after another fifteen years, that I ever got a grasp on its workings.

It was several months later, and the session was in its final days, when I got a somewhat belated note from one of the handful who agreed with my bill that it was on the Senate floor. We were on the floor ourselves in the midst of a roll call, and by the time I could wrench myself free the Senate debate had ended. As I entered the Senate gallery the vote was being read. You guessed it; Finneran had done his job. It was tied up 15–15 and was about to die when the presiding officer, in this case the lieutenant governor, indicated to the clerk that she wanted to cast her vote as accorded by Senate rules. Madeleine Kunin then voted aye. Two days later Governor Snelling, after refusing Finneran's last-minute request for an audience to plead his case, signed it into law.

I had won a championship, but it would be years and a real estate transaction later before I dared belly up to the bar in the Brown Derby again.

The Speaker and the Lobbyists

Not surprisingly, once I became Speaker my relations with lobbyists became much more cordial. But it may surprise you that, as Speaker, I didn't have that much interaction with them. There were reasons for this, probably the most prominent being that they always pretty much knew my position on bills. As I was a liberal Democrat my thoughts on a whole lot of bills didn't have to be guessed at, and the business lobbyists were smart enough not to tip their hand about their wants and political maneuvering in pursuit of their goals by discussing them with me. They stayed away. Perhaps, more strategically, they knew that once a bill was introduced, their efforts, especially if they intended to kill it, were best directed elsewhere. Here I'm referring to the individual committees because, as the 1950s bank robber Willie Sutton once said when the police asked him why he robbed banks, "that's where the money is." The committees were where the action was—or inaction. Finneran had it right. Consequently, lobbyists spent their time sitting in committee rooms trying to win friends and influence people. Their expertise and helpfulness, if forthright and full, were often very much appreciated by the committee members, especially the chairman.

This may be the place to say something nice about lobbyists because they often proved invaluable to the legislature's effort to make law. I respected lobbyists' role in the legislative process, if not the majority of their causes. Most kept their distance, as our causes differed. But there were lobbyists whose company I enjoyed, and I often made attempts to get to know them better. As they tended to segregate themselves in the State House, whether in the halls or the cafeteria, my best chance of sitting and chatting was early in the morning, when I would make an effort to sit and have a cup of coffee. Maybe it was just the chemistry, or just that they knew better than I that we came from different worlds, but conversation always seemed forced. I never really made it with the majority of them. It only got worse when I became Speaker, as they recognized long before I did the potential damage the power of the Speaker's office could do. This distance between us never bothered me very much with the moneyed interests—those representing banks, corporations, insurance companies— but it did with those lobbying on environmental issues, the low income advocates, and other human services. So they were there doing their best to stay out of my way and constantly searching for other avenues to attain their goals. We were the dog and the cat forced to live under the same roof, respecting each other as best we could, but always aware of our differences.

Lobbyists had at least one distinct advantage: they could devote their time to being specialists. As mentioned, each biennium would see perhaps 1,000 or so bills introduced—a number beyond the ability of any one legislator to begin to comprehend. Lobbyists were in the enviable position of being able to focus on the handful of bills that concerned them and accumulate knowledge of those that was most always unmatched by even the most diligent member. If they presented this information in a straightforward and understandable manner to a committee, they became valuable asscts to the committee's efforts to avoid doing something stupid. As a committee member during my first three terms I myself had come to depend on them as providers of often vital information that I had no way of uncovering without great time and effort. As mentioned, we had no staff to do research, and though the Legislative Council was always reliable and willing, it was swamped trying to keep up with the endless requests for assistance. The staff of lawyers often worked long into the night meeting the demands of 180 sometimes impatient members of the legislature. The lobbyist was the well into which we frequently had to dip our cup.

But lobbyists are not just a reservoir of knowledge. They have money, and unfortunately money is the mother's milk of politics.

Shaking the Money Tree

I never asked lobbyists for money for my own campaigns—none, never, not once. I shouldn't be bragging here, as there was a very good reason why not. Of the nine campaigns I had for reelection, my most expensive cost less than two hundred dollars, an amount I could shoulder on my own. It probably led, at least to a slight degree, to my defeat in 1994, but that's another story.

Still, the reader shouldn't get the idea that I never went out grubbing for money from my well-dressed friends. I did, and I did it big time. Though I was a minority Speaker, I was never that much of a minority. Had I been, I never would have won a second term, let alone a third, fourth, and fifth. Consequently I was never forced to raise money for my own campaigns, but I did for the party, more specifically, for my Democrats in the House.

Way back in 1983, when Paul Poirier and I were beginning our campaign to win over the House for Democrats, we understood little about raising money. I'm not sure either party was into shaking the money tree, as Vermont campaigns, for the most part, were low-key affairs conducted pretty much by the individual candidates in the respective districts. And up until we came along as leaders in 1983, the Grand Old Party never had to worry a whole lot about who would control the House because for a century and a half it had had the majority. Consequently the only contest would be in caucus to anoint a Speaker. None of this encompassed expenses or raising money to defray them.

We did, of course, have expenses for our gas and phone bills while we ran around the state recruiting and training candidates, but there was no kitty to help us or any of our recruits with the cost of campaigning. As a minority since before the Civil War we had little hope of tapping lobbyists, even if it had crossed our minds to do so, which it didn't. Our only source of funds was our fellow Democrats. We had gone to our caucus and pled for their help by asking them to cough up fifty dollars each. Of the sixty-five members of the caucus, there were perhaps forty or so who actually thought it a good enough cause to donate. Even some of those had to make it in payments. A few simply handed us what they could afford, ten dollars here, a twenty there.

Our campaign got to be an expensive proposition, and only our commitment to winning the brass ring allowed us to overlook just how expensive. Our wives, who barely tolerated the political world anyway, would have cut us both off at the knees if they had been aware how much we were taking out of our pockets on a daily basis. It was going to take a while before we gained the attributes of power and erudition to shake the money tree.

But learn we did, and I guess I have to take the blame for bringing Vermont politics into the modern world of legislative fund raising. By my second year at the podium I had established an annual event called the "Speaker's Soiree." This was always held in the middle of a week in February, timed to take advantage not only of good attendance but of the period when most bills had already been introduced but not acted on. It was a clear signal to lobbyists that we would enjoy their company at our planned dinner. The affair was broken into two events; the first was a "gala" cocktail party beginning at five o'clock and running until seven. The least expensive of the events, at only fifty dollars a ticket, it would attract perhaps two hundred guests. The big event followed immediately in the form of a "Dinner with the Speaker" by special invitation only. The

At my annual Speaker's Soiree in 1991, I enjoy being spoofed. (Pictured with me is William "Billy" Bulger, then president of the Massachusetts state senate.) I don't believe I ever had more laughs than I had during my sixteen years in the statehouse. Perhaps it was the Irish in me, or just my recognizing that the job was tough enough without taking myself too seriously.

special invitation put you out five hundred dollars a ticket. We might seat fifty at this affair.

Politically, I was careful to have little to do with the sale of tickets and would see to it that the State Democratic Party handled all the details—having the tickets printed, organizing the affair, distributing the invitations to individual lobbyists (and through them their clients), and administering it all through the state party's books. I was careful never to touch a ticket or a check; my only job was to afford the guests the pleasure of my company. It impressed a lot of people, but my wife wasn't one of them.

Staying Humble

As you've probably understood, my wife, Cathy, thought not much of politics and probably less of the vast majority of politicians. She came to

Montpelier only half a dozen times in sixteen years, so I was especially elated when she agreed to drive up and spend a couple of days with me in the capital. Her visit coincided with my Soiree. Knowing that she would be most reluctant to attend I kept it a secret, only suggesting that "we'll have a special dinner tonight" on my way out the morning of the affair. To Cathy a "special dinner" meant I wanted meatloaf and mashed potatoes. And that's what she was preparing as I rushed back to the apartment that afternoon to get prepared for the Soiree.

"What are you doing?" I asked, as she placed the meatloaf in the oven. "We're going out to dinner tonight."

"But, I'm making supper—your favorite meatloaf."

Oh, my! That look came over her face. I knew that look well, and it was not good. Not good! I tried to explain, almost certain of the futility.

"Hon, tonight's my Soiree. I have to go. A lot of people are going to be there. It's my annual fund-raiser. C'mon you'll have a good time. We'll eat the meatloaf tomorrow. Whatta ya say?"

She turned back to the oven, "I'll have the meatloaf. You go." Not good. Not good at all. It was time to get firm.

"Look, Cathy, I have to do this. Fifty lobbyists and their clients have coughed up five hundred dollars each to sit and break bread with the great Speaker tonight. What the hell am I going to do—not show up?"

She turned toward me slowly and with that measure of finality that I knew so well. "Ralph, there were nights, such as this, over the past thirty-five years, when I would have paid five hundred dollars not to have to eat with you." So much for greatness.

8

The Gay Rights Issue

What Motivates a Legislator

THERE ARE THREE primary motivations that bring a legislator to a decision on how to cast their vote on any given issue. Deciphering which is at work in a particular case is a complex matter.

Some members arrive in the statehouse with such extensive political backgrounds or life experiences that there is little guessing where they stand on a whole array of issues. They have spent the better part of their lifetimes following a certain philosophical path, and it is almost always fruitless to hope that they will suddenly discard it all and change direction 180 degrees. These are true believers, and they didn't come this far to sell their soul. They range the political scale from far left to far right, with a big gap in the middle.

A hodgepodge of members are not overburdened by the weight of conscience, nor do they need to be persuaded by argument. They vote according to how they see their action affecting what they are trying to achieve. These are usually people in positions of leadership, wannabes, or people who have other issues equally important to them and see the possibility that to lend a hand here amounts to a chip to be cashed later.

Others come with their finger to the wind, so to speak. It isn't that they believe in nothing; it's just that they are, for the first time, in a position to consider things that had never before taken up a whole lot of their time. Often full explanations of the pros and cons of an issue can win them over or conversely turn them against you. This group is more likely to look for second opinions from sources within and beyond the legislature.

The caveat to this "science" is that it is always dangerous to segregate these three groups into neat piles: there are too many peripheral pressures on members at any given time to predict why a member votes one way today and a totally opposite way a week from now.

I've witnessed members vote both yes and no on the same issue because they got a telephone call from somebody back in the district, the governor jerked them into his office for a little talk, or their seatmate leaned over and murmured something in their ear. These are not the most stalwart of members.

But the vote of the members is only half the story; the issue itself can dictate the route a member takes. The Vermont legislature in any biennium will have upwards of 1,000 bills introduced, and perhaps a couple of hundred will find their way through the legislative maze to become law (see Table 8.1). Bills reaching the floor and requiring a member's vote can be categorized into three groups.

Constituent Votes

The first type involve what I call "finger-to-the-wind" issues. These are bills on which the member uses whatever method is available to figure out what the folks back home want him or her to do. Merrill Perley, a Republican from up in the rural Northeast Kingdom, never cast a vote without rushing to a phone and calling his local selectman back home in Enosburg. At least, that's who he always claimed he was calling; no one was ever able to verify who was on the other end of the line.

Some members are more diligent in their polling and spend as much time as they can attending local meetings, talking to local officials, hanging out in the coffee shop, encouraging correspondence, welcoming evening and weekend telephone calls, paying close attention to their hometown newspaper, and now that the Internet had come into style, I assume reading their e-mail. None of them have the ready access to polls

TABLE 8.1 Bills Introduced and Passed in the Vermont General Assembly, 1959–2002

Year	Bills introduced	Bills passed	Percentage of bills enacted into law
1959–1960	517	331	64
1961–1962	577	343	59
1963–1964	553	307	56
1965–1966	630	320	51
1967–1968	696	392	56
1969–1970	673	307	46
1971–1972	698	268	38
1973–1974	756	276	37
1975–1976	775	264	34
1977–1978	984	280	28
1979–1980	1,003	205	20
1981–1982	1,028	249	24
1983–1984	996	253	25
1985–1986	1,066	294	28
1987–1988	1,145	310	27
1989–1990	1,294	325	25
1991–1992	1,420	296	21
1993–1994	1,265	265[a]	21
1995–1996	1,166	210	18
1997–1998	1,073	172	16
1999–2000	1,185	179	15
2001–2002	1,075	163	15

Source: State of Vermont Legislative Council.

[a] Excludes thirteen bills vetoed by the governor.

or staff that legislators in other states and in Congress have. Thus, at best they are taking a measured guess as to how people in their district look on any given issue.

Complicating this inflow of information is the probability that a member's district contains a rainbow of opinion. My district, for example, had within its boundaries a conservative section that placed Christmas second behind their favorite time of year: deer season. Conversely, Bennington College sat adjacent to my home and housed students and staff who spent their time handing out Green Peace brochures and studying Zen. Any attempt I might have made at finding consensus would have driven me to Prozac.

A second complication to the puzzle of doing the "people's will" was the fact that most people back home didn't have a clue as to what the legislature was doing "up in Montpelier," and a whole lot simply didn't much care. The member, caught up in the intensity of the State House environment, too often unknowingly began refuting Copernicus: The center of his or her universe became the committee room, the fight to win support for a little amendment, or the importance of dining with the governor, along with three hundred others, at some evening freebie in the Tavern Ballroom. Hell, I look back and remember years that presidents got sent packing, wars broke out, walls came down, and communism collapsed, and all the members wanted to talk about in the cafeteria was the Senate conference committee's three appointees to the Appropriations bill. The world beyond Montpelier might as well not have existed. It was too painful for a member's ego to even begin to think that the people back home most likely couldn't have cared less.

"What the Hell! Why Not?" Votes

The second category were throwaway votes: When a member recognized that the bill on the floor didn't affect his district or his conscience, he or she could sit back, relax, and wait for opportunity to come knocking.

Opportunity might present itself in the person of the member in the next seat, who did have a stake in the bill's outcome; in the leadership's plea for support; or in the governor's hinting that his or her help might be appreciated. This "What the hell, throw 'em a bone" response never was accompanied by, "You owe me one" because it was a given that could go unexpressed. The only caveat might be a reminder to the grateful member, who had perhaps wanted a stretch of highway repaved or a bridge in the myriad construction projects in the transportation bill, to "make sure a river flows under it."

The true "conscience issues" were few and far between, but they always set off an alarm that could terrorize the weak of mind or those who shrank before adversity. Even the strong and committed became aroused—often to a frenzy.

These weren't issues on which a member could poll his district. They were so controversial that discretion dictated they were better left unmentioned. But members could be certain that, once they were raised, they would hear from home. Unlike the "what the hell" issues, it was a rare legislator who didn't have a strong interest in the outcome of these measures. The interest was predominately one of "conscience," but in addition, the member could be sure that these issues always would resound with a huge impact back in the district, one way or the other. The most disengaged legislator had to recognize that these questions were of the "damned if you do and damned if you don't" kind and ones that would test his or her resolve to the fullest.

Bills of this kind affected all of us, but those who arrived at their decision from deep-seated beliefs had the easiest time. If a member's convictions rested on sincere religious beliefs or constitutional conviction, they were unshakable—whatever side of the issue they came down on. There might be severe political repercussions for their vote, but these members were doing what they believed to be right, and that was the end of the discussion. Their solace in their convictions was to be envied.

Others labored and fretted night and day over what to do. A vote for the Equal Rights Amendment might be the right thing to do, and even satisfy the biggest doubter's logic, but then what would the guys at Rotary or the coffee shop say?

It seemed so reasonable to notify a parent of a minor's pregnancy. But what if the "father is the father"? I'm sure few back home had ever considered that ugly possibility.

And the mother load of all dilemmas, Shouldn't all Americans have the right to their own sexuality?

"Oh my! Lordy, what to do?"

"Mr. Speaker, can't we table this bill, hide it in Murphy's committee? Mr. Speaker? Mr. Speaker? Mr. Speaker?"

A Storm Hits the House

Ron Squires, D-Guilford, was the first openly gay member in the Vermont legislature. There was no dramatic public confessional; that was not Ron's style. Being gay was no big deal to him, and his "coming out" was osmotic in that Ron never made any efforts to deny who he was. He just let people carry on with their gossip while he carried on with being a damn good legislator. Meanness being a tiring preoccupation, most members came to deal with Ron for what he was—a damn good legislator and a better human being. What the homophobes did I don't know.

So we had one gay member amongst us, and we had one black member, Francis Brooks, D-Montpelier, my Democratic leader in 1991–1992. Both were my friends, and I can say with some assurance that both were friends to mankind. So it was with very limited experience that we in Vermont analyzed new questions of race or sexuality. The whitest state in the nation, Vermont never has had to confront the kind of racial problems that other states had experienced. The same was not true with respect to sexuality. Here we found ourselves dealing with what every state legislature has had to deal with, as sexuality is not a matter of color, nor does it cling to any religion, age, or national origin. If statistics are right that perhaps 10 percent of the world is gay or lesbian, it follows that they are an equal and fundamental part of the American fabric—our family, our neighbors, our co-workers, and our seatmates in the legislature. This meant that in my 150-member House, statistically speaking, there were fourteen more out there in the well not "fessin' up." (Now you know something else about Ron Squires—he had courage.)

This minority had suffered the blows of homophobia from some in the general population and the denial of equal rights in state legislatures across the nation. Vermont was different in only one way—we decided to do something about it.

The Senate had introduced and passed S-131, a bill that called for guaranteeing equal rights in employment and housing for gay men and lesbians. I had sent it into my liberal-leaning Judiciary Committee, and it immediately set out down a road filled with anger and hate. Though it was a simple and straightforward proposition, we were well aware of its emotional and explosive nature, which promised to divide our caucus in two, no matter what our efforts to avoid it.

Even the liberals, who could be counted on to support the bill, were more than a little nervous about being on record supporting gay rights. Other members had religious or conscience objections. The major problem was that a large number in the caucus were simply terrified of the bill; it aroused a homophobic atmosphere that one literally could feel throughout the building. This would be the second time we had brought such a bill out on the floor. Two years earlier the galleries filled to overflowing with guys in checkered hunting jackets, while a handful of gays sat alone up next to the Speaker's rostrum in trepidation. It became obvious that the atmosphere would never allow us to garner the votes needed, and no sooner had we taken our seats than I made a decision: I had the chairman of the committee, set to report the bill, pull it back into committee. I truly felt for the first time in my entire tenure in the legislature that violence was in the air.

This time when the chair of the Judiciary Committee, Sally Fox, D-Essex, notified me that she was set to vote the bill out of committee, I asked her to delay for a day or two in order for the leadership to begin gathering support.

The lobbying against the bill had been overwhelming. Hordes of witnesses filed into the Judiciary Committee over a three-month period determined to push their conviction that to expand equal rights in housing and employment was to bring about the demise of the family and the nation. We also scheduled four public hearings in the evening. The well of the House would be filled to capacity, and the air of animosity could be cut with a knife. I attended those meetings as an observer, and all I can say is they were scary. But the committee, under the steady guidance of Sally, had endured, and the bill was now ready for floor action—and, we hoped, passage. Our support was not overwhelming, but I thought we could muster the votes to get the bill through to passage and onto the governor's desk for his signature.

Normally the process of garnering support for any bill was to run it by the caucus and then let the leader and whip take on the responsibility of gathering up votes. Of all the duties of leaders, counting and gathering votes for the caucus's agenda was the primary one; that's what they got paid for (jesting here, as there is no additional pay for any member of the legislature save the Speaker and the president pro tempore of the Senate). We had discussed this among ourselves and concluded that this was such a hot issue that the leaders were going to have their mettle tested as never before. We believed the result might be that the members' reaction to pressure from them might result in some personal blowups that would be hard for the leader and whip to counter or mediate. We agreed that any loss of control by them could send the caucus into chaos for the rest of the session.

We also agreed that their positions didn't have the inherent power necessary to wedge somebody out of the "No" column and into the "Yes" column on an issue this intense. Should they be forced to make the effort it might jeopardize their ability to lead. We decided that they should quietly withdraw from the task and that I would do what I very seldom had been forced to do in the past—go to my members, one by one, and personally and up close ask them to help me with this.

Though the odds seemed stacked, I had distinct advantages as the person responsible for garnering votes among the members. First and foremost, I believed we were right on the issue. But being right wasn't always enough in the legislature. If we could protect the rights of mass murderers, pedophiles, and other deviants in American society, surely we could protect the rights of 10 percent of the American population who differed on how the rest of us made love. Frankly, I wasn't much interested how one treated another in the privacy of their bedroom, but I was focused on how we treated each other in the workplace and in housing. I believed without an iota of doubt that gays and lesbians were entitled to the same rights as the rest of us "normal" people.

There was another distinct advantage to my leading the charge: I was the Speaker, and I had the leverage to buttonhole[1] each and every member—not because I was better at the task than the leaders but because the members would tolerate from me what they might not from others. That human interaction is part of power, and I intended to use it.

Common sense told me to stay away from some members. I knew their vote was coming from their conscience, and it didn't matter how wrong I felt their conscience was, I still had to respect their right to be wrong. On the other side, an equally large number agreed with the bill, and though they might be nervous about the political fallout, they would vote for it in the end. They knew where they were, and so did I.

The battleground rested with the remaining members, who felt in their hearts that people shouldn't be discriminated against but who were going to vote no because the politics of the situation was so explosive. These were the members I sought to win over. I had two options with recalcitrant members, "Give me some help on this," or at least, "Take a walk." This was a walking type of issue for the weak-kneed.

Within twenty-four hours I was in the mid-sixties in my vote count. Passage required a majority of those present. Sixty-five or so votes weren't going to cut it, as the bill had generated such emotion that few, if any, would be absent. If there was full attendance, seventy-five votes would do it. The Speaker, as one of 150, only voted to break or make a tie (which in the latter case could be the death knell for a bill that the Speaker wanted killed). No one could ever guess correctly what the attendance would be on any given day, but our exercise as a leadership team was to begin a running count of members present the day of the vote. This would begin early in the morning and be updated constantly so we knew who was there and who wasn't, right up to the moment the roll call began. Missing members would be tracked down, assuming they were going to vote with us, and calls would go out to their home, business, or cell phone. We were diligent, and this extra effort often made the difference.

The Pressure Mounts

I wasn't alone in trying to hustle votes. The hallways were filled with opponents of the measure that we were about to bring on the floor. Most of these lobbyists were ministers and other folks who were not strangers to the building. They could be counted on to make their presence felt anytime we considered a controversial issue that centered on such things as expansion of women's rights (ERA), the recodification of the Vermont constitution to include the pronoun "she" wherever appropriate, parental notification of a minor's seeking an abortion, immunization of children prior to entering school (yes, they opposed that, too), home schooling, charter schools, and of course, abortion. I avoided them as best I could because I couldn't rely on controlling my temper with what I considered their profound ignorance. They stepped around me, too, and probably felt much the same. Thus, I was taken aback when Brooksie popped into the Speaker's office and informed me, "I think you're about to have a visitor."

"Who's out there?" I asked, peeking out into the reception room and seeing no one.

"He's not out there, yet, but he's downstairs and he's got quite a crowd following him. It's your bishop, Bishop Marshall. He's on his way up here to speak with you."

Sean Campbell, seeing the humor that I missed in this, interjected, "It's confession time, Mr. Speaker."

I jumped up, leaned through the door, and informed my secretary, Barb, that I was "in conference" and would see no one. I then did what I seldom did during ten years as Speaker: I closed my office door.

I was raised in a very Irish-Catholic neighborhood in the blue-collar suburb of Somerville, Massachusetts, and I often joked that I had never really met a Protestant, or for that matter, a Republican, until I moved to Vermont. There are some traits that, as one matures and grows older, they are able to make more nuanced, to realign with their philosophic growth. But no matter how much they grow and change, they will live and die with certain fundamentals—long ago ingrained in their childhood character—never completely disappearing. I was born Irish, Catholic, Democratic, and a Celtics fan, and that is more than likely how I'll go out. Besides, I was already pretty touchy about the willingness of my Church to let me know that I was being pretty careless with God's commands.

Just the week before at Sunday Mass in North Bennington, where I was a weekly lector and substitute altar boy, I had been confronted by a gauntlet of my fellow parishioners who, while attempting to hand me a rose, shouted their objections to expanding rights to the "sinners." I managed to push through without reacting, but once inside, I notified Father Demasi that if I had to go through this another week he would have to find another lector. Father, being the good man that he is, apologized for the harassment and saw to it that they took their protest elsewhere. My hour each week at my place of worship may have been made safe, but now they were at my place of work.

The bishop appeared and asked if I was available, and Barb informed him that I was tied up and would be awhile (only a venial sin). Bishops aren't accustomed to waiting for sinners; thus he decided to move to his next scheduled event, a mass meeting on the State House steps. I didn't see any of this, but the press reported that the crowd, which had been bused in from the four corners of the state, numbered over a thousand. Some were from my parish back in Bennington, and amid prayers for the souls of sinners could be heard the distant chant, *"Wright is wrong; Wright is wrong; Wright is wrong."* They actually had big campaign buttons depicting this. I still have one.

Twisting Arms

My goal was to get our count into the low seventies, which we needed for any measure of security. The last five or six took all the persuasion and political know-how I possessed.

There were very few members I hadn't bailed out of a tough situation as Speaker. It might have been a choice committee assignment, help moving a bill from a reluctant committee, help in their district, or care and comfort in personal trauma or tragedy.

On occasion this lending of aid and comfort even called for making a short-term loan from the "bank." The bank was a plain white envelope that I kept in the bottom drawer of my desk. It always had a couple of hundred dollars in small bills in it (my personal funds). Members in the habit of running short during the week soon learned that they could procure a short-term interest-free loan in the Speaker's office—no forms, no questions.

A Speaker's day is filled with occasions to use his or her power to be helpful to the members, and a large majority of the delegation never failed to apply when they thought the power and persuasiveness of the office could serve their purpose. I had made it a rule not to let even the most mundane of demands for help go unanswered. As long as it wasn't against the law, didn't require that I go to confession, or wouldn't break up my marriage, I did it. It took a steely-nerved member with a short memory to deny me a request for reciprocal help. This, coupled with the fact that I made it a point to ration the times I would make such a request (that duty normally fell to the leaders), made my pressure all the more effective now.

As I got closer to the magic number, the list of those I felt might be able to turn around grew smaller. Time was growing short and my frustration was building.

"Bob, can I talk to ya for a minute?" I said, as we bumped into each other just outside the Speaker's office.

"Sure, Mr. Speaker," came the less-than-enthusiastic reply. Bobby sensed he was about to be buttonholed.

Now Bobby was one of those "what the hell" voters who never missed an opportunity to ask me to do him this favor or that, and there weren't many members who had plied the trade of enlisting the Speaker's assistance more than he. He was always aware of his district's wants and often brought home not just the bacon but the whole pig. First on any junket list, he could be counted on to get his share and more of the available perks. He also, through asides, had earned something of a reputation as a homophobe.

"C'mon in the office a minute," I said. He followed like a kid headed for Mother Superior's shed.

"Now, Bobby, you know I've been working my ass off trying to get enough votes to pass this gay rights bill and I need your help. I wouldn't ask you, but it's going to be an extremely tight vote. What do you say— can I count on you?"

"Geez, Mr. Speaker, I just can't give you a hand on this one," he said. "My district is dead set against me voting for something like this." He was nervous.

"Oh, for Chrissakes, Bobby, you know as well as I that by the time next election comes around no one's going to remember this vote."

"They'll remember this one, Mr. Speaker. I've been getting a lot of mail and calls. This is a tough one." He said it with the confidence of a man winning an argument.

"C'mon, Bobby, I really need you on this one," I pleaded.

"Mr. Speaker, you've been real good to me, and you know I'd do anything to help you out if I could, but you know it isn't just the folks back home. Frankly, the bill just isn't right."

That was the killer. Nobody had ever remembered Bobby caring a whit about what was right and what was wrong, but he spoke now with the conviction of a used car salesman closing the deal for a lemon with sawdust in the transmission. He repeated this plea.

"It's just not right." Now at his best, his was the voice of an innocent choirboy.

Suddenly my mind flashed back to a rather famous "Tip" O'Neill tale, and I ended the conversation by lashing out at him, paraphrasing the legendary former U.S. House Speaker from Massachusetts:

"Bobby, you asshole, I don't need you when I'm right. I need you now."

I was up to sixty-six.

The Debate Begins

I worked the building right up to the time that we had to go out on the floor, and my efforts paid off in that I felt that if every vote held, we'd win it. Perhaps more vital to our hopes of success was that I had talked six Democrats and five of my Republican hockey team into taking a walk. I breathed a sigh of relief because all would have surely voted against the bill if they were on the floor. Still, I felt the vote was going to be extremely close. There was little margin for error.

The galleries were once again filled with the gnarled-knuckled, breathing their air of hate, and I could feel the wetness wilt my freshly starched shirt. But this time there would be no turning back.

The debate was as contentious as any I had ever heard, and I felt no sense of comfort over the entire two or three hour period. My practice of allowing the members to carry on to their hearts' content probably extended the arguments.[2] Opponent after opponent rose to their feet, repeating over and over their reasons for denying a segment of Americans their rights, their rage often bursting through in their words. A sample of what we listened to for the better part of three hours, these are the exact words of the member from Danville, Mr. Smith (yes, one of my old Republican friends of Smith, Smith, and Smith fame). Insisting that his words be journalized for posterity, he rose on the floor and spoke the following:

Mr. Speaker:

I will vote "no" because I cannot support a bill that contributes to the moral degradation of Vermonters. Chapter II, Section 68 of the Vermont Constitution reads: "The encouragement of virtue and the prevention of vice and immorality ought to be constantly kept in force and duly exercised."

This is a bill attempting to make respectable the lifestyle and degrading and disgusting sexual practices of this special group of people, the same group which introduced AIDS to this country.[3]

The Representative from Essex, Jane Mendicino, who would be my Republican opponent for Speaker in 1993, spoke the following words:

Mr. Speaker:

The people of Vermont refused an amendment that would have given women equal rights under our Constitution. The people felt that rights are granted already and if rights are violated, then as a citizen of this country there is the judicial branch of government to correct the injustice. If we keep *screwing around* [italics mine] with our rights, we will end up with no rights at all. And I love our country and its people too much to let this happen.[4]

Ron Squires rose and spoke these words:

Mr. Speaker:

This bill is not about behavior and conduct, or about sex. It's not about special privileges or rights for one class of people. It's about giving gay men and lesbians the same rights and privileges that the rest of you enjoy. I can't begin to tell you how I've felt as the rest of this body has debated whether or not I have the same rights and privileges as the other 149 members in this body, or the 30 members across the hall. . . .

During March we reported on a sadistic cannibal in Milwaukee, on war, famine, Mafia murders and the heartfelt wish of some gay couple to have their commitment to one another sanctioned and sanctified in religious ceremony. Which topic do you think inflamed the reading public? I don't have to answer. You know.

Mr. Speaker, this debate has been about hate and bigotry and fear and ignorance and I urge you, my colleagues to support S-131 so that we can move beyond that. Thank you, Mr. Speaker.[5]

The eloquence of Francis Brooks, Democratic leader, one of only two black members in the House at the time, I paraphrase from memory, as he spoke that day of the specter of fear, "fear of being judged by others, not for who you were, but for your superficial characteristics. This fear of being judged was a lonely road few had traveled." The quiet that overtook the House said it all. It was apparent that the members were moved by Brooksie's passionate plea. Applause broke out as he sat back down in his seat. I delayed, before gaveling the members back to order.[6]

And Then Rose That Damned Murphy

I was feeling upbeat for the first time, but no sooner had Francis finished than my darkest nightmare came true. Out of the corner of my eye, I saw Murphy jump to his feet and heard the dreaded beckoning, "Mr. Speaker." God damn you Murphy. You promised me that you were not going to speak on this. I don't think I had ever been as upset or felt such an awareness of betrayal as I now felt toward John Murphy. He was going to bring the bill and us down, all by himself.

Those fighting to pass the bill groaned in apprehension as they braced for the anticipated "gay bashing" from Murphy. I stood at the podium and for a moment considered ignoring his request to be recognized. This was out of the question, of course, and I did the only thing left in my repertoire. I stared at him with a long look of anger that he caught and reflected on, all in the same moment. Though we had no concrete agreement that he would stay out of the fight, he was well aware of all the efforts I had made.

A group gathers to witness Governor Howard Dean sign the gay rights bill into law in 1992. Seated left to right are Rep. Vi Luginbuhl (R-Burlington), Sen. David Wolk (D-Rutland), Governor Dean, and me. Rep. Sally Fox (D-Essex), chair of the Judiciary Committee, stands third from the left. Rep. Ron Squires (D-Guilford) stands directly in front of the American flag. The highlight of my career is the effort we made to expand human rights to another segment of the American population.

Murphy had been quiet for over two hours, and I was convinced he was going to pay me the courtesy of letting me win or lose on my own. As close as I knew the vote was, I was certain this was a debate where crucial votes could be swayed by arguments from the floor. This didn't happen often, as members usually make up their minds before debate, but there were rare examples of its occurring in the past, and this was one.

"When Murphy jumped up, I said to myself, 'Oh, no, we're dead,'" Brooksie reflected afterward. As for my thoughts on Murphy, I would have strangled him if I could have reached the little sucker.

"Mr. Speaker," again the request from seat 150.

"Yes, member from Ludlow."

"May I say a few words?" What could I do? I had to recognize him.

"Yes, member from Ludlow. You may"—anger and disappointment in my voice.

"Mr. Speaker," he began, "I've always been a person of courage and conviction. As I listen today, I have searched my soul and found that I've been wrong. Very seldom have I come to that conclusion [roar of laughter from all but the podium]. In the past, I have done everything I could to kill the gay rights bills. In the past, I've been on the wrong side. Mr. Speaker, I've changed my mind. Today I hope to do what is right. I'm going to support this bill. I can assure my colleagues this bill isn't any different than those that I helped to kill in the past. It's me, Murphy, who's different." With that, he plopped back down in his seat.

The entire House sat in stunned silence. And then like a summer cloudburst came a thunder of applause unlike any I had ever experienced in the House. I stood at the podium thinking, "What a wonderful world this is."

And I swore that if I ever got to Ireland, I would fall to my hands and knees and kiss the sod that had grown Johnny Murphy.

We won that day, 71–58, and the bill became law five weeks later. It stands as one of my proudest memories.

Later the press tried to find Murphy's reason for his change of heart. They were half-convinced that he had made a deal with me. Murphy had made a deal—that's a fact. But it was with someone a helluva lot more powerful than the Speaker.

And this one's for you, Ron Squires.[7]

Notes

1. Buttonholing, in legislative parlance, refers to the Speaker's making it known to members that he or she has a commitment to a particular bill. On other occasions, it could mean that the Speaker is seeking out individual members, and with eye-to-eye contact, asking them to help on a particular item. Few members would ignore this type of in-your-face request from their Speaker.

2. Not all Speakers allow unlimited debate. House rules state clearly that for a member to speak a third time on any one issue he or she must ask permission of the House. I always allowed the member to continue on with a simple, "Hearing no objection, the Chair rules 'permission granted'." (There were times when I

would groan quietly with the members over the ruling.) A move by a member to cut off debate would necessitate a vote by the entire body. These seldom passed as they were looked upon as the ultimate insult to even the most obnoxious, long-winded orator.

3. *Journal of the House of the State of Vermont,* Adjourned Session, 1992, 565.

4. Ibid.

5. Ibid., 566–567.

6. Applause, or any outward display of emotion, is strictly forbidden under House rules.

7. Ron Squires passed away eight months later, in January 1993, of AIDS.

9

Working with the Executive Branch, Part 1
Madeleine Kunin, Democrat, 1985–1991

IT WAS A historic year, 1985. Not only did the Vermont House have a Democratic Speaker, but also Vermont voters had elected a Democratic governor, the first since 1972 and only the third since before the Civil War. More important, the governor was a woman—the first ever.

Madeleine Kunin rode into office a nose ahead of the bachelor Republican candidate John Easton. She won by less than 3,700 votes and only managed that thin margin by labeling an "Easton government" as merely a "caretaker government." She painted a picture of status quo if Easton succeeded Richard Snelling, and it worked—if only just barely.

Madeleine Kunin and her big brother, Edgar May, have to be the epitome of what America is all about, truly an American success story.

Madeleine May, aged six, sailed past the Statue of Liberty in 1939, barely escaping the jackboots of evil then overtaking all of Europe. She earned her BA degree from the University of Massachusetts in 1956 and an MS from Columbia in 1957, and after settling in Vermont took another master's degree from the University of Vermont in 1967. Married to Dr. Arthur Kunin, she entered politics as a state representative from Burlington in 1973. Kunin rose to become lieutenant governor in 1978 and served four years under Republican governor Dick Snelling. Now she found herself the first female governor in Vermont history. What a great country!

We were both liberal Democrats, and we would serve together for the next six years. It was to be a very productive six years. Taking advantage

174

of our control of both the legislative and executive branches of government, we managed to push through a multitude of new laws that sent a clear signal to all who would listen that Democrats had the power and were not afraid to use it.

If the people of Vermont wanted a governor who would push to protect Vermont's environment, overhaul how we funded education, or simply deal with the ordinary person's concerns, then Madeleine Kunin was their woman. I was more than happy to help her in her cause.

My relationship with Madeleine, as with all of the three governors I worked with, was based on

Governor Madeleine Kunin acknowledges a standing ovation from an overflowing audience at her inauguration in 1985. I remember whispering to her, "Carry this with you for a lifetime, Madeleine."

respect, if not always for the person most certainly for the office. The relationship was touchy. I felt I had a clear sense of the Founding Fathers' intent regarding the separation of powers among the three branches of government, and I paid careful attention to any endeavor on a governor's part to weaken or abridge the legislature's prerogative to make the law. It was the executive branch's duty to carry out the law. The governor could suggest, lobby, persuade, and cajole, but it couldn't demand, or so I believed. The legislatures in larger states (or Congress) can more easily compete with the power of a full-time executive and staff most of the time. But in Vermont, our part-time legislature, with no staff, forced us to be ever-vigilant to prevent one branch from dominating the other. Thus in spite of our close politics and philosophies, Madeleine Kunin and I were to have our tussles.

The Property Tax Rebate Issue

It didn't take long for the governor and me to cross swords, and it was over an issue about which we both felt strongly: The flagship of my agenda—actually the only boat in my fleet—was property tax relief.

I had made it very public that I intended early in the session to increase the funds available to our property tax rebate program. Under this program the state rebated a portion of the property taxes levied by cities and towns to the taxpayer, based on income. The program not only was extremely effective in providing relief to the hard-pressed home owner and renter, but because it did its job so well, it was by far the most popular relief program that state government offered. Originally put forth by former governor Tom Salmon in the early 1970s, it was credited for the come-from-behind win that catapulted him into that office. Both sides of the aisle now laid claim to its ownership, and thus my proposing an enormous increase in its funding did not come with a whole lot of political risk.

Like every governor, Kunin saw her role as one of protector of the purse. And like every governor she spent a lot of her waking moments worrying about balancing revenues. This never prevented governors from spending every available nickel, and some unavailable ones, but the spending was only justified if it was on their programs.

If a projection said that we could expect a 6 percent increase in revenue in the next fiscal year from the thirty-three tax sources available, then that simply meant to a governor that they could fund all their favorite programs by an additional 6 percent. When you read about the constant congressional squabbles, whether between the parties or between Congress and the president, the fight is over who gets the bag of money, not whether it's going to get spent.

If there were unlimited money—no deficit, or a money-making machine that could pump out coin without any need to raise taxes to give it value—then you would find the old art of compromise clicking in, and each side would find a way to satisfy the other. But we were just coming off the deficit years under Snelling, and there was no oversupply of cash that would allow all sides to spend at will.

It was for this reason that the governor set out to kill my suggestion in a behind-the-scenes assault. If it meant she had to work closely with the Republicans, then so be it; that's what she set out to do.

I had real problems with this thinking, as I looked upon the Grand Old Party as the enemy. Besides, it flew in the face of all I believed. It was a political form of treason for her to simply analyze the situation and decide I was wrong and that she now had license to leave me on the issue and consort with the enemy. Hey! What ever happened to "dancing with the guy who brung ya"? So this was how it was going to be: "If I agree with you, we'll work together and be best buddies. If I don't, we'll work with the Republicans." I took her on.

Dealing with the Power of a Committee Chair

The governor and I had very different backgrounds. Loyalty was embedded in my very fiber. I had been raised in a tough, blue-collar community where you were classified by parish and gang. My hitch in the Marine Corps only hardened my idea of solidarity with those whom you worked and played. To me "loyalty," from my earliest years, had become another word for "love." I couldn't separate the two.

The governor, raised in a more refined and cultured environment, didn't see it quite that way. She set her goals and set about aligning herself with whoever could help her attain them. On the property tax rebate she enlisted, quietly, the efforts of the Appropriations Committee's Republican chair, John Hise (Bristol). To me this amounted to political adultery.

John was a respected member of the Assembly, and his committee members, whether Democrat or Republican, liked him to the point of reverence, as he truly worked for popular consensus and almost never went behind his committee's back to play political games. I say "almost never" because in this instance, that's exactly what he did.

I had a seven-to-four Democratic majority in the committee, and it was clear to them all that my goal to put a couple of million extra into the rebate program was a goal shared by the Democratic caucus. But their love for their chairman kept them from serving notice on him that they were eventually going to use their strength in numbers to push the bill out over his head. Meanwhile they sided with him and went along with his refusal even to bring it up for a vote.

I didn't know what to do. Every time I inquired about how my rebate bill was coming in committee, my buddies would simply shuffle their feet and dust as fast as they could. I tried everything to wedge the bill out, but to no avail. John was telling the press he wasn't the culprit, as he made a habit of never interfering with the will of the majority in the committee. He argued, "We simply haven't found the time to deal with it." What was there to deal with? Simply allocate two million into the fund.

This bit of chicanery went on for several weeks, and I felt the time had come to confront John. I didn't look forward to having this conversation with a man everybody considered equal to their lovable ol' grandpa, but it was something I had to do if I was ever going to get my bill out.

"John," I started the conversation in my office, "I think you're well aware I want the rebate bill taken up and voted on in your committee. I've got the votes and you know that. Up to this point you've relied on your members' love for you to keep it from even coming up. I also want you to know I think what you've been doing is shitty. You're out telling the world that I'm a bad guy and I'm threatening to commit some sort of ethical violation by usurping the committee process and forcing the bill out. My Democrats believe I'm the bully here, and though I haven't said anything to them about your little cabal with the governor, they think I'm a wretch for doing this to their beloved chairman. What they don't know, but I know as sure as I'm sitting here, is you're playing politics with the governor and intentionally killing my bill. You have the best of both worlds; you get to undermine the Democratic caucus's priority while endearing yourself to the governor—a pretty shrewd and behind-the-back move, John. And while everyone in the building believes I would be doing something as sleazy as that, no one believes you're doing the very same thing. I guess I could understand and even tolerate the sleaze ingredient here, but I'm finding it impossible to climb over your unfairness in not telling your committee the truth. You're not going to get away with it. Nor is your new very best friend, the governor."

He sat silent, his eyes unblinking.

OK, I thought, let's push this a little further.

"Do you deny, John, that you're simply trying to kill my bill and that you're misleading people who think that you're above all this?" He moved in his chair, displaying discomfort at the confrontation.

"No," he replied. "I am trying to kill your bill, and I have a very good reason. I don't think the state can afford it."

"We'll let the members decide that," I said.

I then called each of my Democrats into my office and read the riot act to them, emphasizing how they got where they were and my disappointment in their willingness to forsake our commitment to Vermont's public schools, which depended on the state's rebate program to lighten the pressure on ever-increasing local taxes on individual property owners. It worked.

The rebate bill passed out of the committee without testimony, and several of the members broke down in tears at doing in "Grandpa" Hise. It was testimony to the depth of the affection members can have for their chairman and to how far an honest man will go to win a political battle.

I didn't ever mention to the governor what I thought about her willingness to throw me over the bridge if I didn't serve her cause, but I let Liz Bankowski, Kunin's closest aide, know that if she ever did it again I'd file for divorce.

She never did.

We worked well together, at least 99 percent of the time. Kunin was bright and committed to doing the very best she knew how, but I felt she never quite got over being the first woman in what had been a man's world. Politics did not come easily to her, and it took her the longest time to come to grips with the wheeling and dealing that are part of everyday life in the State House. I never thought she had this difficulty in coping with the underbelly of political give-and-take because she was a woman, as females of the world can more than hold their own with the roughest of rogues. I simply thought it was a matter of unwillingness to engage herself in the mundane, day-to-day infighting that was normal in the world of politics. She didn't enjoy it and gave the impression that she was above it all.

This was not true of Elizabeth Bankowski.

Bankowski was from Dorchester, Massachusetts, a tough, blue-collar neighborhood in Boston. A former assistant to Father Drinan, the Jesuit congressman from Boston, she knew her way around and could make comfortable talk with prince and pauper alike. She was Kunin's best friend as well as her most savvy and trusted aide. Every president and governor has a Liz Bankowski.

Just Say You're Sorry

Sometime during Kunin's first term (she served three, two-year terms) we were in an immense struggle to pass one of the half-dozen environmental bills that made it into law that first year. We had gone over our roll call lists a dozen times but still couldn't find the one vote we needed to bring about passage. Out of desperation we combed the list one last time for that reluctant soul whose mind might be changed. This time we went into great detail, having somebody in the group of leaders surrounding my desk explain why each "no" wouldn't join us. We heard all the sound reasons until we got to Frank DaPrato, a conservative Democrat from Swanton, up in Franklin County.

"Why isn't DaPrato coming around for us, Brooksie?" I asked Francis Brooks, the Democratic whip.

"He's mad at the governor," Brooksie said matter-of-factly.

"What the hell ya mean he's mad at the governor? Everybody's mad at the governor; it's the end of the session. What kind of cockamamie reason is that?"

"I don't know. He just says he's mad at her and isn't going to vote for the bill. He didn't lead me to believe it's anything philosophic."

"There's more crazy people in this building than in *One Flew Over the Cuckoo's Nest*," I said, and I bolted out the door to find DaPrato.

I tracked him down in the cafeteria.

"Frank, I gotta talk to you about a problem I understand you're having with the governor. What is it?"

"I don't have no problem. She does," he answered. "She can go to hell, and if you're here, Mr. Speaker, to get me to change my mind, just forget about it. I ain't going to do it."

"Now wait a minute, Frank," I pleaded. "Tell me. What's the problem?"

Frank took five minutes, nonstop. The governor seemingly had snubbed him several months earlier at a potluck supper in his district, and he had not forgotten it. Of course, Kunin had no idea of the affront, and she had gone on about life in the State House without ever being aware that DaPrato was angry at her or that the anger had grown to giant proportions.

"I won't forget it. What goes around comes around. Let her cook; I don't want her damned four-number license plates," he spouted out, getting angrier all the time. I was only sitting and listening, letting him unload, when "four-number license plates" crashed inside my head.

"What about the license plate?" I asked nonchalantly.

"She can stick that, too. I'm never gonna ask her for another thing."

I broke away, saying I'd be back to him, and headed for Bankowski's cubbyhole just off the governor's office.

"Liz, can I see you a minute?" She immediately got up and we huddled in the corner. "Look, Liz, I think I can get the vote we need, but it's gonna take a conversation with one of the members and the governor. She's gonna have to apologize to Frank DaPrato," I said hurriedly.

"Apologize for what?" Bankowski was willing, but wondering.

"Well, I'm not exactly sure what she did to him—didn't recognize him to the crowd at some dinner in his district—but just have her apologize, ya know, sort of generically." Listening to my own conversation, I was beginning to realize how stupid this all was sounding.

"Where is he? Can we get him to see her?"

"I'll get him, but you gotta brief the governor. Oh, by the way, can you see to it he gets a four-number license plate? Apparently somebody's giving him a hard time over it." I was genuinely confused as to why DaPrato hadn't been able to get his own plate. They were available to even the most naive of freshmen, and no special OK from the governor's office was necessary. Hell, Corcoran had most of Bennington riding around with four-number plates. You would have thought, driving into

Bennington's municipal parking lot, that you were in the United Nations garage.

Liz mulled over what I had described as the problem. She thought she knew the solution.

"Mr. Speaker, you sure that's what he wants—the plates and an apology? How am I going to tell a governor she has to apologize for some unknown infraction to a rep from up on the Canadian border? We'll do it. I'll find a way. I'm sure she'll do it because we've got to have this bill. But let's try the low-number plate first, and then, if that doesn't work, we'll get them together and she can apologize for whatever."

It worked. He got his plates and an audience with the governor. Though she didn't have to apologize, she was forced to schmooze with someone she obviously didn't have a helluva lot in common with. And we got our bill, by a margin of victory that totaled one.

The legislature is an interesting place.

Madeleine Kunin did not look at politics as a science but rather as an opportunity to express her vision as to the purpose of government. She achieved a good deal during her six years in office. She signed over a dozen environmental bills into law; mandated that all Vermont children be provided the opportunity to attend kindergarten; raised the minimum wage (though this couldn't have been done without Murphy); nearly doubled the property tax rebate program's funding (as mentioned, somewhat reluctantly); increased state aid to education; established alcoholism as an illness; and made auto insurance mandatory. Last, but not least, she brought an army of talented women into state government.

Separation of Powers

I worked with three governors during my ten years as Speaker, each very different. Madeleine Kunin was probably the most difficult to get close to. Perhaps it was because we were both new to our jobs and neither of us understood our roles in government. We spent the better part of the six years believing in the same things but never seeming able to reach a harmony in our efforts. Looking back, I have concluded that the real kink in our inability to feel comfortable with each other had to do, not just with our very different backgrounds, but with our respective roles in government. I, firmly believing in the separation of powers, resented her intrusion on the inner workings of the legislature, particularly the House. To me, the governor proposed and the legislature disposed. Both of us may have exaggerated where our authority began and ended, but because I looked at my House as family, I took great exception to her meddling in its day-to-day operations or, worse still, working behind the scenes with the opposition.

Both Speakers O'Connor, and Morse had looked to the executive to set the agenda. O'Connor, as I mentioned earlier, never seemed to have an agenda of his own. And Morse's agenda was dictated by the close and dominant personality of Governor Snelling. I felt somewhat different in that I was certain that it was within the legislature's dominion to have an agenda and to push it. After all, it was clear that the legislature made the laws; the executive carried them out.

I wasn't so naive that I wasn't aware that tradition had fully established a governor's prerogative to suggest, through the annual State of the State address, the issues that he or she hoped to see action on. But that address was delivered to a joint meeting of the legislature. It was a request, not a demand. The request was important, but so was the response. The response to me meant that on those issues where our agendas coincided, we could work together; the issues she never mentioned, or on which she differed with what we hoped to legislate in the following two years, weren't necessarily to be conceded or thrown away. As we never talked about this discrepancy in our understandings of authority, we seemed always to be at odds with one another.

It wasn't an outward dislike or display of antagonism but more a failure to make a personal connection. It's probably the normal relationship between an executive and a Speaker, as I was to experience the same with Howard Dean when he became governor. But what seems baffling today, as I write this, is that this disconnect didn't occur with Dick Snelling—a Republican. He would be the only governor that I trusted, shared confidences with, and worked in total harmony with. What's the answer to this puzzle? I'm not sure. But I will say that though I had respect for the office that both Kunin and Dean held, and I never disliked them, that was different than what I felt about Dick Snelling. I not only respected his office, but I respected him, and I believe he felt the same about the office of the Speaker and me. Perhaps more important, I loved the man immensely as a human being.

So Governor Kunin and I spent the first year or two quietly sparring. In the first year we had battled privately over the rebate issue, but we managed to find some semblance of resolve without going public. That was not the case with the Interstate Banking bill.

When Politics Gets Too Personal, Everyone Loses

The Interstate Banking bill was a measure to allow larger banks in other states (Massachusetts and New York, primarily) to move into the state, permitting consolidation—or monopolization—of the banking industry through their purchase of the much smaller—and may I say, more personal—Vermont banks. It was the classic, Darwinian "big things eat little things" situation. I had paid the bill little heed as it came over from the Senate. I probably never would have given it a second thought, but it turned out to be a bill that was in the wrong place at the wrong time.

This was 1986, the second year of my speakership. We were performing the annual, end-of-session ritual, and the normal hostage taking of bills was going on between the House and Senate. It didn't appear to be out of proportion to anything that had happened in the past, and so I felt a measure of confidence in threatening the Senate that we wouldn't move their priorities unless they agreed to move those of the House. In particular we were concerned with an environmental bill that attempted to protect the fast-disappearing open land that symbolized most everyone's idea of what was right about Vermont. Referred to as the Current Use bill, its essence was to encourage farmers and others who owned large tracts of farm and forest to keep them from development by lowering their property tax rate. We thought it was a pretty important bill and had worked hard to push it through the House. It met the crossover deadline and had passed by a huge margin, but it had simply been ignored by the Senate.

The Senate was now making excuses that they didn't have the time this late in the session to deal with the bill properly, and they were refusing to suspend the rules to expedite the matter. The fact was that they had had ample time but had simply tried to kill the measure by not dealing with it. The whole rebuttal to our efforts was led by the presiding officer of the Senate, Lt. Gov. Peter Smith. He was from an old Vermont family that had been in the banking business in Vermont for generations. He was aided and abetted by his Republican minority in the Senate. By refusing to suspend the rules, Smith had managed to hang the bill up on the last day of the session.

I looked at the Senate's actions as a matter of arrogance. I was convinced that Senate members had to have a certain amount of uneasiness with their limp excuse and that they were simply being unfair. This was my first real confrontation with the other body, and I had no intention of letting them get away with it. But they were in a position of strength, since to suspend the rules required a three-fourths majority, and they had the votes to block it. To me, it was a case of tyranny by the minority. In retaliation I threatened to hold up a bill of importance to them.

The press later reported that I had targeted the Senate bill I set out to hold hostage, but it just wasn't true. That was simply a case of the media's having to have a motive behind every story. It was nothing more than coincidence that the next bill moving through the House happened to be the Interstate Banking bill. I promptly took the bill itself out of the "pending box" and stuck it in my pocket. And that's exactly where I intended it to rest until they unlocked the cage that held the Current Use bill.

Unknowingly, I had pocketed the flagship of the entire Republican agenda for that session. It was on the Republican agenda, but it seemed to be everybody's darling. Governor Kunin liked it, seeing it as a token for the business community as partial repayment for the ton of liberal legislation we had passed in our first biennium. There were also more than a few Democratic senators and House members who were in love with it, if only for personal reasons. Many, including some of my very liberal friends, held bank stock that promised to rise, even skyrocket, if certain smaller Vermont banks were given the right to merge or be bought out by the giant banks in Boston. Finally, there was the whole contingent of bank lobbyists and executives who, in anticipation of the surefire passage of this relatively unnoticed measure, watched gleefully as their bank stock rose ever-so-consistently with each stage of the bill's progress through the legislature.

The gleeful atmosphere rapidly faded when I slipped the Interstate Banking bill into my pocket and went off down the back stairs to dinner with Leigh Tofferi, D-Ludlow, one of my close friends, who represented the same two-member district as Murphy.

It probably didn't help that when a reporter told me that the Senate would not cave in to what they considered my act of arrogance, I responded with my best Clint Eastwood imitation: "Make my day."

I had gone too far, pushed the system beyond its boundaries of procedure and protocol into the personal. Here it would morph from civility and compromise to anger and retaliation. But I also felt strongly that the Senate had crossed that same line, into an area unfair to those of us in the House who had worked our tails off to pass a bill that we felt was vital to braking overdevelopment of our rapidly disappearing open land.

Those were my philosophic justifications for hanging tough on the banking bill. But there were also important political reasons why I would not back down: I was very much aware that to turn back on my threat would have signaled that what I said was different than what I intended to do—that I would not fight for what I believed in. It would be like handing your lunch money over to the school yard bully. This type of wavering can end careers in a hurry. But so could what I had just done.

I talked to dozens of people that night. "Don't do this Ralph. It's not worth it," one pleaded.

"It'll be the end of you as sure as I'm sitting here, Mr. Speaker, an end to your speakership." I listened politely, with a sense that what my friend Sen. Harvey Carter, D-Bennington County, was saying was probably true.

Others showed up at my office door angry as hell. They arrived at the same conclusion that my friend had, except they expressed it in a louder tone. As for the governor, I refused to even see her, as there was little I could do, or at least was willing to do, that would make her happy.

As the hours wore on that final Saturday night of adjournment, the pleas from my colleagues seemed unending, and at one point I did waver.

After receiving the banking bill from the Senate, back in March, I had sent it to the House Commerce Committee. When it came time to appoint a conference committee to iron out the differences between the Senate and the House versions I had opted to break my rule of loading the committee with a Democratic majority—I appointed two Republicans and one Democrat. At the time I appointed the conferees the bill was still a rather obscure and unimportant item in the array of bills to be dealt with.

As the stalemate grew more serious during the evening, it came to a head when the chair of the House conferees, a Republican from Proctor, came into my office and announced, "Mr. Speaker, we're going back down into the meeting on the banking bill, and I just wanted you to know that we've reached agreement with the Senate to move the bill."

"Who's reached agreement?" I looked up, glaring at Art Sanborn.

"Myself and Chase" (of White River Junction, the other Republican I had carelessly appointed to the three-member committee of conference), he answered. "This has gone on long enough."

"Well, you can't do that," I said, emphasizing the "you."

"What do you mean we can't? We've talked it over, and we think this is the best we can get out of the Senate. As chair of the conference committee that's what we think is best." He was talking now like this was final.

"You can't do that, Sanborn, because you aren't the chair of the committee. In fact, you're not even on the committee any longer."

"Mr. Speaker, with all due deference, I don't think you can do that"—anger tinting his voice.

"Not only can I do it, it's done." I turned to Tim Van Zandt, from Springfield, one of my Democratic lieutenants. "Van Zandt, you're the new chairman of the Interstate Banking bill."

Sanborn stormed out of the office.

I turned to Van Zandt, handed him the banking bill, and gave him the simplest of instructions, "Get lost, Timmy. If they don't have the bill or the chairman of the conference committee [the originating house always designated the chairman of any conference committee] then they can't discuss it."

Van Zandt, delighted to be part of the whole affair, stuffed the bill in his pocket, snapped me a salute, and about-faced out of the office, down the backstairs, and into the night.

As the evening wore on with no sign of capitulation on the part of the Senate, I began, as I said, to have second thoughts. "OK, someone go find Van Zandt." We searched all over the building and then systematically made calls to all the places where he might be: his room at the motel, his friends, and every watering hole in town. No Tim.

Finally, in exasperation, I asked my secretary to get me his home phone number, even though I couldn't imagine him or anyone else leaving on the last night of the session. The phone rang a couple of times, and a man answered, "Hello."

"May I speak to Representative Van Zandt, please."

"Hey, Ralph, this is me, Timmy," he responded, extremely upbeat. I couldn't believe it. He was home, a hundred miles away, with the bill.

"Timmy, what the hell ya doing home? Where's the bill?"

"It's right here on the kitchen table. You told me to get lost. I always do what my Speaker tells me." And he broke out laughing.

Well, that was the end of any thought of caving in and bringing up the Interstate Banking bill, but it's not the end of the story. Four months later, I received a card postmarked York Beach, Maine, from my good friend Rep. Peter Allendorf, D-Underhill. It read as follows:

Dear Mr. Speaker,

As you can see, we are on our annual trek to the great beaches of Maine. We happen to be stopping at our favorite resort when who did we run into but none other than the member from Springfield, alias Tim Van Zandt. He sends his regards, and asked if you might relay, through me as his intermediary, just when he can come home.

Regards, L. T. Allendorf

P.S. I'll bet you a case of beer that you can't kill the Interstate Banking bill again next year.

We adjourned that Saturday night without the Interstate Banking bill or the Current Use bill. Ego and pride had guaranteed that everybody went home a loser. I hurried home and the next day was driving a big old yellow school bus with my program kids on a prearranged trip to Washington, D.C. Shortly after we got there, I called to tell Cathy we had arrived safely. My son Rick answered the phone, and as it happened to be 6 p.m. on the nose, the Channel 3 news was just coming on. The lead story was the precipitous fall of the stock of all the major banks in Vermont. A lot of people who had anticipated the passage of the Interstate Banking bill had taken a bath. Rick hung up the phone joking that I should check under the hood of the bus before starting it up in the morning. I didn't think he was funny.

And Madeleine Kunin didn't think I was very funny. The whole experience frustrated and angered her, as she had to accept the fact that even the power of the executive oftentimes falls victim to the whims of people who are beyond her control.

The Kunin Years—An Analysis

Madeleine served six years as governor and then, in 1990, stunned a whole lot of people with the announcement that she would not run for a fourth term. That she felt she had done all that she set out to do I doubt. I think she was just tired of the constant demands that being governor, even of a small state such as Vermont, encompasses. The long hours, constant pressures, and unceasing battles to accomplish her goals had taken their toll. She was tired. Her marriage was coming apart, and another campaign loomed like a dark cloud. Why not now? She could leave with her head high and the sense of a job well done.

History will record her as a pretty good governor who accomplished a lot and who smashed forever the glass ceiling between women and the governor's office.

My feelings were mixed. True, her years as governor had produced an amazing onslaught of legislation, much of which now serves as the foundation for Vermont's national reputation as a special place to work, live, and raise a family. Lots of folks in the rest of the nation have come to see Vermont as perhaps the one place in this big country that has held onto its bucolic past. It hasn't been easy, and Kunin can take great pride in having led the drive to preserve Vermont's environment, improve the public education system, protect and expand human rights, and open doors for women in government. But she didn't do it alone.

Much of success, in government or life, is being in the right place at the right time. Madeleine might be loath to admit it, but it was her good luck to take the oath of office in the same week in 1985 that a reemerging Democratic House did. The House had seventy-two Democrats, but the number was not the important fact. The kind of Democrats who took their seats in that biennium and those of the next ten years mattered more. They were liberal in their politics, and they came prepared to work and contribute. They had the courage of their convictions and the vision to want to make things better.

Madeleine had it all, except the ability to overcome her fear that the world would suddenly realize that she was a woman doing what had always been a man's job. She lived in fear of not being reelected, and it limited her ability to use her power to right the wrongs in how America fails to deliver health care for its sick and dying; fails to provide excellence in education for our children; and fails to bring on board all who still live each day with not quite the same rights as the rest of us.

In fairness, she introduced future leaders to these causes, as she pushed issues that buffed the edges. But I never felt she understood the leadership power that a governor commands or the good fortune of having a legislature that was willing to be led.

For six years we clashed silently, always behind closed doors, and when she left I felt little closer to her than when we had begun our journey. I take not a little blame for this disconnect, as our styles were different. Where I was usually willing to plunge ahead in a chase to achieve an end, with finances, at best, an afterthought, Kunin felt a responsibility to measure the cost in pursuit of balancing the budget. Where I spent little time trying to convince or compromise with my fellow Republicans, Madeleine was always much more willing to reach across the aisle. Where I looked upon the future as today, she saw it in terms of the next election. My style eventually led to my demise; hers to a slow erosion of her energy and desire to plug on.

The next governor was going to be much more my style.

10

Working with the Executive Branch, Part 2
Richard Snelling, Republican, 1991

RICHARD SNELLING, A Republican, was the governor I admired most. (The ripping noise you are about to hear is the sound of my Democratic Party membership card being torn in half.) I admired and respected the person he was and the politician he was. He was a good leader and a good man. I know you can hear all the horror stories you want from hundreds, perhaps thousands, of people willing to tell you about his bad temper or his arrogance, but there was a whole lot more to the man than that.

If my only experience with Governor Snelling had been the two years I served with him as Democratic leader in 1983–1984, I would have little more to tell. But as Speaker for my fourth term, I had an additional eight months' experience with him when he returned to the governor's office in 1991. Once again, it was a very difficult time in Vermont's financial history. We were in the throes of a deficit again, and this time it was even bigger than in 1983–1984. We were $91 million in the red, which represented nearly 15 percent of our entire general fund.

Working Together Again

Our fiscal house was in shambles. Snelling was going to get little or no help from his own party, and as usual, we Democrats were going to be asked to ride to the rescue.

There was a different twist here. The 1983–1984 deficit had belonged to the Republicans; this one was the sole responsibility of the Democrats. In our devil-may-care spending during the Kunin years, no matter how deserving the causes, we not only went through the surplus created in those prosperous years, but we spent money we didn't have. Consequently, our bond rating on Wall Street edged towards junk bond status, and we found ourselves once again in the politically devastating position of cutting programs and/or raising taxes. Snelling was the unfortunate inheritor of the mess.

There was never the slightest question whether we were going to cooperate. We would, and that was a forgone conclusion. The question that most concerned us was how the deficit was to be paid. What taxes was the incoming governor going to recommend be raised? Was there going to be a rush to make monstrous cuts? I was no tax or budget expert—far from it, as I was often frightened by how little I knew in these highly complex fiscal matters. The legislative ladder I climbed had most of the rungs missing: I had never even served on a money committee. What little knowledge I possessed had filtered through in the four-month period each year when the legislature was in session. After that it was back to my day job as a teacher. Once again I was reminded how handicapped we were as a legislature made up of part-timers without staff. The only safety net available to us was the dictum, "The governor proposes, and the legislature disposes."

Now we once again had to rely on the executive branch to put together the package that would bail out the state, from both the tax side and the expenditure side. This took a giant leap of faith. We were dependent on the precision and truthfulness of the governor's staff for what a tax would raise in revenues and how the money would be spent. Most important, we had to depend on their guarantee that any proposed taxing and spending would not make matters worse. Our only check on their numbers would be through the small effort that the Legislative Council's fiscal staff could provide our Joint Fiscal Committee, which was made up of three members from the House and three from the Senate who met periodically during the summer and fall. Let me assure you that this was no "think tank" we were using as our only tool.

The bottom line was that only the governor had an adequate level of expertise at his disposal. We simply had to put our trust in a single political force, Dick Snelling, and trust him not to play politics with it. He never let the people of the state down, nor me, and that was a measure of the man's greatness.

When the Common Good Overcomes Personal Politics

When we gathered to open the 1991 session, the governor must have had the same thoughts running through his mind as I had racing through mine, as he did an extraordinary thing. It was an act that was least expected, especially from him. It was an act of humility.

They say a picture is worth a thousand words—in this case it's true. "So, Mr. Speaker, you want a piece of me?" I can imagine Richard Snelling would gibe. Before Snelling's 1991 inauguration the press heralded that he and I would be gladiators duking out partisan battles over the next two years. Their hype couldn't have been further from the truth.

We had just finished the Speaker's election, and I had returned to my office to begin my fourth term as Speaker. I was going through the myriad chores I would have to complete to assign the members to their new committees and prepare for three or four days of ceremony that would take place in the well of the House prior to all the members' heading off to their worlds of making legislation. It was a time of idleness for all but me, but with an aura of excitement.

My office was filled with all my lieutenants, milling around, making phone calls, or simply basking in the afterglow of having won another two years in power. They were sitting around, their feet propped up on desks and coffee tables, shooting the bull. It was too early for them to wander into the bathroom where I had a fridge always well stocked with refreshments, but they didn't need any refreshments to boost their spirits. I looked up from my desk and out through the glass separation, and to my surprise I saw the governor sitting in the far waiting room, thumbing through one of the old magazines. Jesus, nobody ever sat out there waiting for an appointment with me. People just tapped on the open door and walked in.

He could have been a Fuller Brush man for all appearances.

"Nancy, is that the governor sitting out there." I called to Nancy Mason, my secretary.

"Yes," she answered. "I told him, Mr. Speaker, he could come right in and you would see him right away." With that she looked around with disgust. It was one of those looks our mothers gave us, telling us she loved us but perhaps not our friends. Nancy was a very efficient type who brooked no nonsense in her day-to-day chores. She more than frowned on what she considered the crass, good ol' boy ambiance that permeated the office at times like this. She especially took exception to Harris and Corcoran's seeming run of the office.

"But he said it was no problem," she continued, "he'd wait until you had finished with your guests." She peered over once again, with an even more disdainful look at Harris and Corcoran.

"Geez, Nanc, we can't have the governor sitting out there. Let me get rid of these guys and then ask him to come right in." I turned, and in my best I'm-not-fooling-around voice said, "OK, you guys, let's go. Out."

You would have thought I had just cut them out of my will. I got more than one look of indignation, and feeling a little sheepish at my air of disloyalty, tried to explain I had the governor waiting to see me. They got up slowly and began to shuffle out, grumbling under their collective breaths, "Hmmmph! Big deal!"

Well, it was a big deal. No governor yet had gone to this extreme, to visit with me in this manner, while I had been Speaker. Sure, I had had visits in the past, but they were always announced, and I always made sure I was standing at the ready when the governor and entourage entered in a fashion that was missing nothing but the Marine Corps Band playing "Hail to the Chief." This time the governor looked like a forlorn figure, sitting patiently, all alone, in the vacant outer entryway. He hardly looked like a head of state.

I rushed out, embarrassed, and invited him in, making sure to pull together two chairs in front of my desk. Even that seemed inadequate in my effort to accord him what I felt was his proper stature. I sat across from this larger-than-life figure, nervously trying to remain in whatever conversation he had in mind. It wasn't easy, as Dick Snelling loomed over all in his presence, a personality who turned every head when he entered a room. After taking a moment to offer his congratulations on my being re-elected, he got right to the point.

"Mr. Speaker, I didn't want to break in on your meeting with your friends, but it's important we have this meeting as early as possible so we can work together and get this extremely dangerous deficit behind us. It's beyond just our political well-being, Mr. Speaker. The future viability of the State of Vermont is at stake. I know what my role is going to be, and it's going to take all my energy and good will to bring about the solution. But I can't do it without you. That's not rhetoric; I mean that."

I shifted nervously in my chair, realizing I must have looked like a very small figure sitting not two feet from this man.

"I've been reading the papers like you probably have," he continued, "and all this bull about 'finally, the clashing of the titans, Wright versus Snelling.' Well, that simply isn't going to happen. I guarantee there isn't anything that's going to make us start fighting with each other; nothing you say or do is going to make me angry. Nothing. You'll see. We—and I emphasize 'we'—have a job to do. It can't come about without us working together, perhaps against everybody that in the past we might have relied on individually. Somehow, we've got to bring them together to bail us out of this awful dilemma." And then he leaned forward. "I hope you can help me."

Help you? Christ, I'd slay a dragon for you.

The plan Snelling had put together was well laid out, and more important, it was fair. The corporate interests didn't escape their share of the tax levies he proposed, but the bulk of the money raised was through a flat tax across the board. Vermont's personal income tax is one of only two in the country that are tied to the level of federal taxes paid (Rhode Island's is the other). Ours was 25 percent of the federal taxes paid in any year. Snelling proposed that it be raised to 28 percent.

When he appeared in my office that day, I never mentioned what a majority of my caucus had suggested we ask in return for our cooperation in helping the governor over his fiscal hurdle. (Actually, more than a few were advocating that we let the governor "twist slowly in the wind," no matter what he offered in return.) What they wanted was a graduated tax that would be less of a burden on the poor and would saddle the rich with the bulk of the increase. If we could have accomplished this we would have been the only state with such a tax table.

I nearly fell out of my chair when, several weeks into our effort to bring this all to fruition, Dick Snelling once again sought me out, this time at the podium after we had adjourned for the day, and asked if we could talk in private. A private talk in the legislature is almost an impossible task, as everybody feels free to join in on any conversation they come upon and just as free to walk away when they become bored or something of more importance catches their attention. It is a rudeness that is somehow perfectly acceptable in the culture of the State House.

I asked the governor to sit with me in the decorative red seats adjacent to the podium that were reserved for the thirty Senators when we had a joint session. Strangely enough, such a public meeting served as a signal to others that a private conversation was taking place, and they would leave us alone.

"Mr. Speaker, I know you haven't brought this up, and I appreciate your not doing so, but I just want to tell you how great it's been working with you and how much I appreciate your efforts. I also am very aware of all the heat you've taken from the different sources, some within your own party, for doing what you're doing. I, too, have had them screaming and hollering at me, but that's OK; they don't bother me. I hope they don't you."

"I'll be all right," I interjected.

He went on, leaning closer to me.

"I've thought about all this a great deal, so please don't respond until I've finished. I'm here to offer you a progressive income tax—one that puts 28 percent on the lowest rung; 31 percent on the middle group; and 34 percent on the richest Vermonters. The one caveat is that you've got to promise me we sunset it all back down to the present flat rate of 25 percent when the deficit is paid. I know that's more than two years out and a different legislature can do anything it damned well pleases, but I'm just asking that we put it in the bill that it is our intention to sunset back to 25 percent at that time. I think it's the fairest way we can go, and it's a small thank you for helping on this."

I tried to stay calm and responded, "And?"

"That's it. Let me know." He got up and left.

Life never ceases to amaze me, for here was the governor, my partner but still my political opponent in the eyes of the world, offering to do what I had only dreamed of doing. I coulda kissed him!

What the governor didn't go into was that he was taking a terrific amount of heat from members of his own party and especially from the business community, who never publicly let up their cries of anguish at the tax increase. Of course they didn't like any tax increase, but one that had them carrying the bulk of the load was enough to send them into fits. Privately, I later learned, he actually had an audience with a small group of them in an effort to convince them that this was the only fair solution to bailing out the state. Of course, they had little interest in such "do-gooder drivel," and they actually went to the extreme of accusing him of being manipulated by the Speaker.

Snelling did exactly what you would have expected from him. He threw them the hell out of his office.

Taking Things for Granted

I didn't know it then, but it was going to be even more dramatic than anyone could possibly have imagined. Three months later, after the most heated and bitter of debates, the vote on final passage of the largest tax increase in the entire history of the state was tied up 72–72 at the end of the roll call. I was forced to vote and break the tie.

Corcoran screwed me that time, and I ended up throwing him out of the condo. I should have handled my need to get his vote better, but I assumed he'd be there when I needed him, and I paid no heed to how he was going to vote. (Another lesson learned—don't take anything or anyone for granted.) I had exhausted all my reservoir of debts and IOUs to get to the point where I felt we were going to win by a very small margin. Corcoran, being Corcoran, had played his cards close to the vest and never spoke about the tax bill. This was in character, as he could talk all night about unpleasant things happening to others but never talked about things that were unpleasant to him. And raising taxes upset the very core of his conservative soul. I assumed, rather stupidly, that Cork would eventually see my predicament and throw me his vote.

Corcoran had a habit of never being in his seat while the roll was being taken. He would appear magically just as the clerks were repeating the names of those not present the first time through. This time, as he rushed in and took his seat I could see Alice Emmons, D-Springfield, his seatmate, informing him that the vote appeared to be tied up. When they called, for the second and last time, "the member from Bennington, Mr. Corcoran," he voted, without looking up at my glare from the podium, and in an obviously sheepish voice, "No." I was surprised, and the members in their shock, sensing the closeness of the count, all turned to stare over at my friend, the Democrats angry, the Republicans amused.

Roll calls don't offer time to reflect or ponder things. I had to maintain a level of cool, though I could feel my temperature rising as I waited for my clerks to double-check their tally before handing it up to me to be read.

A well-trained Speaker who has overseen thousands of roll calls learns to keep count as the clerks call the roll. If the spread is wide one can relax and pay little heed. If it is close, attention has to be paid to the surprises. The unwritten rule is that if you give your word on a vote, a change of heart requires that you inform the leaders prior to the vote. Failure to do this can earn one the label "Not to be trusted"—a kiss of death in a legislature. But I had never asked Corcoran, and he had never volunteered his support.

I assumed he now knew I was in a jam and that the vote was tied. I was certain that Alice Emmons had informed him of the tie vote. I knew also that Corcoran could count as well as anybody, and I prayed that he would take advantage of the small window of time between the clerk's first count and the recount, rise, and request permission to change his vote. I glared at him waiting for the life preserver. He sat there, head down, his eyes fixed on the cluttered pile on his desk. There would be no rescue this day.

Finally, the clerk handed me the official tally, and I read it to a very attentive body—the Republicans with smirks on their faces, the Democrats with looks of fascination at the irony of the situation. My buddy, so instrumental in steering my political career, was now the lone assassin in a crisis that many thought, and some hoped, would force me to vote and hasten my political demise.

"Listen to the result of your vote." Anticipation broke the excited undercurrent of chatter in the hall. "Those in favor, seventy-two; those opposed, seventy-two. The vote ending in a tie, the chair votes aye. The bill passes."

I went back to the apartment, and in spite of Harold Weidman's pleas for mercy on Cork's behalf, I put his clothes and shaving kit on a chair in the building's hallway. After a couple of weeks, and the pleading on Corcoran's behalf by Weidman, the c'mon home call went out to Cork, and he moved his gear back in. The incident was never mentioned again.

The Loss of a Friend

Four months later Dick Snelling, while home alone and cleaning his swimming pool, fell over with a massive heart attack. He was dead before he hit the ground. I lost a comrade in arms, one I respected immensely. The State of Vermont had lost a true statesman.

In the years since I have often reflected on what we might have accomplished as a bipartisan combo. My last face-to-face meeting with Governor Snelling occurred when I visited with him in his office several weeks before his sudden and tragic death. We were alone, and he was especially upbeat about the upcoming session in January. There was some preliminary kibitzing about his wanting me to join him for a sail on his boat moored on Lake Champlain. Remembering this guy had sailed the Atlantic by himself, I left no doubt that this was something I had not the faintest desire to do. Even his invite to split a bottle of Wild Turkey while aboard only added to my apprehension, as the image of sailing for this captain only conjured up scary memories of my twelve weeks on Parris Island under my old drill instructor. When the conversation finally got around to the issues we could anticipate in the new session, he raced through them as if each was a hurdle easily scaled.

Then, becoming decidedly more animated, he leaned forward and blurted out, "You know Mr. Speaker, we can do something about the funding of the schools." There was excitement in his voice.

I sat up, surprised that he would even raise the issue of school funding. It wasn't something that previous political leaders did anything more about than keep adding money each year in hopes of satisfying the 254 local school districts. Their budgets had become what seemed like bottomless pits. No matter that we continued to send down more money, the state aid percentage of the local communities' school expenditures continued to plunge. It wasn't that we didn't do our best, but the school districts were spending a whole lot faster than they dared raise local property taxes.

Snelling was aware that this was an issue close to my heart, but I had come down on the side of caution, as I was convinced that trying to find a fairer way to fund our public schools would never get off the ground in the legislature. It was a political third rail. Now here was a governor suggesting that we plunge ahead.

"If we did this, Governor, I'm convinced that we'd have to do away with the local property tax altogether." My God, he was nodding in agreement—a huge grin flashed across his face. "It means a statewide property tax on business, local property taxes on second homes only, and some help from other taxes including the income tax. Don't we both have enough enemies, Governor?"

"I'm not concerned with enemies, Mr. Speaker, as long as I get to choose them. But it isn't simply finding fairer methods of funding. On the other end of this problem is cost containment. We have to find a way to keep local costs under control. Simply sending money into the communities without any say on how it's spent doesn't solve anything."

"I think there is a way, Governor."

"How?"

"Have the state negotiate and pay for the salaries and fringe benefits of the six thousand teachers, just as we do the state employers. A single, negotiated teachers contract between the union and the state. Instead of local boards competing with each other to maintain their staffs, it would be the state that does the negotiating for what is fair for all teachers, no matter the affluence of the district."

He sat listening, eye contact unflinching.

"It also gives us the opportunity to deal with the runaway health care costs, in that we would be able to negotiate for teachers throughout the state, in combination with the state employees. The threat of the state creating its own health care HMO would counter the 'privates' from dictating costs or terms."

"You know you're right. I've thought about that; it's just that I hadn't heard it espoused by anyone else. Damn, that would work."

Snelling's death dashed the hopes that this conversation held out, but it was a conversation that epitomized the difference among the three governors that I had the pleasure of working with. With Kunin, the conversation most probably never would have happened, as she was more inclined to seclude her plans within her immediate staff. Whatever role I might play as a representative of the legislative branch would be decided by our common interest in an issue. One as big and politically explosive as property tax reform would probably never be broached. Madeleine knew enough about politics to get herself elected and don the title of "Governor" but never achieved that level of security that allowed her to grasp the fine points of statehouse infighting. When in the legislature, she had achieved a somewhat remarkable ascendancy up the ladder of committee importance, but she was never part of the power structure that determined the agenda in the House. Her years in the body were spent as a double minority—a Democrat and a woman. Though aware, I'm certain, of the inner circle, she was never allowed to be part of it.

Snelling, on the other hand, had spent his years in the House not just as a member of the dominant Republican Party but as its leader. He was well aware of all the chicanery and subterfuge that the House utilized to play the game. He was totally cognizant that a Speaker willing to use his constitutional power was, at the very least, an equal partner in the making of law while the legislature sat in session for those four or five months. He didn't need to be told twice that the power to issue four-number license plates or appoint someone to the plumbing board was no match for the power over committee assignments, the daily calendar, an array of perks, and the very flow of legislation. That's why I got that visit to my office on opening day in 1991. Snelling knew that his success directly correlated with my willingness to stand with him throughout the journey. This display of equality on his part (I looked at it as a magnanimous show of humility) was not just a gesture created for political expediency but a display of savvy about how the legislature worked. Madeleine had a difficult time grasping this nuance of lawmaking. But a doctoral degree in parliamentary procedure was no guarantee of success, no matter how adroit or smart the player. With any joint venture, and making law is certainly that, success comes with much greater facility when the partnership is based on trust. Snelling and I had that added ingredient—Madeleine and I never could achieve it. It is another example, I guess, of the point that politics, stripped to its basics, is a people game.

Howard Dean, D-Burlington, my former whip and the next governor I would serve with, would have done what he later did—cut and run. Political wavering was not to be found in Dick Snelling's makeup. In addition, the problem of property tax reform would have required an enormous bipartisan effort, and that's where Snelling would have been most valuable. Kunin didn't have any more Republicans rooting for her than I did, which is to say, few or none. Because Snelling was "King Richard" to his minority in the House and majority in the Senate, his influence and tenacity would have struck trepidation in the hearts of any fellow Republicans who dared turn their backs on his request for support.

Politics is not just the obvious, but is doors slamming silently. Kunin, if she did tacitly join with me, probably would not have fought openly for the cause against the many guaranteed opponents that the property tax bill would have awakened. To take on the business community, second-home owners, and the all-powerful teachers union, not to mention the many people who shrink from change, would have required a political courage, some might say craziness, that not all elected officials have.

In Kunin's defense, she was a first, being Vermont's only woman governor, and had won her first election by the narrowest of margins. Though her reelections were by much healthier percentages, she still had to deal with powerful political contingents that accepted her as long as the ship of state never veered too far from its customary course. These behind-the-scenes power brokers had a fairly high tolerance level for things that didn't encroach on their comfort level. Their comfort was guaranteed to disappear when anyone messed with their bottom line, that is, their pocketbook or their power. To the business community, exchanging the income tax for the local property tax was a hand in their pockets. As to the teachers union, its power rested at the local level with its property tax. Either would be quick to turn on those who threatened their base of self-importance.

The incoming governor, Howard Dean, was different in that he had accumulated an enormous capital of good will, both as the guy who kept the ship on course after the governor died and for his built-in crib of charm as the doctor-governor. But political capital only has value if one is willing to spend it. Later events would show that Dean was a gatherer, not a spender.

Two years later, when the deficit was just a memory and it was time to return the graduated tax back to a flat 25 percent, I was beseeched and badgered by my caucus to renege on my word and not allow the sunset of the progressive income tax to click in. I tried to explain to my caucus that I had given my word, but my pleading met with nothing but smirks.

"Christ, Ralph, he's dead," a member shouted. I didn't know how to answer this without getting angry, so I made a joke out of it all and answered, "Yeah, I know. But I'm hoping I end up in the same place as Dick Snelling, and if I ever do, after going back on my word, I don't want to spend the shortest moment with him, let alone eternity. He'll tear my ass apart. More important, he would be disappointed in me." Everyone knew there was finality to my answer.

We sunset the taxes as promised.

That one was for you, Captain.

11

Working with the Executive Branch, Part 3

Howard Dean, Democrat, 1991–1995

According to the Vermont Constitution, "Upon the death or the incapacitation of the governor, the Lieutenant Governor shall assume the duties of the Governor."

We had a new governor, and his name was Howard Dean—Dr. Howard Dean.

One Man's View of Howard Dean

Howard Dean never walked into a room with the slightest doubt that everyone gathered there loved him. He just exuded that type of relaxed confidence. (As for me, I never walked into a room without immediately spotting the single figure who hated my guts.)

Howard Dean was a "rich kid," who was successful at everything he had attempted throughout his life. He was raised to achieve, and though he would decide for himself the avenues he would travel, he was not left with any choice between success and failure. Winning starts with the idea that you're not going to lose. Governor Dean had never spent any significant amount of time mulling that possibility. More important, he wasn't afraid to lose. Like everyone else, he was happy to win, but unlike most of the rest of us, he wasn't going to jump off the roof if he lost. (This might be

what my mother was refer-
ring to when I once over-
heard her say in a low voice,
"The rich are different.")
Lack of fear of losing is an
absolute must in a warrior.
And if Howard Dean is
anything, in this respect,
he's a warrior, but one who
selects his wars carefully.

Here's a kid raised on
Park Avenue, who goes to
the best private schools,
summers in the Hamptons,
attends Yale, and after taking a year off skiing to "find
himself" decides he doesn't
want to spend his life hus-
tling stocks with his father
on Wall Street. Instead he
goes off to medical school
and becomes a doctor, to
heal those in pain and ex-
tend life. Horatio Alger's
hero is alive and well, and he was our new governor.

*As U.S. House Speaker Tip O'Neill once ex-
plained to President Ronald Reagan, in politics, we're all friends after six o'clock. In 1996
at a roast in my honor, Governor Howard
Dean (left) and I share an after-six-o'clock
laugh. We didn't share too many of these moments while in the statehouse.*

One might think that this would all lead Dean to be burdened with a
massive ego, but he seldom showed evidence of any.

The new governor was not exactly unknown to me, as he had served as
Democratic whip during his second term in the legislature, my first as
Speaker, in 1985–1986. My earliest recollection of him was during his first
year (1983) when he rose on the floor of the House to argue some losing
cause. He was brief, articulate, and unruffled at his loss. It seemed a strange
response, at least to me, as I never liked losing anything, and as people can
attest, it always showed. I thought then, "This is a different kind of guy."

As whip he tended to be under foot all the time while he was learning the ropes. It was the duty of the party leader to snap a new whip in. I would laugh as Paul Poirier raised his eyebrows to the heavens anytime I would ask, "How's Howard doing?"

Dean still had a medical practice to tend to, and he would leave the State House by mid or late afternoon each day to conduct his rounds at the Burlington Medical Center. We didn't complain, as we were used to running the whole show anyway; actually I think Poirier was always somewhat relieved when the doctor departed for rounds.

The Doctor Has Ambitions

The first serious encounter I had with Dean was when he told the caucus that when I announced my candidacy for the speakership in 1984, he was going to run for whip. This struck both Poirier and me as brazen, as not only had he been in the legislature less than two years, but he announced this before I even began my campaign for the Speaker's office. Poirier, especially, took exception to Dean's move, as it was not at all certain that I was going to overcome the six-vote disadvantage and grab the brass ring in 1985. We had arranged, Paul and I, for the leadership races to be held off until after the Speaker's election, so that if I lost I could rely on the sympathy of my caucus, as their fallen warrior, to at least keep me on as leader. (Of course, this flew in the face of what Corcoran had forced Paul to do four years earlier.) The same was not the case with Poirier, as my defeat would have forced him to run for reelection to his whip's post against Dean, who had already announced.

That this potentially represented a direct challenge to Poirier, who was technically his boss, didn't seem to bother the future governor an iota, as he raced around the state searching out votes from our fellow Democrats, possibly against the very guy he would have to work under if I won. I did win, and the question became moot, but I often wondered what the future would have held for him if I lost, maintained my Democratic leader position, and Poirier had maintained his job as whip by beating Dean in caucus. (No doubt, that would have occurred, as Paul was very well liked and respected by his fellow Democrats.)

What we had learned back in 1985 was that our new, accidental governor was an ambitious man, and we soon realized that the sky was the limit for young Dr. Dean.

The Wolf in Sheep's Clothing

Dean's restlessness and ambition led him to run for the open lieutenant governor's office in 1988, and he it won rather handily against a less-than-strong Republican opponent. He won reelection in 1990 and was but eight months into his second term when the call came from the State Police commissioner that a trooper would arrive within minutes at his medical office in Shelbourne to whisk him to the State House to be sworn in as governor. Richard Snelling had succumbed to a massive heart attack.

Howard dealt with his new role as governor much as I imagined he did his role as doctor: He did the best he could and didn't get fancy. He played with the cards that were dealt him by keeping most of the same appointees Snelling had brought on to ride out the deficit. This was an obvious sign to the Democrats that the momentous changing of the guard was not going to bring about a cleaning of the political house or a change in the agenda. Dean found new opportunities for the late governor's friends and allies—Republicans all. It soon became obvious that the "new king" wasn't going to make any waves. He retained all the sitting commissioners and department heads and told them to go about their tasks. He needed their "special effort under these tragic circumstances. We've got a government to run." He did bring in Cathy Hoyt, a trusted friend who would provide experience and political know-how to this awkward transition of power, as she had for Madeleine Kunin as her administration secretary for six years.

For my part, I was as shocked as anyone. I had lost a trusted friend in Dick Snelling, and in politics one can never get enough of those. I attended the memorial service held in the well of the House and was moved by the outpouring of testimony to this extraordinary man. The state had lost its steady captain, and what lay in front of us was anyone's guess.

As the ceremony broke up the new governor asked if we could have a few words in the privacy of his office. We talked, Dean and I, about his new role and how all of us would have to work together to get the state through the unexpected change of leadership. The conversation turned to the vacant lieutenant governor's office, and he asked me if I would take the post. I smiled and thanked him and then reminded him that that probably wasn't such a good idea. First, there was some question as to whether the office was in fact vacant. The Republicans would be sure to argue that Dean's new title would be "Acting Governor" and that the lieutenant governor's post was not vacated. More important, at least in my mind, was that my becoming lieutenant governor would leave the speakership vacant.

"Howard, that wouldn't be a smart move because the House would have to hold an election to name a new Speaker. We're the minority party. We'd lose the House because my Republican support probably isn't transferable to another Democrat. Neither of us needs that."

He smiled, perhaps with relief at avoiding the personality problems that would come from having me as his second in command, or maybe just at the political sense it made. "You know, you're right, Mr. Speaker. I hadn't thought of that." Later I was asked by a reporter if the new governor had offered me the job. I answered truthfully and was somewhat taken back when Dr. Dean denied it. After I confronted him about making it appear that I was not telling the truth he finally, I'm sure with some reluctance, informed the reporter that he had made the offer. The matter faded from public view, as it was really not an issue, but there was something about it that stayed in the recesses of my mind.

"Steady as she goes" became the modus operandi for the next year and a half. The deficit problem had stemmed the normal flow of liberal largesse that might have put forth dozens of ideas and programs in a normal session of the legislature. When you're broke there aren't many places one can go or things one can do. As far as having to deal with the deficit,

Dean simply had to sit back and wait for the medicine that Snelling had administered to kick in. If it worked, the new governor could receive credit not only for carrying on the deceased governor's plan, but also for doing so in his memory. Should it fail, there would be time enough to admit failure (not Dean's, but perhaps mine) and venture forth with a "Dean plan." That never came to pass because the Snelling deficit retirement package was to prove adequate to move the state from the red to the black. It would take time but no drastic changes in the course set by Snelling.

Dean wasn't going to risk failure by the slightest show of tinkering, no matter how much the disappointed liberal wing of the party longed for creativeness and vision. He was the stockbroker's son, the offspring of sound investments and slow dividends. It was during this last year and a half of what would have been Snelling's term, had he lived, that the liberal Democrats first suspected that perhaps this was a wolf in sheep's clothing, while Republicans raised their tolerance level for a Democratic governor who began to look a lot like themselves.

This was a different kind of Democrat, to be sure. Several weeks after he was thrust into the highest office in the state, Dean's popularity rating topped 70 percent, and it was to go up from there.

By 1993 all the pieces had fallen in place. For the first time since the Civil War, the Democrats had gained control of the House. We did so not by any slight margin as, having learned the art of recruiting and taking advantage of a changing Vermont, we had eighty-six Democrats take their seats at the sound of the gavel in January 1993. The election of three Progressives from what was frequently referred to as the "Republic of Burlington" enhanced our numbers in support of any liberal measures that we might decide to include in our agenda. The Republicans had managed to hang onto a slight majority in the Senate, with the potential to veto any legislation we might send over, but that was not on my mind as I took my oath as Speaker for my fifth term.

All we needed was an agenda.

Governor Dean provided it when he announced in his inaugural address that he would introduce a bill that would bring comprehensive health care to all Vermonters. It was a show of vision that we all were awaiting from the doctor-governor. And because of him Vermont was to move as close to achieving this goal as any state in the nation. None of it would have happened without Dean's unique relationship with the president of the United States. Ironically, I was the matchmaker who first got them together.

A Call from Arkansas

My connection to Bill Clinton came out of the blue.

Obviously, I had heard of Clinton, but it was a rather obscure awareness of a small-state governor who I remembered carrying on for what seemed hours at the 1988 Democratic National Convention. The convention crowd actually cheered upon hearing the words, "In conclusion . . . ," and later the press jumped all over him. But I had actually listened to what he had to say and came away impressed with his grasp of issues, if not his brevity. After that rather sorry effort, I had not given him another thought until the phone rang one Friday evening in December 1991.

I was sitting in my den watching the Celtics. It was early in the second period, and I couldn't believe that someone actually had the nerve to disturb me during a Celtics game. The call couldn't be from anyone who knew me well. Maybe it was a nuisance call, and it was in that frame of mind that I answered with a rather terse, "Hello." Larry had the ball.

"Hello. May I speak to Speaker Wright, please?" The person on the line had a thick southern drawl.

"Speaking. Who is this?"

"Mr. Speaker, this is Governor Bill Clinton, and I'm calling from down here in Little Rock. I wonder if I might have a moment of your time, if you don't mind?" And as if he had a premonition of just how much I minded, he added, "I hope I'm not bothering you at this hour at home."

Absolutely convinced that this was one of my friends screwing around, I jumped right on his case. "Who is this?"

"My name's Bill Clinton. I'm the governor of Arkansas and I'm running for president."

Yeah, sure! And I'm going to be the next pope—pro choice and all.

He added quickly, "I believe we have a mutual friend in Boston—Peter Lucas, the former newspaper columnist from the *Boston Globe.* It's my understanding you met with him recently, and according to a friend of mine, you let him know you might support my candidacy for president. At least, I hope my friend heard it right. I'm calling in hopes I might get your support."

Still assuming the person on the other end was a joker, I reacted in a voice containing little patience, "You know I'm trying to watch the Celtics, here."

"I'm a big Celts fan. How's my friend Joe Klein doing?" Joe Klein was the University of Arkansas grad who was the Celtics' backup center. I knew Cork and Harris wouldn't have had the faintest idea who Joe Klein was. Sports weren't their thing. Christ, I was really talking to the governor of Arkansas. And the poor guy must have wondered what lengths a candidate has to go to in talking to some rude nut from Vermont who happened to be Speaker. I hit the mute button on the TV remote and apologized.

"Jeez, I'm sorry, Governor. It's just that I have these friends."

"Well, Mr. Speaker, I know it's early and I haven't announced my candidacy officially, and there are still lots of people that aren't aware I'm running. But I'm just trying to touch base with as many state Democratic leaders as I can and hopefully get them on board early. Peter informed me you endorsed Governor Dukakis in 1988 from the well of the House. Would you be willing to do that for me?"

"Sure, no problem, but I've got to warn you—I did that for Dukakis and he immediately fell twenty points in the polls." Clinton laughed and said he wasn't worried about that happening again, but he did want to know about my governor.

"Do you think you might be able to get him to support me?"

"Well, I don't know, Governor. I don't know that he has endorsed anyone, since it's still pretty early in the game, but I'll be seeing him when we reconvene in three or four weeks, and I'll be happy to see what I can do for you. All he can say is no."

That was it. I was committed to a little-known governor from a small, backwater state, and the only hedge I had that I wasn't publicly backing another loser was that he probably was going to prove so inept a candidate that his campaign would fold before it got off the ground, hopefully before I had to tell everyone he was my man. So much for what I know about politics, right?

I got Dean to jump off Sen. Bob Kerrey's ship and onto Bill Clinton's in January, and we both agreed to announce our endorsement at my annual fund-raiser in February. This seemed convenient since Clinton would be campaigning in the New Hampshire primary almost daily. It would be fairly easy for him to skip up to the evening gathering in Montpelier. Besides, we argued, it was likely that he would have dropped out by that time, and our hectic lives wouldn't have to be interrupted by this inconvenient and potentially embarrassing sideshow. In fact, it would be worse than that by the second week of February 1992, as not only was Clinton's campaign in deep trouble but George Bush's post–Gulf War poll numbers skyrocketed to over 90 percent favorable. I didn't know it then, but I was standing with a guy who "plays through" during thunderstorms.

My "Speaker's Soiree" was scheduled for a Wednesday night in the second week of February, and though I invited Governor Clinton to be my special guest, I was relieved when his staff called to say that because of the heavy hits the governor had taken over the Genifer Flowers fiasco and his deferral from the Vietnam-era draft he wouldn't be able to make it to my fund-raiser, and his endorsement. That was the good news. The bad news was that his wife, Hillary, would be there on her husband's behalf. Terrific!

I teased Dean a lot the week or so before the event about how he had finally allowed himself to be dragged into a no-win situation. I reminded him just how bad the kidding and abuse would be about our timing in supporting a guy who was dropping off the charts in neighboring New Hampshire. Sometimes he thought it was funny; sometimes he didn't.

But the Soiree turned out to be more fun than anyone could have imagined. Hillary Clinton showed up in the Montpelier Tavern Ballroom that evening with her head high. It was a wonderful display of public courage, and she knocked them dead. I made sure that I stood on one side of her and Dean stood on the other the entire evening. Nobody there that cold and dark winter night could have left without feeling the highest admiration for Hillary. Unfortunately, only about three hundred Vermonters were there to witness to this profile in courage. The rest of America saw only a candidate who looked like he was down for the count. "If you can keep your head high when all about you are losing theirs and blaming it on you . . ."

The next morning when I went into the office, I asked my secretary to pick up a one hundred dollar money order (I never had a checking account) at the post office when she went to lunch. I sat down and wrote, in longhand, this note:

Dear Governor Clinton,

I just wanted to write a brief note of thanks to you and Hillary for making my fund-raiser such a success last evening. I know how difficult it must have been for you and your wife to be concerned about other people's matters at such a time as this. I also feel certain this must surely be the low point in your political career. Nevertheless, simply let me say, "don't let the bastards get you down." You are going to be the next President of the United States come November. Take my word for it, and the proof is I'm willing to put my money where my mouth is with the enclosed check for the entire Wright estate, $100. Spend it wisely.

Warm regards,

Ralph G. Wright

P.S. Hillary knocked them dead. You can be proud of her, especially under fire.

The rest is history.

12

The Health Care Issue

The Governor Proposes a Health Authority

If the new president of the United States had a favorite governor, it was Howard Dean. Within months of being inaugurated in 1993, President Bill Clinton announced it was time to do something about the health care problem in America. And he meant to do it.

Dean, meanwhile, had already prepared Vermont for sweeping health care reform by proposing, a year earlier, a bill creating a Health Care Authority. Its purpose was to study ways to begin reforming a health care system that was delivering less and costing more. Upon completing its study, it was to deliver its results to the legislature. I had sponsored the bill, an unusual move for a Speaker, and the momentum with which it flew through the legislature surprised all of us. The bill didn't do anything to change the antiquated and costly health care system that America had learned to live with, nor did it provide a single additional Vermonter any trace of a health care package. It simply ordered the creation of a Health Care Authority whose mandate was to study the issue from soup to nuts and return with a choice of plans that the legislature could act on the following year, 1994.

Subsequently, the House grabbed the opportunity to prepare for the forthcoming recommendation by the Health Care Authority come opening day of the new session. As passed, the bill had authorized the governor to appoint the members of the authority. Dean assigned a diverse group representing the different segments of the health care field, and several legislators.

The House Picks Up the Ball

To accommodate this initiative I had created a "special" Health Care Committee of members of the House and provided funding for them to meet between legislative sessions. And though it caused some hard feelings with the chair of the Health and Welfare committee, Peg Martin, D-Middlebury, I named Sean Campbell, my Democratic leader, the chairman of the new committee. It wasn't that Peg wasn't sufficiently committed to radical reform to push the bill, and certainly she was bright enough. It was just that we felt strongly that the lobbying and pressure from forces that didn't want this to happen would grow exponentially to full-scale attacks. I felt much more comfortable with a hard-nosed veteran of political combat overseeing the platoon. Campbell, having served three years in leadership, was that.

Sean was extremely bright and had been a valuable and loyal lieutenant on the Appropriations Committee before winning the post of whip and then two years later Democratic leader. We had worked together for three years and had become close and trusting friends. Whatever handicap he was strapped with in the beginning by never having served on the Health and Welfare committee was overcome by his high energy and his reputation as a quick study. He was perfect for the job. I then surrounded him with ten other members of high caliber, including Peg; Republican leader Rick Westman, of Cambridge; Tom Little, of Shelburne, another Republican and a lawyer; and my roommate Harold Weidman. I then filled the remaining slots of the eleven-person committee with reform-minded Democrats. Westman, Little, and Weidman, to their credit, realized the severity of the problem and throughout the process showed a willingness to work in cooperation with the committee.

The Plan

The Health Care Committee worked well together, and come opening day they had a plan. It called for a complete revamping of the delivery of health care to Vermonters, and it was radical. I don't think that this was really what Dean had in mind a year earlier when he called for his study.

He wasn't the type to rock a smooth-sailing boat, and this was sure to create some giant waves. I knew from the beginning that our proposal, now in the form of a bill, wasn't one that pleased him.

To be fair to Dean, I never felt that he recognized the sweeping impact that the initiative that he proposed a year earlier would have on Vermont's largest industries, insurers, hospitals, medical practitioners, and small businesses, especially if the legislature chose the most sweeping of the reform choices. Backroom gossip was a bit harsher on the governor; there were some that felt his initiative was nothing more than an act of political grandstanding. I paid little heed, as a door had opened, and it didn't matter to me who opened it or why. The opening was there and we intended to take it.

And that, of course, was exactly what we did. The "single-payer" system, copied from the Canadian system of universal health care, provided a guaranteed, comprehensive health care package to all Vermonters. The bulk of the cost was to be divided between employer and employee payroll tax deductions, which would come to more than $750 million a year. This was a phenomenal sum that was very near equal to the state's total general fund budget. If it made me a little uneasy, I could only imagine what it was doing to the stockbroker's son.

The single-payer plan presented no philosophical problem for me. I had no compunction about laying those astronomical costs squarely on the shoulders of those who should be paying for the services, the guy with the lunch pail and his boss. Both parties, I believed, had responsibilities: the worker to provide a basic need for himself and his family; the employer to understand that with wealth came social responsibility. A cost study of the current expenditures on health care showed that to convert to a single-payer plan would be cheaper. More important, it would finally allow us to get a handle on runaway cost increases through state control of the delivery system. We were aware that thousands of Vermonters were presently covered—Medicaid recipients with a full package of health insurance and seniors through Medicare—though they still had gaps in their coverage, pharmaceuticals being the most obvious. Thus it wasn't as if we were creating something entirely new or as if government wasn't already a player in this endeavor.

Still, the plan would require a lot of money, and the payroll tax was the only place one could raise the bulk of $750 million. We had numerous other, splinter tax increases in the financing package, but the majority of the dollars would come from the weekly paycheck. Like my friend Willie Sutton, we went where the money was.

Dean, a fiscal conservative, didn't feel as I did. He could break out in a rash at the mere mention of the smallest increase in the most innocuous tax. To propose raising over $700 million via the one tax that had an impact on all working Vermonters probably brought him to the edge of a stroke. He seldom said anything about it, but it was clear he was regretting that he had even suggested the idea of creating a health care authority. But the captain had issued the order to turn the ship, and now the slow movement was under way. There was no hope of changing direction without making waves—something our governor was to show a great distaste for in the years to come.

Dean's dilemma was that he was gaining national prominence as the extraordinary young governor in the little state of Vermont who was poised to set the pace for the entire nation in the quest to bring universal health care to its citizens. And we in the House were primed and ready to see that it happened.

This was a period of existential highs. Our governor was appearing on national news shows on a fairly regular basis, and he always handled himself extremely effectively. He could be a klutzy sort from time to time (the "scream"), in the privacy of his office or when excited, but became pretty sophisticated in front of a camera most of the time. I recall his startling me with the less-than-informed legal opinion that once the cell door slammed shut behind the convicted "they had no rights as an American." I warned him he probably ought not say that at his upcoming press conference.

But he needed little advice from the likes of me as to how to present himself in front of a camera. Once the klieg lights flickered on, he became the handsome young doctor who happened to be the governor of the rustic little state of Vermont. I once told Sean Campbell, over dinner one evening, that it was not impossible to envision Howard Dean in the White House. Once we had chuckled at envisioning him in the governor's office, too.

But popularity wasn't going to be enough to bring about the radical change we were proposing in delivering health care to Vermonters. I say "we," but in reality my governor was quietly placing more distance between himself and the push to get the bill through the House. It wasn't his nature simply to come out and state that he was getting nervous about the stiffening resistance we were encountering from pressure groups that saw our efforts as the final nail in capitalism's coffin. We had stirred a hornet's nest, for sure. The American Medical Association, insurance conglomerates (not just in state; they were swarming from all over the nation), the American Manufacturers Association, state Chamber of Commerce, leagues of cities and towns, and smaller groups such as the Grocer's Association were apoplectic over the plan.

The bigger the lobby interest, the easier it was to combat the negativity. That didn't stop them from spending huge sums on lobbying, advertising, mailings, and so forth, but their effectiveness was measured by their ability to reach out to the everyday Vermonter in a personal way. Receiving a glossy brochure from Blue Cross/Blue Shield or the Prudential Insurance Company from some distant metropolis wasn't the same as getting an earful while picking up the local newspaper and a gallon of milk each evening at the local country store. This was our big advantage—it was not difficult to disparage our "big-city" adversaries in the Brooks Brothers suits. We didn't know it then, but our disadvantage, which was going to do us in, came from much closer to home—the Vermont Grocer's Association. These folks were dressed a lot like Vermonters.

These were not distant "suits" that were easy to ignore, but our neighbors—our local selectmen and school board members and the hosts of the gathering places where we could chat with constituents, hang up leaflets, or leave candidate petitions on the counter. They were the eyes and ears of hundreds of small Vermont towns and villages, and it was the rare pol who could get himself or herself elected without at least their tacit support. We awakened a sleeping giant when, without any thought, we threw into the financing package a host of small taxes, one of which was an increase in the beer and wine tax.

Although we were never certain how the Vermont public assessed our campaign, no grassroots outcry had erupted up to this point. But here was a tax that affected the price of a bottle of wine or a six-pack. Who would have guessed? The Vermont Grocer's Association went bonkers.

The weekend before our scheduled vote on the bill the association took out full-page ads in the daily newspapers around the state denouncing the universal health care plan. The same ads appeared in the numerous weeklies that arrived at tens of thousands of Vermont doors during the week. Through the phone lines went hundreds of calls admonishing House members for what they were about to do. Amazingly, I received not a single call. But this was part of their strategy not to forewarn me of what was occurring.

This onslaught was coupled with an adroit political move by Blue Cross/Blue Shield, which announced that its increase in health plan costs would be a paltry 4 percent for the coming year, compared to previous years that had witnessed double-digit rises in premiums. This was received as a pleasant surprise and suggested to folks that perhaps the worst of the crisis in health care had passed.

It had taken all of January, February, and the first two weeks in March to fine-tune the bill. Because it contained both tax changes and appropriation adjustments it had to be looked over by the respective committees. But by mid-March the baby was ready for delivery on the House floor, and it would meet the crossover deadline. Now all we needed was seventy-six votes. My weekend on the phone had garnered, by my count, eighty-eight votes for the bill.

Of course, I wasn't the only one on the phone that weekend as, unbeknownst to me, the neighborhood grocers were burning up the lines, too.

Getting the Bad News

We sensed the softening of our supporters' commitment almost the moment we returned to the State House on the Tuesday morning before the bill was to come up for second reading. Something had to be done to shore up the members' support. I asked Sean if I might address the caucus scheduled that morning. It was not my custom to ask to speak to the caucus, or even attend it, as I felt that frequent participation in the weekly gathering bred a familiarity that diluted Sean's authority and effectiveness, as well as mine. But this was a special time, and I felt a personal appeal was vital to keep us on track.

When I entered the standing-room-only caucus I could sense the change in the air. (All our caucuses are open, to the public and the press.) I told them that I had spoken to each and every one of them over the weekend. It had taken me perhaps forty hours to dial and talk to each of them personally. They had committed to voting for the single-payer system.

"Now we've got to put up, or shut up," I implored. "I know you've been lobbied with a fierceness never seen in this State House, but we've run out of time. We've survived that and I'm proud of you for it. But now, in just a few hours, we'll be going upstairs to decide if we're going to get run over by the special interests, or we're going to do what's right by the people who sent us here. I've got to know if we still feel strongly about what we're about to do. I say this because several of you have come and asked if we can't find another option. But I have to know how the rest of you feel. I don't want to go up on the floor and be embarrassed. Do you want to go on?"

A few of my more liberal members stood to speak in favor of pushing the single-payer system. The rest sat silent. They said nothing, revealing everything with their silence. They were terrified of the radical nature of what we were about to do, and they didn't want to vote to do it. But they were creatures of that special institution, the legislature, one of whose fundamental principles says, "If you give your word, you keep your word." They weren't going to risk embarrassing themselves in front of their colleagues here in the caucus; they would wait until they could catch me or Sean at a more private time. Sensing this, I ended by saying, "If you've changed your mind, please, let Sean or me know before we go on the floor."

Within an hour, thirty or forty members came to us, and the number of votes we could count on dropped into the mid-forties. The chance to bring significant change to the way we deliver health care—effectively to

As the saying goes, success has a thousand parents, while defeat is an orphan. In a lonely moment at the podium in 1994, I listen to the roll call and await the imminent defeat of the universal health care bill. The chair I'm holding tight is the ceremonial seat of the Speaker—I never sat in it the entire ten years I presided over the House.

some and not at all to others—was lost, defeated not by faraway corporate moguls but by forces just down the road—our friendly neighborhood grocers.

The next day we passed a much-watered-down bill. I had been forced, after garnering only thirty-eight votes for the original bill, to rescue it by recommitting it to the Appropriations Committee. Even that vote to recommit was by a narrow margin, as the Republican opponents, sensing the kill, argued that it should be voted up or down right then and there. It was my saddened but much relieved Democrats who came to the rescue and allowed at least recommittal to committee. There it was altered to but a skeleton of its original sweeping intent. The version passed kept the patient alive, but it was now on life support. The dike being shattered, it was a simple matter for the Republican Senate to drag the measure under for the third time.

The End Finally Comes

I wasn't smart enough to realize that the jig was up, as I hoped the die-hard Senate supporters of significant change would be able to get done what we in the House had failed to do. I hung onto the aspiration that somehow we might still pull it all together, for even though we didn't have a majority of Democrats in the Senate, the public support still seemed to be there, and our ace in the hole was the doctor-governor who had gotten the whole thing started.

We were ten thousand feet above New Jersey when the end came.

The governor and I were sitting across from each other on the way to Washington to attend a fund-raiser for him hosted by the president. It was a corporate plane, made available to the governor by the largesse of the Grand Union Corporation—his connections, not mine. Dean was reading the *New York Times,* and he seemed to be a man without a worry in the world. I was holding on for dear life. He must have noticed my intensity, as he looked up from his paper and asked, "I thought you didn't fly, Mr. Speaker?"

"I fly, but I don't like it much."

"Well, there's nothing to it. It's safer than driving the New Jersey Turnpike." He smiled faintly and slid behind his paper once again.

This time I interrupted him.

"Governor, what are we going to do with the health care plan in the Senate?" I was prepared for a lengthy dialogue on a strategy for an advance to final victory. I didn't have such a plan, of course, but this was the governor's baby, and I had the hope of a child that its father would now outline how to get the job done right.

He barely looked up from his reading and he nonchalantly answered, "Nothing. It's dead."

That's it? It's dead? Two years of grinding and fighting and it's dead? Everything went out of my mind except the slow-motion visual I had of the governor in his white coat, stethoscope around his neck, pulling another sheet up over a patient's face and then casually turning to look at the charts of the patient in the next bed.

I guess this was the one thing I never could understand about Howard Dean: He was so ready to abandon his cause at the first sign of defeat. Maybe it was the medical training that toughened him to the certain failures that awaited us all. Maybe it was that credo of the rich that I had heard so long ago, "Never complain, never explain." Maybe it was what I always had suspected—that Howard had no cause at all, at least no cause for which he was willing to risk his political skin.

It was a surprise that he abandoned health care, the one cause he could justifiably have taken credit for. Even in defeat, he could have held his head high. But to me a whole lot of the pride and glory were sapped from the whole affair by his willingness to forgo fighting to the very end. He was too quick to run up the white flag. It wasn't just causes he was willing to abandon; he was capable of acting the same with people.

We sat in silence the rest of the flight, he in his *Times,* I in my thoughts.

The Dean Years—An Analysis

I had learned the lesson my mother had tried to push across a long time ago, "The rich are different," or at least the children of the privileged seemed to be. As time passed over the years, I struggled to some understanding of my doctor-governor. He was a warrior, to be sure, as he never failed to enjoy participating in the political arena, but a warrior only when the risks favored his survival. It is clear to me now that Howard never really intended his Health Care Authority to do anything more than produce a program to tinker around the edge of the health care problem. He certainly didn't want anything to do with wholesale reform of how we deliver health care to citizens. As long as he had the ear of the president of the United States he must have felt a high degree of security and protection from the forces mustering to defeat it. Once the cannons began firing, first in Washington and then in Montpelier, he began distancing himself from the front lines.

I could only look back with admiration of how Dick Snelling would have reacted. I'm convinced that the first shots fired across our bow by the lobbyists for the health care providers would only have incited him to charge forward to confront the foe. Snelling was a wealthy man by any modern standards, as he owned Shelberne Industries, but he was no child of privilege. He had suffered defeat both in the business world and in politics (he lost races for governor in the 1960s, and for the U.S. Senate in 1986 against Vermont's present senator, Patrick Leahy), and he was not a good loser. Like most of us in politics, his identity and self-worth were connected intimately to victory or defeat. Losses would be gotten over but not without a whole lot of soul searching and gradual rebuilding of self esteem.

With Howard, things were different. He never doubted that he was special. He lived in special places, went to special schools, and grew into manhood overachieving at every level. Defeat, which he never experienced politically until his fall from grace in the Iowa caucuses in 2004, was not something that put any sizable dent in his ego. Defeat was accepted with the same lack of emotion as victory, with the exceptions that he always somehow managed to distance himself from defeat but glad-handed victory as it came through the door.

Health care was not the only issue that he was quick to abandon during the biennium of 1992–1994. We were to suffer an inglorious whipping when in 1994 we finally introduced the property tax reform bill that Snelling and I had held out so much hope for back on that wonderful summer day in 1991. Again Howard managed to slip the noose, and many of us walked our political mile without the doctor present. He did what I believe Governor Snelling never would have done. He cut and ran.

To be sure property tax reform would have required an enormous bipartisan effort, and that's where Snelling would have been most valuable. When she was governor, Madeleine Kunin didn't have any more Republicans rooting for her than I did, meaning few or none. Dean had a lot more Republican friends than he ever cared to admit, and those friendships were based on the shared political philosophy that when it came to jeopardizing power or money, they were in harmony. Even if he had remained with us on either of these issues, the Republican majority in the Senate weren't going to tolerate any arm-twisting from a Democratic governor. They were partners of comfort with no fear of divorce. Snelling was "King

Richard" to his minority in the House and majority in the Senate. His influence and tenacity would have caused trepidation in the hearts of any fellow Republicans who dared turn their backs on his request for support. You didn't deny him without fear of retribution.

Howard Dean was different in that he had accumulated an enormous capital of good will, both as the guy who kept the ship on course after Snelling's death and because of his built-in reservoir of charm as the doctor-governor. But political capital only has value if one is willing to spend it, and events proved that Dean was a gatherer, not a spender.

Dean fled the scene when I finally introduced the legislation to revamp public school funding and health care. Whether he failed to anticipate the explosive backlash from all the forces against these changes but didn't want to go against the House's determination to get something done, or whether he had thought they would never get off the ground and thus he would never have to risk any political capital I don't know. But the result was the same with the education bill and the universal heath care bill—Dean grabbed the first life preserver in sight and went over the side. A whole lot of us went down with the ship come election day 1994, but Howard Dean wasn't one of them. He lived to sail another day and captain another ship.

So my reflections lead me to believe that with Madeleine we would have never left port. With Howard we would have set to sea, but once in troubled waters the ship's crew would have to search for another captain—not a good situation when in any storm—at sea or in the state capital.

Dick Snelling was a very different breed of cat who didn't need to look any farther than the mirror for his captain. And though I might have been a reluctant shipmate had we been able to sail in the turbulent waters that property tax reform and universal health care promised, I would have, without hesitating, placed my faith in my captain to see us through—aided, I'm sure, by more than a brace of that Wild Turkey. And we just might have pulled it off, if not for that moment by the pool.

Epilogue
Saying Good-bye

NINETEEN NINETY-FOUR WAS a disaster. Nothing had gone right. The two issues—health care and property tax reform—that we had worked so long and hard for had gone down to defeat, and with them went a whole lot of my credibility. To my Democrats, I had steered a ship that had crashed on the rocks; to the House Republicans I had shown a crack in my armor and all the possibilities that implied. To my constituents I had shown a disregard for our local relationship and too much concern with broad issues that they had difficulty relating to.

Perhaps more destructive to my political future was that I had stubbornly kept the legislature in session the second-longest time in Vermont history, until June 12, and the press had had a field day with repetitive stories about the "never-ending session."

Adjournment came at dawn on a Sunday morning in June 1994. The building had emptied, as exhausted legislators had gathered their belongings and headed off to their homes and some well-deserved sleep. I sat in my dark office sharing a beer with my Democratic leader, Sean Campbell, our silence saying it all. I don't know what Campbell's inner thoughts were that morning, but I couldn't help reflecting that this would be the last time we would enjoy each other's company in this surrounding.

We said good-bye as we exited into the empty parking lot, and I went back to my apartment to grab a few hours' sleep before heading down the road, home to Bennington. I awoke around ten-thirty and stopped on the way out of town to pick up the morning newspapers. The news was not good. Both statewide newspapers' front pages barely mentioned our long and bloody fight over the two most important issues facing Vermont. Instead, they mocked and ridiculed the long session and by inference the souls who had been so much a part of it. God, we had come so close.

Now I Know How "Little Joe" Felt So Many Years Ago

I got beat that November for the same reasons that "Little Joe" had lost his seat sixteen years earlier—I had forgotten my roots. Montpelier had become more important than my district, and like an army that outruns its supply line I had outrun my reservoir of good will back home. My heart wasn't where it should have been, and my constituents, sensing the end of a relationship, filed for divorce. It was an amiable if sad separation brought about by my failing to remember that the politics of Vermont was as personal as any love affair.

I wave good-bye to my orchestra for the final time, in June 1994. The day brought to a close the longest session since 1965 and marked the end of my political career. I wasn't aware at that moment that it would be my last hurrah inside the statehouse.

The years since have been kind, and I have often looked back on my sixteen years in the Vermont General Assembly, seldom trying to analyze what I might have accomplished but more often fondly reminiscing about the many friends and the times that we shared.

It has been harder to reflect on the less-than-enjoyable moments. Each required great efforts of mental research to recall the sequence of events. It has been easier and much more fun to recall my adventures with the Murphys, Corcorans, Harrises, Snellings, Kunins, Deans, Poiriers, Campbells, Brooksies, Cillos, Freidans, Powdans, and so many others who made it such an enjoyable period in my life.

Almost eleven years have passed, and I have never revisited the legislature. I prefer to remember it as it was. You, the reader, have now forced me to reflect on the question, Did my ten years as Speaker matter? It shouldn't surprise you that I find that a most difficult assignment, much more so than the actual writing of this book.

The interim years have not been fruitless, just so much less exciting. There is nothing like a legislature and setting out to make this a little better world to renew one's spirit. Each day, each hour, is full of the intent of getting something done; always anticipating the battle; being forced to deal with the results.

There was never a day, not one, that I did not believe, on entering the well of the House, that I was in a place where I belonged. It was a job where I mattered, and for that I shall be ever grateful to the people who for sixteen years entrusted it to me.

But I would be less than honest if I didn't admit that I experienced some hard times during my time in the legislature. A leader's task is never an easy one. There were rough intervals when the spotlight was on the podium, and as hard as I tried I could find no one to turn to for rescue. Success or failure hinged on the ability to stay as cool as possible while attempting to evaluate the problem, understand the options, and have the courage to make the decision. Sometimes the decisions were wrong, and I paid the price. That I weathered those stormy times I now take some pride in, for whatever may be said about my tenure, I was never missing in action, and of that I am proud. The arena was where you could find me.

Every leader has their own code of conduct, and to stray from who you are must inevitably lead to your discovery by others as less than sincere. I don't want to talk about qualities that make a leader that, unfortunately, I'm not smart enough to define. I'm not sure I could explain my election five times as Speaker, the House members accepting both my assets and liabilities, but I will say that I never tried to be anyone I wasn't. Personal character is a lot like describing events: wandering from reality can only lead to confusion, and confusion does not lead to success. Character does count.

If I had any advice for someone entering politics, it would simply be, "Don't venture into neighborhoods that are unfamiliar." One can get lost, and that is why it is so important to surround yourself with people who know what they are talking about. A legislator has to pay attention and absorb as much as is humanly possible. Information, as Murphy said, is power. But it can be so much more.

The best speeches I ever made were always about subjects in which I was well versed and, most important, that I believed in. The worst, always and inevitably, were on topics I didn't know a damn about and of course, didn't believe in. What you think is who you are, and honest leaders don't diverge too far from that. Certainly being myself got me into a lot of trouble, but I was never confused as to how or why I had come to those difficult situations.

That's as good a starting point as I can offer.

When the Phone Stops Ringing

At the time of my defeat for reelection, I was sure my world had come to an end. I was no longer a player, an instrument of change. The phone stopped ringing, and new kings had been crowned. I was without a title, and more important, for the first time in my life I was without a job, or any source of income other than a small and inadequate teacher's retirement check, hardly enough to pay a mortgage, college debts, and electric bills.

Perhaps had I been more accommodating to the corporate interests or more controllable to Governor Dean I would have been "taken care of." But that wasn't the case. As Dean had once confided to me, his corporate friends looked upon me as a "dangerous man." It may have been a reflection of how he felt also.

As I still had a family to look after, I was forced to do what I never believed I would do—I became a lobbyist, and though I made more money than I had ever made in my life, I hated every moment of it.

And I was a terrible lobbyist, as I was a lobbyist who refused to lobby. I wouldn't appear in the State House; I wouldn't even make calls to the State House. But my clients still insisted on paying me outrageous money just to be registered as their lobbyist and advise them on occasion. It was perhaps the loneliest and unhappiest year of my life. I searched desperately for some way to escape.

It was President Clinton who rode to my rescue with a call out of the blue asking if I would be interested in joining his administration. He was carrying one of his wounded off the battlefield. Needless to say, I jumped at the opportunity to become a special assistant to the secretary of education. I would work out of the regional office in Boston and represent the U.S. Department of Education throughout the six New England states. It was a lifesaver. Not only was I working in a field that I knew something about, but I had a salary that allowed me to get on with living, doing something that I wasn't ashamed to be doing.

The job wasn't the most exciting I had ever done, as my position was a good way down the bureaucratic food chain in the Department of Education. I spent a whole lot of time on the road visiting schools in New England, always without a whole lot of purpose. Maybe it was just me, but I soon became bored because so little was demanded of what I felt I had to offer. In 2000 when Cathy suggested that I consider retirement and we move to Florida, I agreed. The time had come to finally let go.

Reflecting

It was also the time to look back on all that had happened, and as difficult as it is, I've tried to reflect on and analyze what my experience in the legislature meant, not just to me, but to Vermont, its politics, and its people.

Longevity counts for something, and my ten years as Speaker established a record for years served by anyone in Vermont history. That I was a minority Speaker for all but my last term is certainly outside the norm of most state legislatures. But just hanging around can often symbolize nothing more than that—just hanging around. I like to think that something worthwhile was accomplished during that decade between 1985 and 1995.

Vermont was in the midst of a tidal change in politics during these years and the twenty years preceding them. Phil Hoff ("King Philip") had shocked all the pundits in 1962 when he upset the Republican "boy governor," Ray Keyser, and became the first Democratic governor since before the Civil War. I rode that same wave of change when I upset Bob Kinsey in 1985.

Hoff's election had changed the politics of the governor's office, and mine changed the politics of the legislature. With the influx of down-country professionals relocating to the Green Mountain state, Vermont was in the process of changing from one of the most conservative to one of the most liberal states in the Union. Our elections were the result, not the cause.

Once ensconced in the job, I liked it and worked to keep it. If keeping it meant professionalizing campaign financing, I was more than willing to learn the process. As for recruiting and electing more Democrats, there was no secret formula. I've always maintained it was desire, more than any political magic, that made us so successful at it. Find a good candidate; train him or her; lend support (and later money); and hope for the best. Simply put, we just out-hustled the Republicans by knowing what we wanted to accomplish and keeping at it until it got done. Not surprisingly, the Republicans finally caught on, and in 2000 they took back the House after sixteen years of Democratic rule. A few have jokingly credited their success to reading my memoirs and learning the secret.

More important, I hope, we used our newfound political power to get things done. The record attests that we passed a whole lot of legislation that made Vermont an even better and more caring place to live.

Vermont does not have a professional legislature. True, some enter searching for self-glory, but most come to get things done. None come for the money or the benefits, as there's little of the former and none of the latter. Once there, the vast majority of legislators settle into working toward righting what they see as wrongs. Among my colleagues and me, our goals may have been vastly different, but seldom our motivation.

Though we never managed to accomplish a complete overhaul of the way the state funds public education, we did pour millions into state aid to education. Under Act 60, enacted four years after my exit, in 1998, Vermont has begun the long road to finding a source and manner of funding public education other than the local property tax.

Something similar occurred with health care. Even though we suffered a crushing defeat on providing a statewide health care system in 1993, Vermont has, under Madeleine Kunin, Howard Dean, and a concerned legislature, incrementally moved toward a more inclusive array of programs that provide basic health care for 98 percent of all Vermont's children under age eighteen, as well as entitlements aimed at preventive medical care for all its citizens. They're not there yet, but they've (as they say) moved on down that road.

We passed into law nearly 1,600 bills over the ten-year period, including landmark environmental legislation (Vermont is one of the most beautiful states in America, in part because of Vermonters' insistence on stringent development laws), mental health care entitlement, social service expansion, aid for agriculture, minimum wage increases, and judicial reform. The struggle to pass the gay rights bill I hope had some effect on the momentous decision in 2000 to authorize civil unions.

Critics might argue that all of this represented the problem exactly: We did too much. But that would not be so if you believed that election to the legislature was a responsibility conferred on you by constituents to get up there and get something done. For better or worse, that's exactly how I interpreted my task: "Don't sit there—do something."

To be sure there were measures that we failed at, but as is often the case, we may have planted the seeds of future progress in making Vermont an even better place to live and raise a family.

None of it would have been possible if Dick Snelling had not had the courage to do what was right rather than what was political by—not once, but twice—righting a deficit-laden ship in the midst of economic storms. That we were smart enough to lend him our support, when politics afforded us the excuse to let him twist slowly in the wind, I take some pride. It was government at its best when the public had every right to expect the worst.

And finally, you have to be lucky. Nobody pulls themselves up by their own bootstraps. Somebody has to make the boots, and more important, anticipate the need for straps. I've always marveled at what good fortune I had to serve with so many talented "boot makers." I think how lucky I was to have the likes of Paul Poirier during those first six years of leadership. All who were there will testify that there was never a more tenacious or talented floor leader than Paul. Even Republicans will agree as to the measure of the man.

But he wasn't alone.

The House that I was privileged to preside over was filled with bright, issue-oriented Democrats who were almost always unmatched in debate and never outworked. They were often joined in the trenches by Republicans like Tom Little, Harold Weidman, and Rick Westman, who took the heat and did what they believed to be right. My problem was never a lack of talent to fill the important committees but an overabundance of extremely capable people, some of whom I had to disappoint.

And they were more than just decent and hard working; they had brains. Any leader would have envied my caucus. I got a lot of the credit for what they made possible, but there are those who know the real truth.

And Regrets

I would be remiss if I left the reader with the idea that it was one long road to success. It wasn't. I have my regrets.

Foremost I regret my lack of understanding of how to get the most out of leadership. I led—I don't think anyone will question that—but not always with the greatest of humility. I can't help thinking of Samuel Johnson's observation that "power corrupts, and absolute power corrupts absolutely." His words forcefully say to me that the difference between good leaders and great leaders is how they react to success. Good leaders see success as a victory over a foe; great leaders see it in its purest form— as a simple victory.

Too often I enjoyed my foe's defeat when I should have been admiring his courage to do battle and his right to be wrong. Often the result was personal—stature accrued from another's diminution, sometimes dangerously close to bullying—and my mother taught me better. For such reasons I wish I could do it over.

Finally, the exercise of writing this book has closed off every exit I have desperately sought to avoid defining what part I played in making laws. I don't normally converse with former adversaries, but if you were to take the time to hunt them down you can be sure that they would be happy to give you an earful.

I have never returned to the legislature, but I do take the time to try and keep up with current Vermont politics and occasionally talk to a few old friends who shared those times with me. Most of the time we agree that we did a ton of legislating. We always agree that we had fun. When I ask what it all meant, they have the same trouble answering that I have. What they do express clearly, time after time, is how important they felt, how vital, how much they felt they mattered.

But I'm still avoiding the question. You can't just come out and ask, How great was I? Greatness isn't something to be solicited, even from old and still-loyal lieutenants.

As time goes by I have begun to hear myself referred to as a "legend." But a legend is a myth, a fable, an old wives' tale. I wasn't that at all. I was real, a living person who simply enjoyed the political arena; someone who believed that this can be a better world if we dare confront our mistakes and search for measures to correct them; someone who is well aware that for every step forward the inevitable setback is around the corner and, with this always in mind, stays in the fight.

I guess this finally takes us, with all my rambling, back to the beginning when I defined the single ingredient necessary for running for office: Go ahead—give it your best—just don't let the fear of losing keep you out of the arena.

Carpe diem.

Where Are They Now?

Francis Brooks continues to represent his district in Montpelier.

Sean Campbell left the legislature in 1998 to become commissioner of taxes for the governor, and later Dean's secretary of administration. He is now chief financial administrator at Vermont Academy—the private prep school from which he graduated.

"Little Joe" Caracciola is deceased.

Timmy (the Cork) Corcoran got elected Bennington town clerk in 1995. His son, Timothy, ran and won my old seat. Dad now keeps an eye on him and everybody else from the Bennington Town Hall.

Gov. Howard Dean left the governor's office in 2002 after eleven years to run for president of the United States. For a moment in history, the party faithful fell in love with this new "liberal" knight on a white horse, but he was defeated in the Democratic primaries. He is presently head of the Democratic National Committee.

Jim Douglas, who once sadly presided over my election as Speaker, now presides over the state as governor.

Mary Evelti left the legislature in 1988 and did what raising nine children and the early death of her husband had earlier prevented her from doing: She went to college and received her bachelor's degree. She died in 2002—a mother, a legislator, and a great, great human being.

Jim Finneran is deceased. The Brown Derby now belongs to a family from India.

Sara Gear has left the legislature but remains a player in the Vermont Republican Party.

The talents of **Barbara Grimes** led her from the legislature to state government as a department head, and today she is president of the Burlington Cooperative Electric Company.

Bob Harris is deceased.

John Hise is deceased.

Gov. Philip Hoff now spends his days promoting the same liberal causes he fought for while in the governor's office in the 1960s. He is still "King Philip" to Democrats who remember.

Bob Kinsey returned to his farm in Craftsbury after losing a Republican primary for his long-held seat and then, switching parties, being defeated as the Democratic candidate in the general election in 2000. He died in 2005.

Gov. Madeleine Kunin chose not to run for a fourth term in 1990. President Clinton named her deputy secretary of education and later ambassador to Switzerland. She is presently a guest lecturer at St Michael's College in Winooski, Vermont.

Edgar May left the Vermont Senate in 1991. He then enrolled in chef's college because that addressed a talent he had never explored. He spends his time raising funds for a regional recreational center in Springfield, Vermont, writing, consulting, and cooking for pleasure.

Speaker Stephen Morse retired from the legislature in 1985 and became administrator of the Windom Foundation.

John Murphy left the legislature in 1990, undefeated after thirty years. He retired to a life of tying flies, reading, and spending several winter months in Florida at the request of Flora Belle. He tells me he'd "rather be sitting in a snowbank at the base of Ludlow Mountain," but, he explains, "it's now Flora Belle's turn to make those decisions."

Speaker Tim O'Connor never returned to politics and practices law in Brattleboro, Vermont.

Virginio "Max" Perrotta is deceased.

Paul Poirier left the House in 1988 to run unsuccessfully for Congress. He returned to the Vermont House in 1996. After two terms he decided to run for the Vermont Senate. Defeated, he now works as an advocate for mental health.

Larry Powers is retired and lives in North Bennington.

Bill Russell is still chief of the Legislative Council.

Wally Russell is deceased.

Dr. Jim Shea is deceased.

Smith, Smith, and Smith—I don't have a clue what became of them.

Gov. Richard Snelling is deceased.

Ron Squires is deceased. His mother still walks in fund-raisers to eliminate the dreadful disease AIDS.

Nancy Wright received a Neiman Fellowship to Harvard University on the strength of her investigative reporting. She later had a falling-out with the *Rutland Herald* and left the world of journalism. She was last reported to be a nurse at a hospital in New Hampshire.

Ralph Wright left Vermont in 2000. He now resides in Florida, where he writes, teaches, and struggles to break eighty.

Index

Note: Tables, figures, photos, and notes are indicated by *t, f, p,* and *n,* respectively.